Advanced Technologies in Hydropower Flow Systems

Advanced Technologies in Hydropower Flow Systems

Editors

Adam Adamkowski
Anton Bergant

MDPI • Basel • Beijing • Wuhan • Barcelona • Belgrade • Manchester • Tokyo • Cluj • Tianjin

Editors
Adam Adamkowski
Polish Academy of Sciences
Poland

Anton Bergant
Litostroj Power d.o.o. &
University of Ljubljana
Slovenia

Editorial Office
MDPI
St. Alban-Anlage 66
4052 Basel, Switzerland

This is a reprint of articles from the Special Issue published online in the open access journal *Energies* (ISSN 1996-1073) (available at: https://www.mdpi.com/journal/energies/special_issues/advanced_technologies_hydropower_flow_systems).

For citation purposes, cite each article independently as indicated on the article page online and as indicated below:

LastName, A.A.; LastName, B.B.; LastName, C.C. Article Title. *Journal Name* **Year**, *Volume Number*, Page Range.

ISBN 978-3-0365-4693-3 (Hbk)
ISBN 978-3-0365-4694-0 (PDF)

© 2022 by the authors. Articles in this book are Open Access and distributed under the Creative Commons Attribution (CC BY) license, which allows users to download, copy and build upon published articles, as long as the author and publisher are properly credited, which ensures maximum dissemination and a wider impact of our publications.

The book as a whole is distributed by MDPI under the terms and conditions of the Creative Commons license CC BY-NC-ND.

Contents

Kai Zhang, Xinkuo Jiang, Shiyang Li, Bin Huang, Shuai Yang, Peng Wu and Dazhuan Wu
Transient CFD Simulation on Dynamic Characteristics of Annular Seal under Large Eccentricities and Disturbances
Reprinted from: *Energies* **2020**, *13*, 4056, doi:10.3390/en13164056 . . . . **1**

Adam Adamkowski, Waldemar Janicki and Mariusz Lewandowski
Measurements of Discharge through a Pump-Turbine in Both Flow Directions Using Volumetric Gauging and Pressure-Time Methods
Reprinted from: *Energies* **2020**, *13*, 4706, doi:10.3390/en13184706 . . . . **23**

Zhiyan Yang, Zirui Liu, Yongguang Cheng, Xiaoxi Zhang, Ke Liu and Linsheng Xia
Differences of Flow Patterns and Pressure Pulsations in Four Prototype Pump-Turbines during Runaway Transient Processes
Reprinted from: *Energies* **2020**, *13*, 5269, doi:10.3390/en13205269 . . . . **51**

Hamid Arionfard and Sina Mohammadi
Numerical Investigation of the Geometrical Effect on Flow-Induced Vibration Performance of Pivoted Bodies
Reprinted from: *Energies* **2021**, *14*, 1128, doi:10.3390/en14041128 . . . . **71**

Martin Polák
Innovation of Pump as Turbine According to Calculation Model for Francis Turbine Design
Reprinted from: *Energies* **2021**, *14*, 2698, doi:10.3390/en14092698 . . . . **87**

Erick O. Castañeda Magadán, Gustavo Urquiza Beltrán, Laura L. Castro Gómez and Juan C. García Castrejón
Application of CFD to the Design of Manifolds Employed in the Thermodynamic Method to Obtain Efficiency in a Hydraulic Turbine
Reprinted from: *Energies* **2021**, *14*, 8359, doi:10.3390/en14248359 . . . . **101**

Madhusudhan Pandey, Dietmar Winkler, Kaspar Vereide, Roshan Sharma and Bernt Lie
Mechanistic Model of an Air Cushion Surge Tank for Hydro Power Plants
Reprinted from: *Energies* **2022**, *15*, 2824, doi:10.3390/en15082824 . . . . **121**

Article

Transient CFD Simulation on Dynamic Characteristics of Annular Seal under Large Eccentricities and Disturbances

Kai Zhang [1], Xinkuo Jiang [2], Shiyang Li [1], Bin Huang [3], Shuai Yang [1], Peng Wu [1,*] and Dazhuan Wu [1,4]

1. College of Energy Engineering, Zhejiang University, Hangzhou 310027, China; zhangkai612@zju.edu.cn (K.Z.); lishiyang@zju.edu.cn (S.L.); shuaiyangzju@zju.edu.cn (S.Y.); wudazhuan@zju.edu.cn (D.W.)
2. China Tianchen Engineering Corporation, Tianjin 300400, China; jiangxinkuo@zju.edu.cn
3. Ocean College, Zhejiang University, Hangzhou 310027, China; binhuang@zju.edu.cn
4. State Key Laboratory of Fluid Power Transmission and Control, Hangzhou 310027, China
* Correspondence: roc@zju.edu.cn; Tel.: +86-1373-543-5349

Received: 17 June 2020; Accepted: 3 August 2020; Published: 5 August 2020

Abstract: Annular seals of turbomachinery usually suffer from various degrees of eccentricities and disturbances due to the rotor–stator misalignment and radial loads, while the discussion of annular seal under both large static eccentricities and dynamic disturbances is relatively limited. In this paper, the applicability of linear assumption and reliability of nonlinear dynamic model for eccentric annular seals under large eccentricities and disturbances is discussed based on the investigation of seals with various rotor motions through computational fluid dynamics (CFD). After the validation of transient CFD methods by comparison with experimental and bulk theory results, the dynamic behaviors of annular seal are analyzed by adopting both direct transient simulations and the nonlinear Muszynska model. The results show that the nonlinear dynamic model based on rotor circular whirls around seal center can predict the fluid excitations of different types of rotor motions well under small static eccentricities, while it is limited severely with large static eccentricities, which indicates that the dynamic characteristics of annular seal under large eccentricities are related with the rotor's motion ways. The paper provides a reference for studies of rotor–seal system with complex rotor motions considering radial loads or running across the resonance region.

Keywords: annular seal; CFD; dynamic coefficients; fluid forces; nonlinear dynamic model; static eccentricity

1. Introduction

Hydraulic machinery such as pumps and turbines is widely applied in various energy fields, playing a significant role in energy development, utilization and transformation. The vibration caused by the fluid forces generated in gap seals of hydraulic machinery tend to have important effects on the efficiency and vibration of rotor system [1]. Due to the rise of safety and efficiency concerns, dynamic characteristics of various annular seals have been studied by researchers [2–5]. Almost all of these studies are based on the assumption of small perturbation, hence linear dynamic characteristics of annular seals can be investigated. Generally, the annular seal is not the supporting element in design. Under the condition of static equilibrium, the rotor is normally concentric with the annular seal. Due to the axial-symmetry of seal geometry, as shown in Figure 1, the force coefficients of concentric seals show symmetric or skew symmetric features, as shown in Equation (1), where F_x, F_y are the X and Y components of fluid forces respectively; K and k denote direct and cross stiffness coefficients, respectively; similarly, direct and cross damping coefficients are expressed as C and c, respectively; and M is direct mass coefficient. These five coefficients can be numerically computed by using the bulk flow model [6], CFD simulations by introducing moving reference frame [7,8] or transient method [9] and measured by perturbing the rotor or the stator [10].

$$-\begin{Bmatrix} F_x \\ F_y \end{Bmatrix} = \begin{bmatrix} K & k \\ -k & K \end{bmatrix} \begin{Bmatrix} x \\ y \end{Bmatrix} + \begin{bmatrix} C & c \\ -c & C \end{bmatrix} \begin{Bmatrix} \dot{x} \\ \dot{y} \end{Bmatrix} + \begin{bmatrix} M & 0 \\ 0 & M \end{bmatrix} \begin{Bmatrix} \ddot{x} \\ \ddot{y} \end{Bmatrix} \quad (1)$$

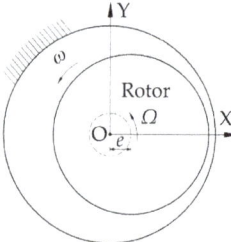

Figure 1. The circular whirl around seal center.

However, under actual condition, the static eccentricity of the rotor may exist in annular seal due to the misalignment during assembly process or the effects of various side loads (e.g., impeller weight). The dynamic characteristics of eccentric annular seals, as shown in Figure 2, were also investigated based on the bulk flow model by Nelson and Nguyen [11]. The fluid force increments (ΔF_x and ΔF_y) induced by the small perturbation around static eccentricity position are similarly expressed in linearized rotordynamic form, as shown in Equation (2) [12].

$$-\begin{Bmatrix} \Delta F_x \\ \Delta F_y \end{Bmatrix} = \begin{bmatrix} k_{xx} & k_{xy} \\ k_{yx} & k_{yy} \end{bmatrix} \begin{Bmatrix} \Delta x \\ \Delta y \end{Bmatrix} + \begin{bmatrix} c_{xx} & c_{xy} \\ c_{yx} & c_{yy} \end{bmatrix} \begin{Bmatrix} \Delta \dot{x} \\ \Delta \dot{y} \end{Bmatrix} + \begin{bmatrix} m_{xx} & 0 \\ 0 & m_{yy} \end{bmatrix} \begin{Bmatrix} \Delta \ddot{x} \\ \Delta \ddot{y} \end{Bmatrix}, \quad (2)$$

where Δx and Δy define the rotor motion relative to the equilibrium position. Unlike concentric seals, the force coefficients of eccentric seals are no longer symmetric or skew symmetric due to rotor misalignment. This brings difficulties to the numerical solutions of force coefficients. Arghir and Frene [13] compared the bulk flow model of concentric seals and eccentric seals, the results showing that the terms of circumferential partial derivatives emerge in all bulk flow equations due to the static eccentricity of flow field. This can result in the coupling effect between circumferential momentum equation and continuity equation and make the solutions of both bulk flow equations and their perturbation equations very complex. As to the CFD method, the seal flow field disturbed by rotor circular whirl is not axisymmetric, as shown in Figure 2, and the steady-state simplified treatment by introducing moving reference frame is no longer applicable [8]. This means that transient simulations are necessary for evaluating force coefficients of eccentric seals.

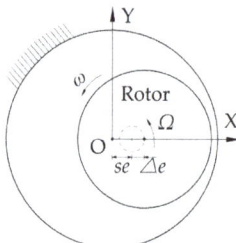

Figure 2. The circular whirl around equilibrium position.

To overcome numerical difficulties in eccentric seal research, Venkataraman and Palazzolo [14] determined the circumferential derivatives through a cubic spline interpolation method and simplified the bulk flow equations of eccentric seals. Athavale and Hendricks [15] presented a small perturbation CFD method for calculation of rotordynamic coefficients of concentric and eccentric seals, and the SCISEAL code along with a modified SIMPLEC algorithm was adopted. Wu et al. [16] developed a new transient CFD method, which is based on rotor's variable-speed whirl; the results show that this new method can keep good accuracy of traditional transient method and save much computational time and cost in the meantime.

The research for fluid force presented above has mainly focused on linear fluid force analysis, and it was performed under the strict restriction and assumption that the whirl amplitude is relatively very small compared to the seal clearance (within 0.1 C_r; C_r denotes the seal clearance). While large amplitude vibration often occurs during the passage of the critical speed of actual turbomachinery, the linear bulk flow analysis may not be applicable for the accurate fluid force characteristics in such situations with large amplitude. To describe the fluid forces of annular seal induced by large disturbances, the nonlinear dynamic model should be established. San Andres and Jeung [17] presented an orbit analysis method based on extended Reynolds equation to investigate force coefficients valid over a wide frequency range of a squeeze film damper bearing with large amplitude and static eccentricity. Ikemoto et al. [6] investigated the nonlinear fluid forces for the concentric seal with large whirl amplitude up to about a half of the clearance by using extended perturbation analysis of the bulk flow theory. Currently, the Muszynska's model proposed by Bently and Muszynska [18] is commonly used by researchers as a nonlinear dynamic model. Li and Chen [19] adopted the Muszynska's seal force model with the empirical parameters to investigate the 1:2 subharmonic resonance of labyrinth seal–rotor system. These empirical parameters obtained by employing the CFD analysis are used in the subsequent nonlinear analysis, regardless of whether the whirl amplitude is around the concentric position or not. He and Jing [20] indicated that Muszynska's model will not describe the dynamic characteristics of the rotor–seal system well when the rotor–seal system has larger eccentricity ratio. However, the present paper is devoted to develop nonlinear dynamic models of concentric seal with large whirl amplitude or eccentric seal with large static eccentricity and rather small whirl amplitude. The applicability of linear assumption and reliability of nonlinear model for seals under large static eccentricities and disturbance amplitude is rarely discussed in the literature. Thus, an investigation on the applicability of nonlinear Muszynska's model under large eccentricities and disturbances is wished for, particularly in nonlinear rotor–seal system research considering radial loads.

In experimental studies of eccentric seals, Marquette, Childs and Andres [21] measured the force coefficients of a plain liquid annular seal under different static eccentricities, and the results show that the force coefficients were more sensitive to the changes of static eccentricity than theoretically predicted. Childs, Arthur and Mehta [22] measured the net reaction forces of gas annular seals as the eccentricity ratios increased; negative stiffness created by unanticipated eccentricities may lead to over prediction of critical speeds, which illustrates the importance of concentric assembly of annular seals.

In this paper, three-dimensional (3D) transient CFD simulations based on dynamic mesh method are performed to evaluate the static and dynamic characteristics of eccentric annular seals. The obtained force coefficients and leakage rates are compared with Marquette's experiment [21] for validating the reliability of the transient CFD method. The effects of rotor disturbance amplitude on the dynamic characteristics of eccentric annular seals are analyzed to investigate the linear ranges of seal dynamic characteristics. In addition, transient CFD simulations and a nonlinear dynamic model are adopted to study the fluid excitations of annular seals induced by different rotor large motions. The nonlinear dynamic model is based on the famous Muszynska's model [18,23,24] and is obtained by fitting the "nominal" force coefficients of concentric annular seal under different whirl amplitude, as shown in Figure 2. With nonlinear model and transient CFD simulations, fluid excitations under various large disturbances are computed. Based on these fluid excitations, seal dynamic characteristics under large eccentricities and disturbances are investigated in detail, which provides a solid basis for the research of seal–rotor system analysis by using Muszynska' model as nonlinear seal force.

2. Numerical Methods

2.1. Geometry Model and Grid

The plain annular seal adopted to perform the studies in this paper is applied in high speed hydrostatic journal bearings, which is tested in the apparatus and facility in Marquette's experiment. The work medium is water at 20 °C. The geometric and operating parameters of the seal are listed in Table 1. As shown in Figure 3, the structured grids are generated in the concentric annular fluid domain by the CFD Preprocessor Gambit, which is geometry and mesh generation commercial software for computational fluid dynamics (CFD) analysis.

Table 1. Parameters of plain annular seal.

Main Parameters	Symbols	Values	Units
seal length	L	34.93	mm
seal diameter	D	76.29	mm
seal clearance	C_r	0.11	mm
rotating speed	ω		rpm
pressure difference	ΔP	5.52	MPa
length-diameter ratio	L/D	0.46	

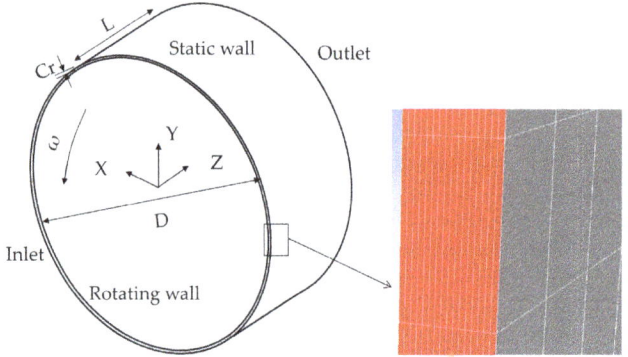

Figure 3. Numerical model of concentric annular seal.

The grid independence is checked by comparing the several grids with different radial grid densities. Under 80% eccentricity ratio, the radial and tangential components of fluid force are evaluated according to different grid models, as shown in Figure 4. The curves of "Fr refined" and "Ft refined" represent the radial and tangential fluid force of refined grid model, which has 36 radial layers with more than 10 layers near the both walls to keep y+ less than 5. The grid model of 16 radial layers is adopted considering the accuracy and computational time. With respect to the tangential and axial density, it can be seen in Table 2 that the results of fluid force show good convergence at Grid 3 (16 × 318 × 1448, i.e., there are 16 layers of grids generated along seal clearance in radial direction, 318 layers in axial direction and 1448 layers in circumferential direction) as the grid density changes to 1.25 or 1.5 times. This indicates that the present grid resolution (16 × 318 × 1448, 7,358,770 grid cells) is suitable for this research considering about the accuracy and efficiency of simulations.

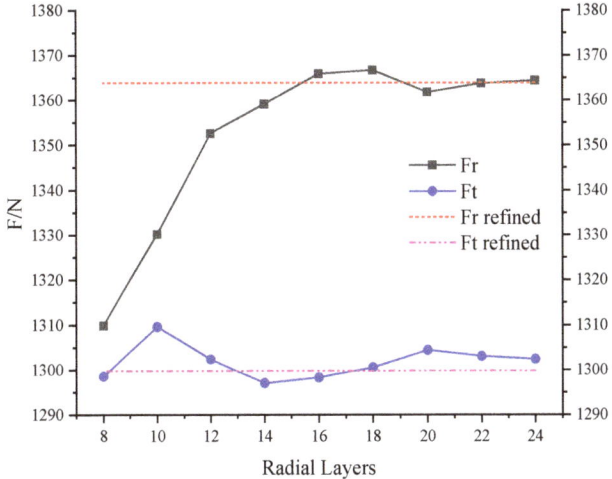

Figure 4. Radial grid density study.

Table 2. Tangential and axial grid density study.

Name	Grid Density	Fr/N	Relative Error [1]	Ft/N	Relative Error [1]
Grid 1	16 × 204 × 1448	1331.43	2.53%	1278.62	1.52%
Grid 2	16 × 254 × 1448	1358.79	0.52%	1289.26	0.70%
Grid 3	16 × 318 × 1448	1365.92	-	1298.33	-
Grid 4	16 × 397 × 1448	1367.51	−0.12%	1299.54	−0.09%
Grid 5	16 × 477 × 1448	1367.86	−0.14%	1300.15	−0.14%
Grid 6	16 × 318 × 926	1344.51	1.57%	1276.36	1.69%
Grid 7	16 × 318 × 1158	1360.28	0.41%	1290.79	0.58%
Grid 8	16 × 318 × 1810	1366.09	−0.01%	1298.65	−0.02%
Grid 9	16 × 318 × 2170	1365.82	0.01%	1298.93	−0.05%

[1] Note: by comparing with Grid 3 (16 × 318 × 1448, radial × axial × tangential layers).

2.2. 3D Transient Solutions

Under various rotor disturbances, the static and dynamic characteristics of plain annular seal are investigated by simulating the transient flow in seal clearance. In this paper, the commercial CFD solver, ANSYS Fluent, is chosen to solve the 3D Reynolds-averaged Navier–Stokes equations. To achieve transient simulations, dynamic mesh problem should be firstly settled. As shown in Figure 2, the motion of rotor (i.e., rotating wall) can change the shape of fluid domain, and grids will change accordingly. However, due to high aspect ratio of grid cells in the clearance, the three types of dynamic methods in Fluent—spring-based smoothing, local remeshing and dynamic layering methods—tend to cause bad orthogonality or negative volume of grids.

To ensure good grid quality, the dynamic mesh model based on interpolation method [9,25] is adopted in this paper, which can effectively control the movement of the girds. First, nodes on rotating wall (i.e., rotor surface) are controlled to move according to the motion equation of the rotor and nodes on static wall keep stationary. Then, the ratio of nodes in the clearance is deduced according to the geometric relations of position of nodes in the clearance and movement of rotor. After that, the motions of grid nodes in the domain are determined by using the interpolation method based on the distances of the nodes from rotor and stator walls. Finally, the positions and velocities of grid nodes in the domain are obtained after the movement of rotor.

Figure 5 shows the grid nodes moving in the clearance of annular seal. As illustrated in the figure, pf^0 (x^0_f, y^0_f) and pb^0 (x^0_b, y^0_b) represent the nodes of rotor surface and stator surface, respectively, when the rotor is at the concentric position. pi^0 ($x^0{}_i$, $y^0{}_i$) is an arbitrary node in the clearance domain of annular seal along the line between pf^0 and pb^0. θ denotes the initial angular coordinate of node pf^0. The superscript denotes the moving step of nodes and the subscript denotes the position of nodes. $d^1(x^1{}_d, y^1{}_d)$ represents the motion vector of moving rotor in Cartesian coordinates. di^1 denotes the vector from pi^0 to pi^1 ($x^1{}_i$, $y^1{}_i$). Then, the new coordinates ($x^1{}_f$, $y^1{}_f$) of pf^0 (current node pf^1) are defined as Equation (3).

$$x^1_f = x^0_f + x^1_d, \quad y^1_f = y^0_f + y^1_d, \tag{3}$$

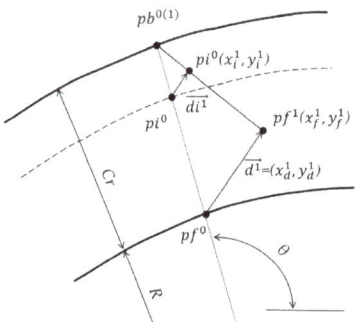

Figure 5. Schematic diagram of moving grid node.

The node of stator surface is assumed to stay still, the movement distance between rotor and stator is determined by the interpolation algorithm. Then, the new position coordinates ($x^1{}_f$, $y^1{}_f$) of pi^1 could be expressed as Equation (4).

$$x^1_i = x^0_i + ra \times x^1_d, \quad y^1_i = y^0_i + ra \times y^1_d, \tag{4}$$

where ra denotes the ratio of the distance between the nodes in the clearance domain and the static outer wall to the clearance. When the rotor is in concentric and eccentric position, the initial angular coordinate θ of pf^0 and the ratio of ra can be expressed by known parameters R and C_r and the coordinates of pf^0, pi^0 and pb^0 according to collinear geometric relations of pf^1, pi^1 and pb^1. Then, the new position of pi^1 in the clearance after the movement of rotor can be obtained by substituting ra to Equation (3).

The displacement of each node is restricted and calculated by mathematical procedures, which strictly ensures the movement coordination of adjacent grid nodes. The whole dynamic mesh process is implemented by adopting a subroutine linked with the CFD solver. This algorithm has been tested and the results show that, when the rotor whirled from the concentric position (with exaggerated seal clearance C_r), as shown in Figure 6a, to the eccentric position, as shown in Figure 6b, the grid distortion rate will increase but there is no negative volumes and highly distorted elements. The maximum grid aspect ratio will not exceed 200 even with eccentricity ratios (e/C_r, e denotes the rotor eccentricity) of 80%, which indicates that this dynamic mesh algorithm is suitable for the transient simulation with large eccentricity.

Due to rotor eccentricity, one side of the grids is compressed and the maximum aspect ratio of the grids increases on basis of the initial grid model in Figure 6a. Considering the extreme thin grid layers, numerical computations are performed under double precision to ensure the stability and reliability of the result. The boundary conditions of 5.52 MPa total pressure and 0 Pa static pressure are, respectively, adopted at inlet and outlet. Both walls are set as no-slip walls and the rotating wall possesses a rotation speed which equals to r/min. The wall y+ of flow field under various disturbances is generally located in the range of 20–40 and the Realizable k-ε model with enhanced wall function is suitable to handle the situation [9,16]. The first-order implicit scheme is used for the discretization of time term. The chosen time step is equal to the wall rotation for 1 degree so that the courant number in most regions can be confined within 5 for stability. More than 360 steps are performed to ensure the stability of transient simulation according to different rotor motions. The second-order up-wind scheme with numerical under-relaxation is adopted to the convection term in the equations. The central-differencing scheme is employed to discretize the diffusion. The velocity–pressure coupling is solved by using the well-known SIMPLE strategy. Each simulation case for one revolution costs about 50 h on the platform of CPU is Intel® Xeon® Gold 6240 @ 2.60GHz with an average 16-parallel-processes solver.

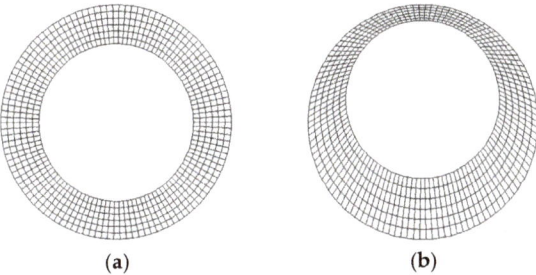

Figure 6. Diagram of cross section of the meshed rotor: (**a**) initial grids; and (**b**) moved grids.

2.3. Computing Static and Dynamic Characteristics of Eccentric Annular Seals

Transient CFD simulations are used to compute the static and dynamic characteristics of eccentric seals. The six cases with different static eccentricity ratios (se/C_r, where se denotes the static eccentricity of rotor) are investigated, respectively, 0%, 10%, 20%, 30%, 40% and 50%. The eccentric direction in +X direction is shown in Figure 2. The leakage rates of eccentric annular seals can be obtained by simulating the steady-state flow fields without rotor disturbances. The dynamic characteristics of eccentric seals can be analyzed by considering small rotor perturbations. The adopted perturbation is the circular whirl with a small whirl amplitude Δe (termed as dynamic eccentricity), as shown in Figure 2. The whirling speed Ω is constant. Given the suitability of small perturbation assumption, dynamic eccentricity ratio ($\Delta e/C_r$) should be very small (1% in the study). The small whirls are described by Equation (5). The fluid force increments (ΔF_x and ΔF_y) induced by perturbations are expressed by Equation (6).

$$\begin{cases} \Delta x = x - se = \Delta e \cos(\Omega t) \\ \Delta y = y - 0 = \Delta e \sin(\Omega t) \end{cases}, \tag{5}$$

$$\begin{cases} \Delta F_x = F_x - F_{x0} \\ \Delta F_y = F_y - F_{y0} \end{cases}, \tag{6}$$

where F_{x0} and F_{y0} represent fluid forces at equilibrium position. Substituting Equations (5) and (6) into Equation (2), F_x and F_y can be expressed as the harmonic functions of time, as shown in Equation (7):

$$\begin{cases} F_x = F_{x0} + A_1 \Delta e \cos(\Omega t) + B_1 \Delta e \sin(\Omega t) \\ F_y = F_{y0} + B_2 \Delta e \cos(\Omega t) + A_2 \Delta e \sin(\Omega t) \end{cases}, \tag{7}$$

where

$$\begin{cases} A_1 = -k_{xx} - c_{xy}\Omega + m_{xx}\Omega^2 \\ B_1 = -k_{xy} + c_{xx}\Omega + m_{xy}\Omega^2 \\ A_2 = -k_{yy} + c_{yx}\Omega + m_{yy}\Omega^2 \\ B_2 = -k_{yx} - c_{yy}\Omega + m_{yx}\Omega^2 \end{cases} \tag{8}$$

By simulating the transient flow field with rotor perturbation, the time histories of F_x and F_y can be recorded by integrating the fluid pressure at each time step. Then, they are used to evaluate F_{x0},

F_{y0} and the four constant coefficients (A_1, B_1, A_2 and B_2) in Equation (7) by curve fittings. A_1, B_1, A_2 and B_2 are composed of a known whirling speed Ω and three unknown force coefficients, as shown in Equation (8). To obtain all the unknown force coefficients, A_1, B_1, A_2 and B_2 under at least three (generally five is desired considering the fitting error) whirling speeds should be determined. Hence, at least three transient CFD simulations should be performed.

2.4. Fitting Nonlinear Dynamic Model

Force coefficients of annular seals can only be used to describe fluid forces induced by rotor small perturbations. The Muszynska's model is adopted to describe the fluid forces of annular seal induced by large disturbances. It is derived based on a serial of experiments and adopts nonlinear dynamic parameters similar with force coefficients to associate fluid forces with rotor motion, as shown in Equation (9):

$$\left\{ \begin{array}{c} F_x \\ F_y \end{array} \right\} = -\left[\begin{array}{cc} S - m_f \tau_1^2 \omega^2 & \tau_1 \omega D \\ -\tau_1 \omega D & S - m_f \tau_1^2 \omega^2 \end{array} \right] \left\{ \begin{array}{c} x \\ y \end{array} \right\} - \left[\begin{array}{cc} D & 2\tau_1 \omega m_f \\ -2\tau_1 \omega m_f & D \end{array} \right] \left\{ \begin{array}{c} \dot{x} \\ \dot{y} \end{array} \right\} - \left[\begin{array}{cc} m_f & 0 \\ 0 & m_f \end{array} \right] \left\{ \begin{array}{c} \ddot{x} \\ \ddot{y} \end{array} \right\}, \quad (9)$$

where $S = S_0(1-\varepsilon^2)^{-n}$, $\tau_1 = \tau_0(1-\varepsilon)^b$, $D = D_0(1-\varepsilon^2)^{-n}$, for $\varepsilon = \sqrt{x^2+y^2}/C_r$

n, τ_0 and b are empirical factors for certain seal structure; S_0, D_0 and m_f can be computed using Black–Childs formulas [26]. When the seal is under steady working condition (constant ω and ΔP), the S_0, D_0, m_f and empirical factors in Muszynska's model become constant values. Namely, nonlinear dynamic parameters in matrices are only related with eccentricity ratio ε. Thus, Equation (9) can be expressed in a simplified form, as shown in Equation (10):

$$\left\{ \begin{array}{c} F_x \\ F_y \end{array} \right\} = -\left[\begin{array}{cc} K(\varepsilon) & k(\varepsilon) \\ -k(\varepsilon) & K(\varepsilon) \end{array} \right] \left\{ \begin{array}{c} x \\ y \end{array} \right\} - \left[\begin{array}{cc} C(\varepsilon) & c(\varepsilon) \\ -c(\varepsilon) & C(\varepsilon) \end{array} \right] \left\{ \begin{array}{c} \dot{x} \\ \dot{y} \end{array} \right\} - \left[\begin{array}{cc} M(\varepsilon) & 0 \\ 0 & M(\varepsilon) \end{array} \right] \left\{ \begin{array}{c} \ddot{x} \\ \ddot{y} \end{array} \right\}, \quad (10)$$

The Muszynska's model under constant working condition is very similar to the linear dynamic model of concentric annular seal in Equation (1). The only difference is that dynamic parameters in Equation (10) are nonlinear functions of ε and can be used to describe fluid forces induced by rotor large disturbances. The expressions of nonlinear dynamic parameters can be determined based on the formulas in Equation (9), but proper empirical factors need to be chosen. In addition, the nonlinear expressions can be fitted based on the "nominal" force coefficients of concentric seal under different eccentricities (as shown in Figure 2). These "nominal" force coefficients can be computed by using CFD methods [8,27]. Rotor perturbation is the circular whirl around seal center. Usually, whirl amplitude (i.e., rotor eccentricity) is controlled within $0.1C_r$ for satisfying the linear assumption. To obtain "nominal" force coefficients under different eccentricities, the limitation is broken here, and the adopted whirl amplitudes are located in the range of $0.01C_r$–$0.8C_r$ (i.e., ε in 1%–80%).

Transient CFD simulations are conducted to solve the flow field disturbed by constant-speed circular whirls, and fluid-induced forces can be obtained. Based on these fluid forces, the "nominal" force coefficients of concentric annular seal can be evaluated [8] and used to generate the nonlinear dynamic model. With respect to the Muszynska's model, the new nonlinear model does not need any empirical factors. Theoretically, it can describe fluid forces (seal forces) induced by various rotor motions within eccentricity ratio 80%. Its reliability and suitability are discussed in Section 3.

3. Results and Discussions

3.1. Dynamic Characteristics of Different Static Eccentric Seals and Comparisons

The leakage rates and force coefficients of annular seal under different static eccentricity positions and same whirl amplitude ratio ($\Delta e/C_r = 1\%$) are computed using the numerical scheme based on transient CFD simulations (see Section 2.3). They are, respectively, shown in Figures 7–12 along with the results from San Andres' bulk flow method and Marquette's experiments.

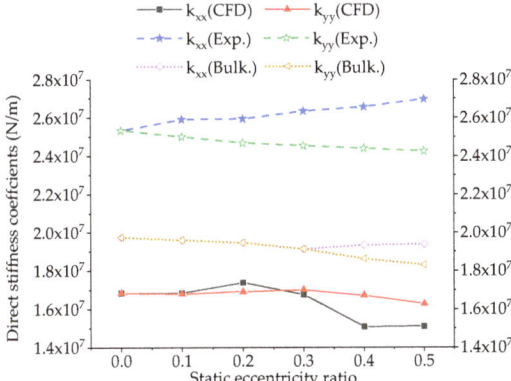

Figure 7. Direct Stiffness coefficients of eccentric annular seals.

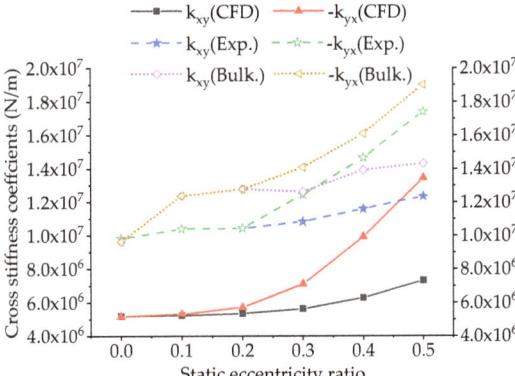

Figure 8. Cross Stiffness coefficients of eccentric annular seals.

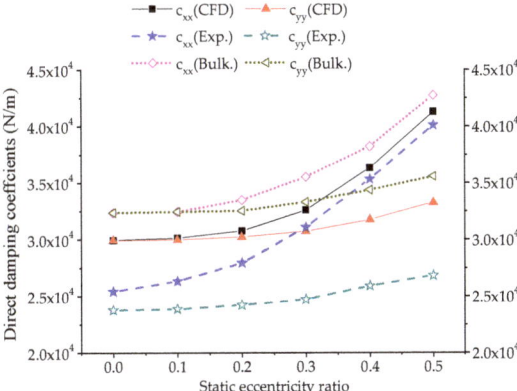

Figure 9. Direct damping coefficients of eccentric annular seals.

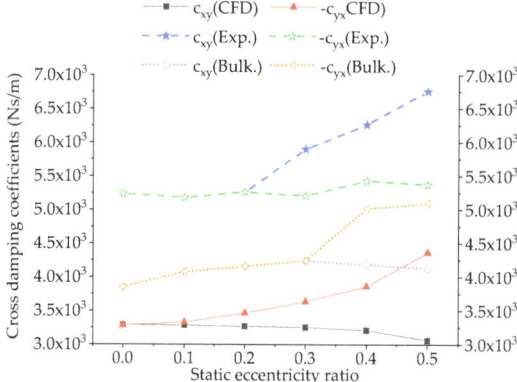

Figure 10. Cross damping coefficients of eccentric annular seals.

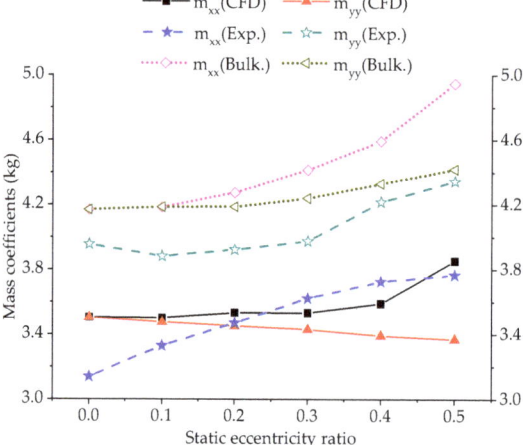

Figure 11. Mass coefficients of eccentric annular seals.

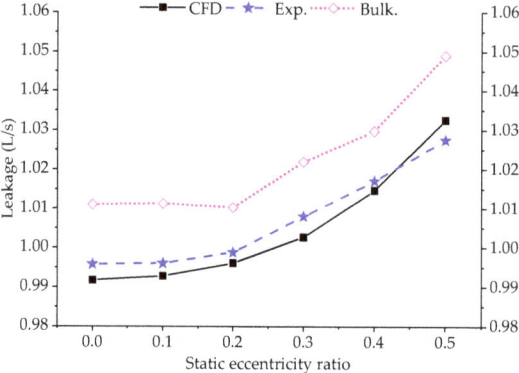

Figure 12. Leakage rates of eccentric annular seals.

In Figures 7 and 8, the measured values of direct and cross stiffness coefficients are larger than numerical values from transient CFD simulations. The test apparatus of Marquette's experiment does not include any device to control or measure the inlet swirl, and the non-uniformity of incoming flow is not considered during the testing procedure, which may lead to variations of stiffness coefficients with eccentric directions according to Wu's research [28]. The boundary condition of seal model illustrated in Marquette's research is only pressure condition for inlet and outlet. There is no geometry information or measurement of inlet, which is also mentioned by the authors as a drawback. The reason of the lower accuracy is that it is much difficult to ensure the boundary condition of CFD analysis, especially for the inlet, consistent with the Marquette's experiment. Tae Woong Ha's study [27] shows the similar difference between the stiffness results of CFD analysis and the experimental results. Despite the differences of values in Figure 7, it shows a high level of consistency between results of transient simulations and measured values as static eccentricity ratio increases.

In Figures 9 and 10, direct damping coefficients from transient simulations and bulk flow method are both a little higher than measured values, and CFD results are closer to experimental values. Cross damping coefficients from the three approaches are all close in size. As shown in Figure 11, although numerical results of mass coefficients do not coincide with measured values in variation trend, they are close in size.

Figure 12 shows the variations of seal leakage rate with the eccentricity. As rotor eccentricity increases, seal leakage rate just slightly rises. In Figure 12, leakage rates computed by transient simulations are very close to measured values, which further indicate the reliability of CFD method. This also shows that leakage rates of annular seals mainly depend on sealed differential pressures and are not sensitive to flow status at seal inlet, unlike force coefficients [28].

On the whole, rotor eccentricities change the static and dynamic characteristics of annular seals to some extent; the behaviors of annular seals should be specially considered when the rotor is far away from seal center. By comparing with experimental data, transient CFD simulations are effective in computing the static and dynamic behaviors of eccentric seals.

3.2. Effects of Disturbance Amplitude on Force Coefficients of Eccentric Annular Seal

The force coefficients of eccentric seals in Figures 7–12 are computed using a very small dynamic eccentricity (eccentricity ratio 1%). To study the effects of disturbance amplitude, two more dynamic eccentricity ratios, 5% and 10%, are separately adopted to evaluate force coefficients of eccentric seals. The results are presented in Figures 13–17 for comparisons.

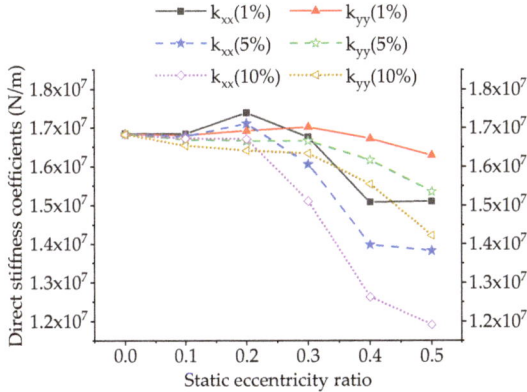

Figure 13. Direct stiffness coefficients under different dynamic eccentricities.

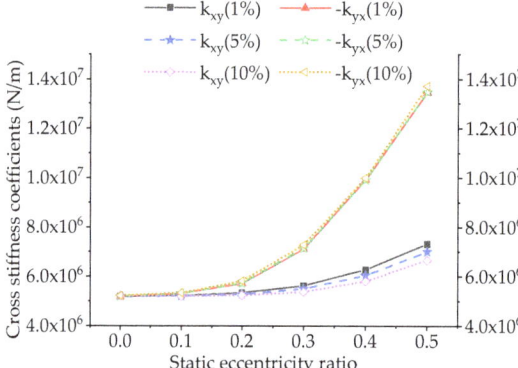

Figure 14. Cross stiffness coefficients under different dynamic eccentricities.

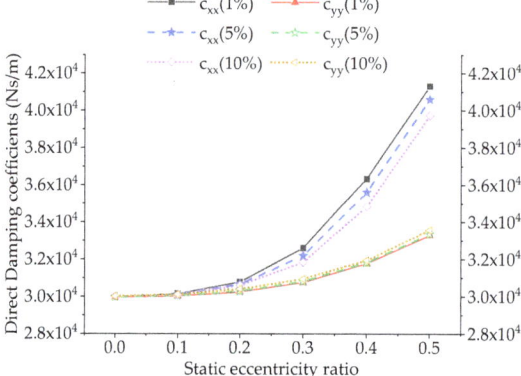

Figure 15. Direct damping coefficients under different dynamic eccentricities.

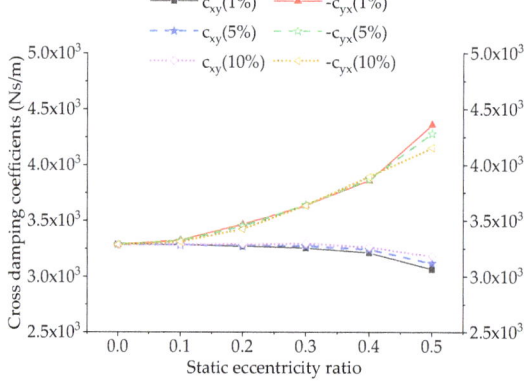

Figure 16. Cross damping coefficients under different dynamic eccentricities.

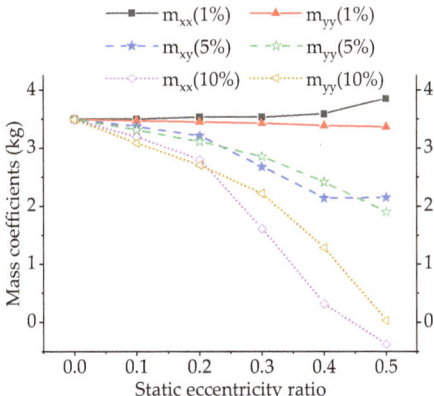

Figure 17. Mass coefficients under different dynamic eccentricities.

As shown in Figures 13–17, force coefficients based on three dynamic eccentricities are not the same. Their differences grow gradually as rotor static eccentricity increases, especially the coefficients k_{xx}, k_{yy}, k_{xy}, c_{xx}, m_{xx} and m_{yy}. For the concentric seal with static eccentricity zero, its force coefficients are generally unchanged with varying dynamic eccentricities. Namely, the dynamic characteristics of concentric annular seal are still linear when dynamic eccentricity ratio reaches 10%, which has been widely recognized by researchers [7,8,29]. However, as to the eccentric annular seal, its force coefficients tend to be sensitive to dynamic eccentricities (i.e., disturbance amplitude). As rotor static eccentricity increases, the sensitivity to rotor disturbances strengthens gradually and the linear range of seal dynamic characteristics narrows. With respect to the concentric seal, the annular seal under large eccentricity is more likely to show nonlinear characteristics.

3.3. Nonlinear Dynamic Model

As discussed above, force coefficients of eccentric seals can only be used to describe fluid forces induced by very small perturbations due to their strong sensitivity to disturbance amplitude. To express seal forces under large eccentricities or large disturbances, the nonlinear dynamic model is determined based on the thought in Section 2.3. The "nominal" force coefficients of concentric seal are computed based on different whirl amplitudes. They are presented in Figure 18 along with polynomial fitting curves. Piecewise fittings are used for direct stiffness K and cross damping c. As shown in Figure 18, the fitting effects of five force coefficients are satisfactory. The nonlinear expressions of these coefficients are listed as follows:

$$K(\varepsilon)(\times 10^6) = \begin{cases} 2.71\varepsilon^2 - 0.703\varepsilon + 16.9, & \varepsilon \leq 0.1, R^2 = 1 \\ 1.70\varepsilon^3 - 8.67\varepsilon^2 + 4.21\varepsilon + 16.5, & 0.1 < \varepsilon \leq 0.8, R^2 = 0.9911 \end{cases} \quad (11)$$

$$c(\varepsilon)(\times 10^3) = \begin{cases} -16.2\varepsilon^4 + 10.8\varepsilon^3 - 2.20\varepsilon^2 + 0.0767\varepsilon + 3.29, & \varepsilon \leq 0.4, R^2 = 0.9995 \\ -2.28 + 6.15\varepsilon^2 - 5.43\varepsilon + 4.58, & 0.4 < \varepsilon \leq 0.8, R^2 = 0.9997 \end{cases} \quad (12)$$

$$M(\varepsilon) = -5.28\varepsilon^4 + 6.63\varepsilon^3 - 3.58\varepsilon^2 + 0.36\varepsilon + 3.50, \quad \varepsilon \leq 0.8, R^2 = 0.9905 \quad (13)$$

$$k(\varepsilon)(\times 10^7) = 14.5\varepsilon^5 - 24.2\varepsilon^4 + 15.5\varepsilon^3 - 3.22\varepsilon^2 + 0.250\varepsilon + 0.517, \quad \varepsilon \leq 0.8$$
$$R^2 = 0.9999 \quad (14)$$

$$C(\varepsilon)(\times 10^4) = 10.7\varepsilon^4 - 11.6\varepsilon^3 + 5.57\varepsilon^2 - 0.682\varepsilon + 3.01, \quad \varepsilon \leq 0.8, R^2 = 0.9994 \quad (15)$$

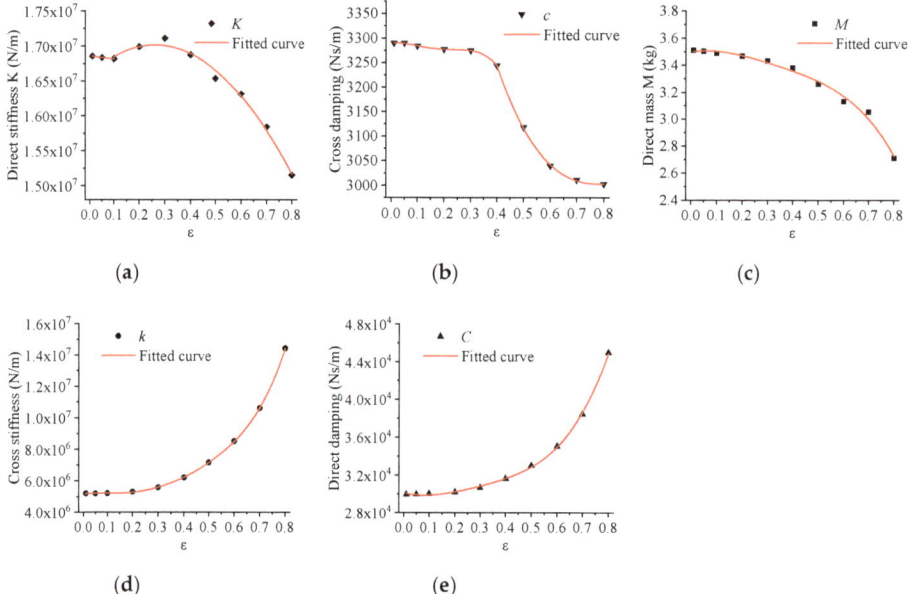

Figure 18. "Nominal" force coefficients of concentric annular seal: (**a**) direct stiffness; (**b**) cross damping; (**c**) direct mass; (**d**) cross stiffness; and (**e**) direct damping.

Substituting these nonlinear expressions into Equation (10), the nonlinear dynamic model is obtained. It will be used to evaluate fluid forces induced by rotor large disturbances along with transient CFD simulations.

4. Fluid Excitations under Large Disturbances

The fluid forces of annular seal under rotor large motions are computed by nonlinear dynamic model as well as transient CFD simulations. The suitability of nonlinear dynamic model for various rotor disturbances is investigated through comparisons with direct transient simulations. Several typical rotor motions are chosen for the investigation.

4.1. Constant-Speed Circular Whirl Around Seal Center

The rotor performs circular whirl around seal center with speed 10,200 r/min (Figure 1) and the whirl magnitude is 55% C_r. The motion equation is shown as below. Substituting Equations (11)–(16) into Equation (10), the induced fluid forces (F_x and F_y) are obtained by the nonlinear dynamic model. They are shown in Figure 19 along with the results from transient CFD simulations.

$$\begin{cases} x = e\cos(\Omega t) \\ y = e\sin(\Omega t) \end{cases} \quad (16)$$

Because the prescribed initial solution is not absolutely accurate, the transient CFD computation needs passing a period of time to eliminate its effects. Fluid forces computed at initial some time steps are not true and can be ignored. In Figure 19, fluid force curves from nonlinear dynamic model and transient CFD simulations are in good agreement. Maximum differences are only 16.5 N for both F_x and F_y, and they are mainly caused by fitting and computing errors. This indicates that the present nonlinear dynamic model is adequate to describe seal fluid excitations induced by circular whirls around seal center.

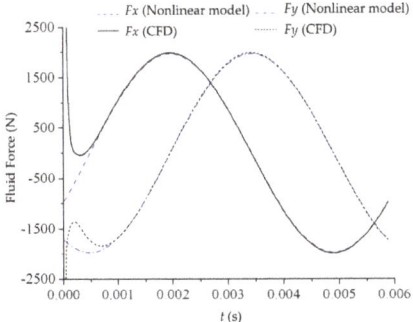

Figure 19. Fluid forces induced by the circular whirl around seal center.

4.2. Constant-Speed Circular Whirl Around Static Position

The rotor is assumed to perform circular whirl around static eccentricity position, as shown in Figure 2. The dynamic eccentricity ratio is 10%. Two whirl centers correspond to static eccentricity ratio 20% and 50%, respectively. The whirling speed is same with the rotating speed, 10,200 r/min. Rotor movements (x, y) can be expressed by Equation (3). Substituting Equations (3) and (11)–(15) into Equation (10), fluid-induced forces (F_x and F_y) are obtained by nonlinear dynamic model. They are compared with the forces from transient CFD simulations, as shown in Figures 20 and 21

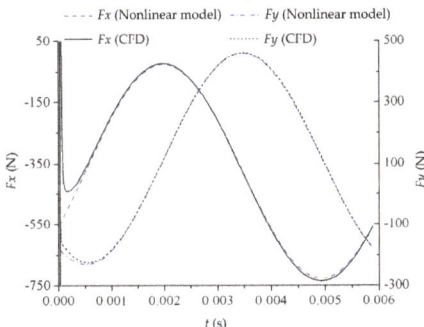

Figure 20. Fluid forces induced by the circular whirl around seal center (se/C_r 20%).

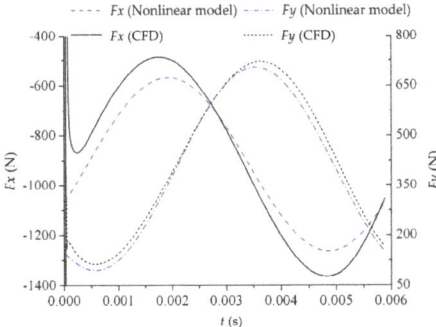

Figure 21. Fluid forces induced by the circular whirl around seal center (se/C_r 50%).

As shown in Figure 20, for the circular whirl around the static position with eccentricity ratio 20%, fluid forces from nonlinear dynamic model and transient CFD simulations agree well.

Maximum differences are 9.42 N for F_x and 4.65 N for F_y. However, when the static eccentricity ratio increases to 50%, fluid force curves obtained by these two approaches are no longer consistent, as shown in Figure 21. The maximum differences are 111 N for F_x and 36.7 N for F_y. This indicates that the nonlinear dynamic model has low reliability for rotor disturbances under large eccentricity. However, the circular whirl around concentric position is an exception (see Figure 19). The nonlinear dynamic model can deal with it well. The two rotor motions corresponding to Figures 19 and 21 are both under large eccentricities. The only difference is their motion ways. The rotor motion corresponding to Figure 19 is the whirl around seal center, and "nominal" force coefficients used for generating the nonlinear dynamic model are based on this motion way. Therefore, it is understandable that the nonlinear model applies well. From this point of view, the reason that nonlinear dynamic model does not suitable for circular whirls around large eccentricity position (as shown in Figure 21) can be assumed to be that the force coefficients (or dynamic characteristics) of annular seal under large eccentricity are related to rotor motion ways.

4.3. 1D Harmonic Shaking Motions

To validate the assumption proposed above, the circular whirl around the static position with eccentricity ratio 50% is divided into two separate 1D shaking motions, as shown in Figure 22. One is the shaking motion in X direction; the other is in Y direction. The Y direction is also the tangential direction of the concentric whirl. Namely, the Y-directional shaking is somewhat similar to the circular whirl around seal center. The expressions of two shaking motions are, respectively, presented in Equations (17) and (18). The amplitude A is 10% C_r and the harmonic frequency Ω corresponds to the speed 10,200 r/min.

$$\begin{cases} x = se + A\cos(\Omega t) \\ y = 0 \end{cases} \quad (17)$$

$$\begin{cases} x = se \\ y = A\sin(\Omega t) \end{cases} \quad (18)$$

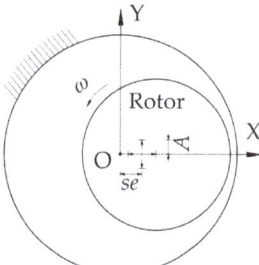

Figure 22. Two harmonic shaking motions.

According to motion equations of two harmonic shakings, fluid-induced forces can be obtained by nonlinear dynamic model and transient CFD simulations. They are shown in Figures 23 and 24. The comparison with transient CFD simulations shows that the reliability of nonlinear dynamic model is low in predicting fluid forces induced by X-directional shaking. Maximum differences of two approaches are 119 N for F_x and 30.8 N for F_y. However, as to the Y-directional shaking, the reliability of the nonlinear model is obviously improved, as shown in Figure 24. This can be attributed to the slight likeness of Y-directional shaking with the circular whirl around seal center. In Figure 20, maximum differences of two approaches are 18.5 N for F_x and 17.7 N for F_y, and they are much smaller than those in Figure 23. Namely, the nonlinear dynamic model is more applicable to rotor disturbances similar to the circular whirl around concentric position. The assumption proposed in Section 4.2 is confirmed and can explain the low reliability of nonlinear dynamic model. Under large eccentricity, the dynamic characteristics of seals are varied with the motion ways of the rotor, and the nonlinear dynamic model based on a specific motion way is incompetent in dealing with all kinds of rotor disturbances.

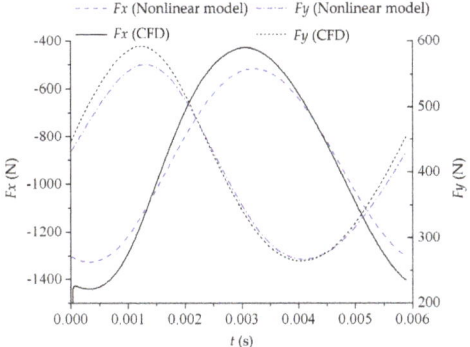

Figure 23. Fluid forces induced by X-directional shaking.

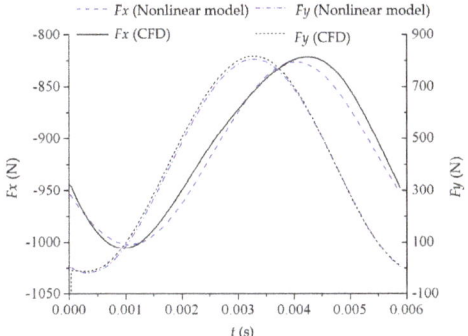

Figure 24. Fluid forces induced by Y-directional shaking.

4.4. Quasi-Circular (Spiral) Whirl

In this section, the rotor is assumed to perform the circular whirl around seal center with growing whirl radius, i.e., the spiral whirl, in order to validate the suitability of nonlinear dynamic model for quasi-circular whirls no matter eccentricity magnitudes. The whirling speed is r/min and the rotor eccentricity ratio rises linearly to 60% within six whirl periods. The whirl equation is presented in Equation (17) and the whirl orbit is shown in Figure 25.

$$\begin{cases} x = f \cdot t \cos(\Omega t) \\ y = f \cdot t \sin(\Omega t) \end{cases}, \tag{19}$$

where T is the whirl period and $f = 60\% \, C_r/(6\,T)$, indicating the eccentricity speed of the rotor.

In actual applications, the spiral whirl in Figure 25 represents the destabilizing process of the rotor. Fluid forces induced by the destabilizing whirl are obtained, respectively, by nonlinear dynamic model and transient CFD simulations. They are shown in Figure 26. The rise of rotor eccentricity with time leads to the increasing fluid force (i.e., the resultant force of F_x and F_y). The F_x and F_y from nonlinear model are in good agreement with those from transient CFD simulations. Maximum differences of two approaches are 42.7 N (i.e., relative error 2.3%) for F_x and 35.7 N (relative error 2.3%) for F_y. Namely, nonlinear dynamic model is reliable in evaluating fluid forces induced by the quasi-circular whirl around seal center without special limitations on eccentricity magnitudes.

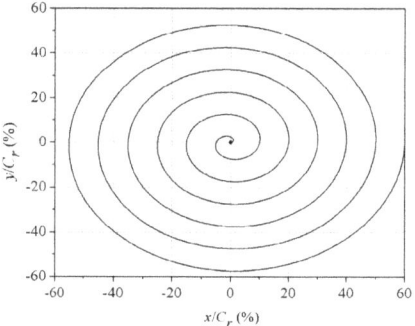

Figure 25. Spiral whirl orbit of the rotor.

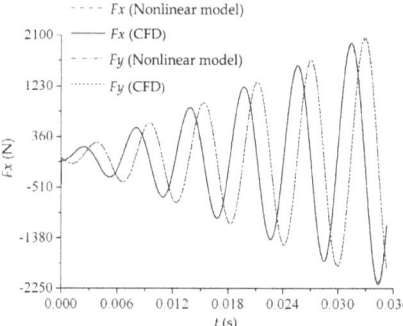

Figure 26. Fluid forces induced by the spiral whirl around seal center.

5. Conclusions

In the paper, dynamic characteristics of the annular plain liquid seal under various large rotor disturbance motions are studied using the transient CFD method based on dynamic mesh technique and nonlinear Muszynska' model.

Force coefficients and leakage rates of annular seal under different static eccentricities are evaluated. The reliability of transient CFD simulation is validated by comparing the force coefficients and leakage rates with those from the Marquette's experiment and bulk flow method. With increasing static eccentricity, these force coefficients show clearly asymmetric behavior and obvious changes. The force coefficients from transient CFD simulations show a high consistency with experimental values despite the different values of stiffness. The error sources are mainly form the influence of upstream and inlet boundary condition due to the drawback of the experimental apparatus for absent inlet control. Leakage rates computed by the CFD method fit better to measured values than those from the bulk flow method, which indicates that leakage rates are insensitive to static eccentricity.

As to the concentric annular seal, its dynamic characteristics are usually supposed to be linear (namely, constant force coefficients) when the rotor disturbance is within 10% C_r. However, this conclusion is not suitable for the eccentric annular seal, especially the seal under large static eccentricity. As rotor static eccentricity increases, the force characteristics of annular seal become more sensitive to whirl amplitude, in other words, the linear range of dynamic characteristics narrows gradually. With respect to the concentric seal, the annular seal with large eccentricity is easier to show nonlinear characteristics.

According to the Muszynska's model, a nonlinear dynamic model is presented in the paper for describing nonlinear seal forces induced by rotor large disturbances. The suitability of the nonlinear model for all kinds of rotor disturbances is studied through four forms of rotor motions.

The nonlinear dynamic model is suitable for various rotor disturbances when the rotor is under small static eccentricity (e.g., eccentricity ratio under 20%). However, when rotor static eccentricity is large (e.g., eccentricity ratio 50%), the nonlinear dynamic model based on circular whirls around eccentric center becomes incompetent and unsatisfactory. It shows high reliability only for circular or quasi-circular whirls around concentric center. This means that dynamic characteristics of annular seal under large disturbance are related to rotor motion ways. For the annular seals under large dynamic eccentricity (whirl amplitude) and rather small static eccentricity (e.g., static eccentricity ratio under 20% in this case), the nonlinear Muszynska's model performs well when dealing with large rotor disturbances. The range of capability of this nonlinear model depends on the typical parameters of annular seals. It can also explain why Muszynska's model is out of action when rotor–seal system has a large eccentricity ratio in He's research.

On the whole, dynamic characteristics of annular seals under large disturbance are very complex. They are very sensitive to various rotor motion ways including whirl amplitude and static eccentricity. For the seal with large disturbances motion of a small static eccentricity, the nonlinear Muszynska's model performs reliably, which provides a solid basis for the seal–rotor system analysis using nonlinear seal force model. The capability and limitation of nonlinear dynamic model under large disturbances needs further investigation.

Author Contributions: Conceptualization, K.Z. and D.W.; methodology, K.Z., X.J. and P.W.; validation, D.W. and P.W.; formal analysis, K.Z. and X.J.; investigation, K.Z., S.L. and P.W.; resources, D.W.; data curation, K.Z., X.J. and S.Y.; writing—original draft preparation, K.Z. and X.J.; writing—review and editing, S.L. and S.Y.; visualization, K.Z.; supervision, P.W. and D.W.; project administration, B.H. and D.W.; and funding acquisition, B.H. All authors have read and agreed to the published version of the manuscript.

Funding: This research was funded by National Natural Science Foundation of China, grant numbers 51706198 and 51839010.

Conflicts of Interest: The authors declare no conflict of interest.

Nomenclature

C: c	Direct and cross damping coefficients of concentric annular seal (N·s/m)
$c_{xx}, c_{yy}, c_{xy}, c_{yx}$	Damping coefficients of eccentric annular seal (N·s/m)
C_r	Seal clearance (mm)
e	Rotor eccentricity or whirl radius (mm]
f	Eccentricity speed of the rotor
F_x, F_y	Fluid forces in X and Y directions (N)
F_{x0}, F_{y0}	Fluid forces at equilibrium position (N)
$\Delta F_x, \Delta F_y$	The increments of fluid forces relative to F_{x0} and F_{y0} (N)
K, k	Direct and cross stiffness coefficients of concentric seal (N/m)
$k_{xx}, k_{yy}, k_{xy}, k_{yx}$	Stiffness coefficients of eccentric annular seal (N/m)
M	Direct mass coefficient of concentric annular seal (kg)
m_{xx}, m_{yy}	Direct mass coefficients of eccentric annular seal (kg)
ra	Ratio of the distance between the nodes in the clearance domain and the outer static wall to the clearance
se	Rotor static eccentricity (mm)
se/C_r	Static eccentricity ratio
t	Time (s)
x, y	The displacements of rotor center (mm)
$\Delta x, \Delta y$	Rotor displacements relative to equilibrium position (mm)
Δe	Rotor dynamic eccentricity (mm)
ε	Eccentricity ratio (e/C_r)
ω	Rotating speed of the rotor (rpm)
Ω	Whirling speed of the rotor (rpm)

References

1. Du, Q.; Zhang, D. Numerical investigation on flow characteristics and aerodynamic performance of a 1.5-stage SCO2 axial-inflow turbine with labyrinth seals. *Appl. Sci.* **2020**, *10*, 373. [CrossRef]
2. Wang, X.; Liu, M.; Kao-Walter, S.; Hu, X. Numerical Evaluation of Rotordynamic Coefficients for Compliant Foil Gas Seal. *Appl. Sci.* **2020**, *10*, 3828. [CrossRef]
3. Xia, P.; Chen, H.; Liu, Z.; Ma, W.; Yang, B. Analysis of Whirling Motion for the dynamic System of Floating Ring Seal and Rotor. *Proc. Inst. Mech. Eng. Part J J. Eng. Tribol.* **2019**, *233*, 1–15. [CrossRef]
4. Awad, H.; Parrondo, J.; González, V. Vibrations in Leaking Spherical Valves with Annular Seal. *Proceedings* **2018**, *2*, 1444. [CrossRef]
5. Zhai, L.; Wu, G.; Wei, X.; Qin, D.; Wang, L. Theoretical and Experimental Analysis for Leakage Rate and Dynamic Characteristics of Herringbone-Grooved Liquid Seals. *Proc. Inst. Mech. Eng. Part J J. Eng. Tribol.* **2015**, *229*, 849–860. [CrossRef]
6. Ikemoto, A.; Inoue, T.; Sakamoto, K.; Uchiumi, M. Nonlinear Analysis of Rotordynamic Fluid Forces in the Annular Plain Seal by Using Extended Perturbation Analysis of the Bulk-Flow Theory (Influence of Whirling Amplitude in the Case with Concentric Circular Whirl). *J. Tribol.* **2018**, *140*, 1–15. [CrossRef]
7. Gao, R.; Kirk, G. CFD Study on Stepped and Drum Balance Labyrinth Seal. *Tribol. Trans.* **2013**, *56*, 663–671. [CrossRef]
8. Untaroiu, A.; Hayrapetian, V.; Untaroiu, C.D.; Wood, H.G.; Schiavello, B.; McGuire, J. On the Dynamic Properties of Pump Liquid Seals. *J. Fluids Eng.* **2013**, *135*, 051104. [CrossRef]
9. Li, F.; Cui, B.; Zhai, L. Research on Rotordynamic Characteristics of Pump Annular Seals Based on a New Transient CFD Method. *Processes* **2020**, *8*, 227. [CrossRef]
10. Childs, D.W.; Arthur, S.P. Static Destabilizing Behavior for Gas Annular Seals at High Eccentricity Ratios. In Proceedings of the ASME Turbo Expo 2013: Turbine Technical Conference and Exposition, San Antonio, TX, USA, 3–7 June 2013; Volume 7A, pp. 1–7.
11. Nelson, C.C.; Nguyen, D.T. Analysis of Eccentric Annular Incompressible Seals: Part 1—A New Solution Using Fast Fourier Transforms for Determining Hydrodynamic Force. *J. Tribol.* **1988**, *110*, 354. [CrossRef]
12. Andres, L.A.S. Analysis of Variable Fluid Properties, Turbulent Annular Seals. *J. Tribol.* **1991**, *113*, 694–702. [CrossRef]
13. Arghir, M.; Frene, J. A Bulk-Flow Analysis of Static and Dynamic Characteristics of Eccentric Circumferentially-Grooved Liquid Annular Seals. *J. Tribol.* **2004**, *126*, 316–325. [CrossRef]
14. Venkataraman, B.; Palazzolo, A.B. Thermohydrodynamic Analysis of Eccentric Annular Seals Using Cubic Spline Interpolations©. *Tribol. Trans.* **1997**, *40*, 183–194. [CrossRef]
15. Athavale, M.M.; Hendricks, R.C. A Small Perturbation CFD Method for Calculation of Seal Rotordynamic Coefficients. *Int. J. Rotating Mach.* **1996**, *2*, 167–177. [CrossRef]
16. Wu, D.; Jiang, X.; Li, S.; Wang, L. A New Transient CFD Method for Determining the Dynamic Coefficients of Liquid Annular Seals. *J. Mech. Sci. Technol.* **2016**, *30*, 3477–3486. [CrossRef]
17. Andres, L.S.; Jeung, S.H. Orbit-Model Force Coefficients for Fluid Film Bearings: A Step beyond Linearization. *J. Eng. Gas Turbines Power* **2016**, *138*, 1–11.
18. Muszynska, A.; Bently, D.E. Frequency-swept Rotating Input Perturbation Techniques and Identification of the Fluid Force Models in Rotor/Bearing/Seal Systems and Fluid Handling Machines. *J. Sound Vib.* **1990**, *143*, 103–124. [CrossRef]
19. Li, Z.G.; Chen, Y.S. Research on 1:2 Subharmonic Resonance and Bifurcation of Nonlinear Rotor-Seal System. *Appl. Math. Mech. (English Ed.)* **2012**, *33*, 499–510. [CrossRef]
20. He, H.J.; Jing, J.P. Research into the Dynamic Coefficient of the Rotor-Seal System for Teeth-on-Stator and Teeth-on-Rotor Based on an Improved Nonlinear Seal Force Model. *J. Vib. Control* **2014**, *20*, 2288–2299. [CrossRef]
21. Marquette, O.R.; Childs, D.W.; San Andres, L. Eccentricity Effects on the Rotordynamic Coefficients of Plain Annular Seals: Theory Versus Experiment. *J. Tribol.* **1997**, *119*, 443. [CrossRef]
22. Childs, D.W.; Arthur, S.; Mehta, N.J. The Impact of Hole Depth on the Rotordynamic and Leakage Characteristics of Hole-Pattern-Stator Gas Annular Seals. *J. Eng. Gas Turbines Power* **2013**, *136*, 042501. [CrossRef]

23. Muszynska, A. Whirl and Whip—Rotor/Bearing Stability Problems. *J. Sound Vib.* **1986**, *110*, 443–462. [CrossRef]
24. Muszynska, A. Improvements in Lightly Loaded Rotor/Bearing and Rotor/Seal Models. *J. Vib. Acoust. Stress. Reliab. Des.* **1988**, *110*, 129–136. [CrossRef]
25. Li, Q.; Liu, S.; Pan, X.; Zheng, S. A New Method for Studying the 3D Transient Flow of Misaligned Journal Bearings in Flexible Rotor-Bearing Systems. *J. Zhejiang Univ. Sci. A* **2012**, *13*, 293–310. [CrossRef]
26. Childs, D.W. Dynamic Analysis of Turbulent Annular Seals Based On Hirs' Lubrication Equation. *J. Lubr. Technol.* **1983**, *105*, 429–436. [CrossRef]
27. Ha, T.W.; Choe, B.S. Numerical Simulation of Rotordynamic Coefficients for Eccentric Annular-Type-Plain-Pump Seal Using CFD Analysis. *J. Mech. Sci. Technol.* **2012**, *26*, 1043–1048. [CrossRef]
28. Wu, D.; Jiang, X.K.; Chu, N.; Wu, P.; Wang, L.Q. Numerical Simulation on Rotordynamic Characteristics of Annular Seal under Uniform and Non-Uniform Flows. *J. Cent. South Univ.* **2017**, *24*, 1889–1897. [CrossRef]
29. Yan, X.; Li, J.; Feng, Z. Investigations on the Rotordynamic Characteristics of a Hole-Pattern Seal Using Transient CFD and Periodic Circular Orbit Model. *J. Vib. Acoust.* **2011**, *133*, 041007. [CrossRef]

© 2020 by the authors. Licensee MDPI, Basel, Switzerland. This article is an open access article distributed under the terms and conditions of the Creative Commons Attribution (CC BY) license (http://creativecommons.org/licenses/by/4.0/).

Article

Measurements of Discharge through a Pump-Turbine in Both Flow Directions Using Volumetric Gauging and Pressure-Time Methods

Adam Adamkowski, Waldemar Janicki and Mariusz Lewandowski *

The Szewalski Institute of Fluid-Flow Machinery, Department of Hydropower, Polish Academy of Sciences, Fiszera 14, 80-231 Gdansk, Poland; adam.adamkowski@imp.gda.pl (A.A.); waldemar.janicki@imp.gda.pl (W.J.)
* Correspondence: mariusz.lewandowski@imp.gda.pl

Received: 13 July 2020; Accepted: 28 August 2020; Published: 9 September 2020

Abstract: This article presents the original procedures for measuring the flow rate using the pressure-time and the volumetric gauging method in the case of performance tests of a reversible hydraulic machine in either turbine or pump modes of operation. Achieving the lowest possible measurement uncertainty was one of the basic conditions during implemented machine tests. It was met using appropriate measuring procedures and high-class measuring equipment. Estimation of the uncertainty for both methods was made on the basis of an analysis consistent with current requirements in this respect. The pressure-time method was supplemented by the computational fluid dynamics (CFD) analysis that allowed reducing the impact of the pipeline complex irregular geometry on the uncertainty of flow measurement. Appropriate modifications of the calculation procedure enabled accurate measurements of flow during the pump mode of operation of the tested machine as well. The volumetric gauging method, thanks to a special procedure used for accurate measurement of the water level in the upper reservoir of the power plant, allowed measuring the discharge through the tested reversible machine with very low uncertainty. The obtained results allowed for a detailed comparison and mutual verification of the methods used to measure the discharge of the tested reversible machine in both modes of its operation. The most possible causes of obtained results are discussed and summarized in the paper. The need for further research was pointed out to explain the differences obtained and their influence on the accuracy of discharge measurement using the pressure-time method in pump operation mode.

Keywords: reversible hydraulic machines; penstocks; pressure pipelines; performance tests; flow rate measurements; volumetric gauging method; pressure-time method; water-hammer

1. Introduction

Fluid flow rate measurements are one of the most complex measurements that are carried out in engineering practice. These measurements, due to the need to maintain a very narrow uncertainty band, usually require the use of sophisticated, precise measuring equipment and the use of appropriate rigorous measurement procedures [1–3].

Liquid flow rate measurements in closed conduits or open channels of small size, for instance up to 1–2 m of diameter, are usually carried out using standard measuring devices such as measuring orifice plates, nozzles, Venturi tubes, measuring weirs, electromagnetic and ultrasound flow meters, calibrated bends, and others. Such devices are usually installed in properly prepared measuring sections of conduits or channels and provide a relatively easy and fairly accurate method of measuring the flow rate.

The situation is definitely more complicated when the liquid flow rate is to be measured in large-size conduits with a diameter of several meters or more. Measurements of the flow rate in this type of structure, usually used in hydropower, are very difficult and expensive, especially when it is necessary to ensure the lowest possible uncertainty of measurement results.

According to international standards [4–6], a few primary methods for flow rate measurement can be used in hydropower plants:

- The velocity-area method—utilizing the distribution of local liquid velocities, measured using propeller current meters (especially in cases of large conduit diameters) or Pitot tubes (for smaller diameters and flow of liquids free of sediments). The volumetric flow rate is determined by integrating the velocity distribution over the entire area of the measuring cross-section.
- The pressure-time method (often called the Gibson method [7,8])—consisting of measuring the time course of changes in the pressure difference between two cross-sections of a closed conduit while stopping the liquid stream by means of a shut-off device. The volumetric flow rate of the liquid at the initial conditions, prior to the stoppage of the flow, is determined by appropriate integration of the change in pressure difference measured during the stoppage of the flow.
- The tracer method—consisting of measurements of the passing time, or concentration, of the radioactive or non-radioactive marker (e.g., salt) between two cross-sections of a conduit. The method requires long conduits and suitable conditions for good mixing of the marker.
- The volumetric gauging method—consisting of determining the variation of the water volume stored in the headwater or tailwater reservoir on the basis of the variation of the water level in this reservoir over time.
- The acoustic method—based on vector summation of the sound wave propagation speed and the average liquid flow velocity—it uses a difference in frequencies or passing times of the emitted and received acoustic signal.

It can be concluded that the first four methods on the above list belong to the group of traditional methods, while the acoustic method is relatively new and has been recently the object of numerous research activities oriented on its improvement and validation [9,10]. This method has not yet reached proper acceptance among the specialists. Standard [4] suggests conditional use of this method, i.e., in case of mutual agreement between interested parties. Its basic advantage is that it can be used for continuous flow rate measurement and monitoring. Such a feature is impossible or extremely hard to achieve using other primary methods of measuring absolute flow rate.

The volumetric gauging method and tracer method are those which are less frequently used in hydropower engineering. The first method is characterized by a very limited application, mainly to hydropower plants with artificial reservoirs, especially in pumped-storage plants. The second one requires very long measuring segments of flow conduits and special conditions facilitating the mixing process of the injected markers (e.g., the use of turbulizers).

The velocity-area method and the pressure-time method are primary methods that are the most commonly used for measuring the flow rate in the pipelines of hydraulic turbines [3,11–13]. It is also worth noting that the velocity-area method using propeller current meters, very popular in the past, nowadays is being replaced by the pressure-time method in hydropower plants equipped with pipelines longer than 10–20 m. One of the main reasons for this is the much lower cost of preparing and performing flow measurements using the pressure-time method and the use of computer techniques in recent years, which facilitate measurements and give the possibility for getting higher accuracy of results obtained with this method.

For low and very low head power plants, particularly with short intakes of hydraulic turbines, (with no penstocks) the situation is different. Up to now, generally only the velocity-area methods, especially current meter method, are basically available in such kind of plants. Flow rate measurements with this method are still quite expensive and alternatives are being sought. One such alternative is the acoustic scintillation technique, under development [14,15].

Relative (index) methods are also used to measure the flow rate in hydropower plants. For example, the Winter–Kennedy method and the methods utilizing non-standardized pressure difference devices, non-standardized overflows (weirs), some simple variants of the acoustic method or local velocity measurement, which can be used for determining the relative value of the flow rate, or even the physical value, provided that calibration has been done on site by comparing with the results of measurements using the primary method [16–18].

As is the case concerning every measurement technique, obtaining the appropriate measurement precision is of the utmost importance. This is absolutely necessary wherever there are low uncertainty requirements, e.g., in the case of performance tests of hydraulic machines. The measurement conditions occurring in the flow systems of these machines require experience and knowledge about the flow phenomena prevailing in these systems, and also force the search for additional, unconventional techniques to ensure sufficiently low measuring uncertainty.

The bases of the analysis presented in the paper are measurement examples of flow rate through a high-head reversible hydraulic machine. Measurements were conducted using the volumetric gauging method and the pressure-time method, recommended (as mentioned earlier) by international standards [4–6] as the primary methods for discharge measurements used for performance tests (warranty, acceptance) of hydraulic turbines, pump turbines, and storage pumps. However, there are some restrictions on applicability as in the case of the pressure-time method, but work is continuously ongoing to expand and update these standards (A. Adamkowski, one of the authors of this work is a member of the PTC 18 Committee that is currently developing a revision to the ASME Performance Test Code PTC 18-2011 "Hydraulic Turbines and Pump Turbines").

The simultaneous application of the pressure-time method and the volumetric gauging method to measure discharge through the tested hydrounit with reversible Francis turbine opened the possibility of their peer verification, which was the main goal of the work.

As part of this task, the suitability of the pressure-time method for measuring flow rate in the pump mode of operation was tested. The use of this method in such conditions is not recommended by standards [4–6], therefore the obtained results are of particular importance for the development of this method.

The tests were performed ensuring a low level of measurement uncertainty. It required a number of procedures, some of which are innovative solutions, such as:

- Applying a special procedure for measuring of water level changes in the upper reservoir using the volumetric method.
- Taking into account the complex geometry of measuring section of the pipeline and its impact on flow phenomena using techniques based on computational fluid dynamics (CFD) and applying these results in the pressure-time method.

Moreover, in order to reliably estimate the measurement uncertainty of the applied methods, a procedure that takes into account general requirements concerning uncertainty assessment gathered in [19] has been proposed. This task is an attempt to systematize the problem of estimating measurement errors with the use of the analyzed methods.

Comparison concerning results obtained using chosen flow measurement methods, which is an example quite rarely seen in the literature concerning this subject, provides a unique source of knowledge about the features of the methods and the possibilities of their practical use.

2. Materials and Methods

2.1. The Research Object

Both discussed methods for discharge measurement—pressure-time and volumetric gauging method—were used for performance tests of a reversible hydrounit in a Polish pumped-storage power plant (PSPP). The considered plant is equipped with four similar reversible hydraulic machines (pump-turbines) working under the head of approximately 440 m and generating/consuming power over 120 MW.

The artificial head water reservoir is connected to pump-turbines using two underground penstocks, branching close to the inlets of the pump-turbines, prior to the shut-off ball-valves. The pump-turbines are connected via the tailrace tunnel with the surge tank to the tail water tank. A schematic diagram of the PSPP flow system with its main dimensions is shown in Figure 1.

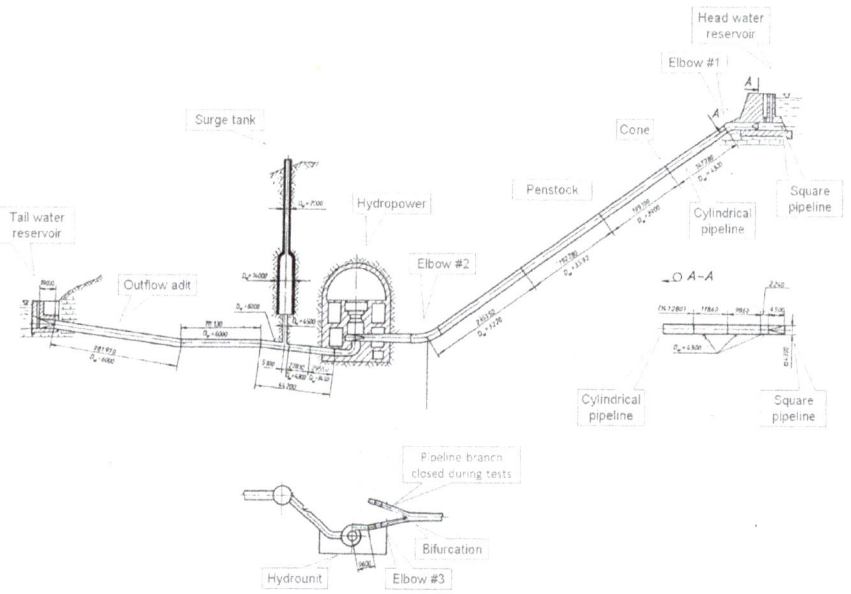

Figure 1. Flow system of the pump-turbine.

2.2. The Volumetric Gauging Method

Determining discharge using the volumetric gauging method consists in measuring the volume of water ΔV flowing through the tested hydraulic machine during time Δt. The discharge is determined using of the following formula:

$$Q_V = \frac{\Delta V}{\Delta t} = \frac{V(z(t_f)) - V(z(t_0))}{t_f - t_0} \qquad (1)$$

where ΔV [m^3] stands for measured increase or decrease in volume of water in the head water reservoir, $\Delta t = t_f - t_0$ [s]—the time interval in which the increase/decrease in water volume occurred, and z—level of water in the head reservoir.

When using the volumetric gauging method, there are several issues that can significantly affect the accuracy of the measured flow rate [11,18]. The main task is to determine the relationship between the volume and the water level of the reservoir $V(z)$. This relationship should be determined on the basis of precise reservoir geometry measurements (particularly useful for artificial reservoirs) or accurate bathymetric scanning. The issue of determining the reservoir volume also involves measuring the water level in this reservoir.

In common situations, transmitters designed to control this level usually included in the power plant equipment are not suitable for use in the volumetric gauging method as they have a wide measuring range and low accuracy class. In order to achieve low uncertainty of measurements, the change in the water level in the reservoir should be determined using special methods. The schematic diagram of the proposed method is shown in Figure 2. Its most important element is measuring the increase in water level Δz in the power plant reservoir by means of a precise transducer measuring the pressure difference in the reservoir and a constant pressure level set using small auxiliary tank, hung at the appropriate height. The configuration of such an installation should ensure the possibility of carrying out an approximately one-hour measurement at a fixed operating point of the tested hydrounit.

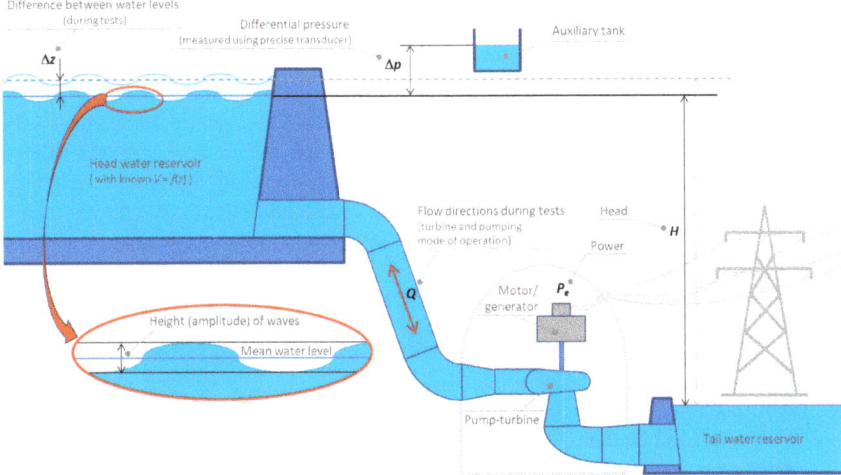

Figure 2. The water level change measurement technique used in the volumetric gauging method.

The proposed method allows for the significant reduction of the measurement uncertainty giving an additional possibility for taking into account the unfavorable phenomenon of water surface waving occurring during the tests. This phenomenon can affect the results of the measured flow rate in the most significant way. Traditional ways for measuring the water level used in the volumetric gauging method cannot ensure required accuracy of discharge measurements. Using a measuring system with appropriate characteristics and applying linear regression for the results of measuring the level of water in the reservoir leads to eliminate the effect of water waving on measurement results (Figure 3). It's worth pointing out that it is very important to base the regression line on the boundaries selected at the extreme points of the peaks or valleys of the differential pressure signal. This is a prerequisite for obtaining the correct final flow measurement results.

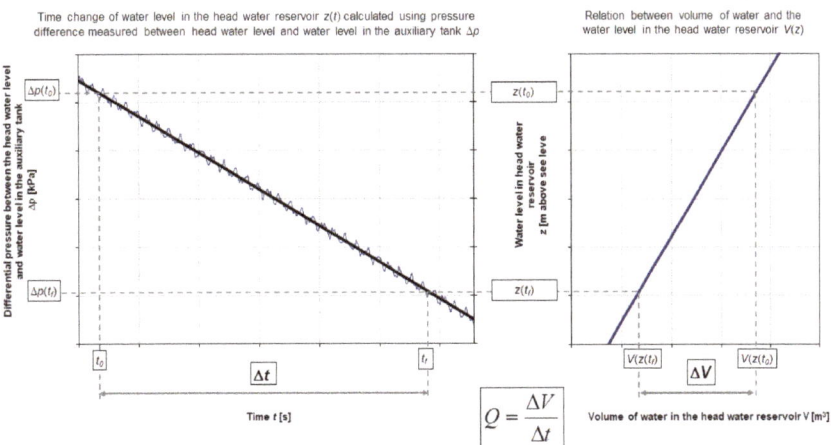

Figure 3. The volumetric gauging method—basic rules of flow rate determination.

Owing to the solutions applied, a very narrow uncertainty range was possible to achieve and the results of its estimation are presented in the next chapter of the paper. The uncertainties (standard and expended) were estimated according to the procedure described in Appendix B that was developed basing on the general recommendations presented in [19].

2.3. The Pressure-Time Method

2.3.1. Basic Information

The pressure-time method is based on the relationship between flow rate at steady state conditions and pressure-time change occurring in the pipeline during cutting off the flow [7,8]. The value of Q_0 indicating the discharge at initial liquid flow conditions is calculated using the definite integral over a time interval in which the flow varies from initial conditions to conditions after the flow is completely shut off [4,6,11]:

$$Q_0 = \frac{1}{\rho F} \int_{t_0}^{t_f} (\Delta p(t) + \Delta p_d(t) + \Delta P_r(t)) dt + Q_f \qquad (2)$$

where:

ρ is the density of a liquid,
t_0 and t_f are the initial and final time-limits of integration, respectively,
Q_f is the discharge under final steady-state conditions (after complete closing of the shut-off device) due to the leakage through the closed shut-off device,
Δp is the difference in pressures measured between the pipeline measuring cross-sections B-B and A-A, which geometrical centers are at level z_A and z_B, respectively (Figure 4):

$$\Delta p = p_B + \rho g z_B - p_A - \rho g z_A \qquad (3)$$

Δp_d is the difference in dynamic pressures between the pipeline measuring cross-sections with area of each section equal A_A and A_B:

$$\Delta p_d = \alpha_2 \frac{\rho Q^2}{2A_B^2} - \alpha_1 \frac{\rho Q^2}{2A_A^2} \qquad (4)$$

where:

α_1, α_2 are the kinetic energy correction factors for A-A and B-B sections (the value of the kinetic energy correction factor for fully developed turbulent flow in the pipeline, dependent on *Re* number is within the limits from 1.03 to 1.11 [20,21]);
ΔP_r is the pressure loss caused by hydraulic resistance in pipeline between the measurement cross-sections—quantity calculated as proportional to the square of flow rate (accounting for its direction):

$$\Delta P_r = C_r \cdot Q|Q| \qquad (5)$$

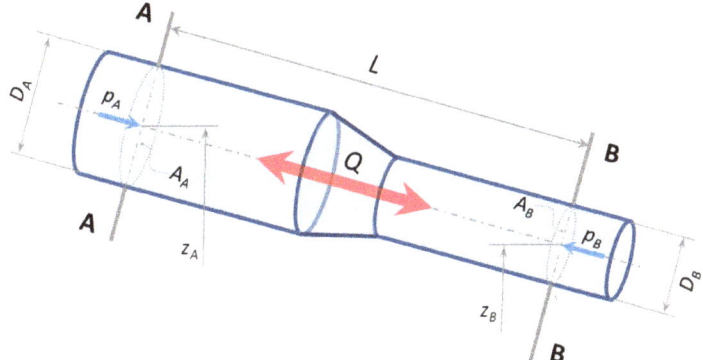

Figure 4. Scheme of the penstock measuring section with markings.

One of the most important parameters in Formula (2) is the *F* factor. Its value depends on the geometry of the pipeline flow system between the pressure measurement cross-sections. The following formula can be used to calculate the *F* factor in case of the pipeline segment with length *L* and *j* sub-segments with different sizes:

$$F = \int_0^L \frac{dx}{A(x)} = \sum_{j=1}^{j=J} \frac{\Delta x_j}{A_j}, \quad \text{with} \sum_{j=1}^{j=J} \Delta x_j = L \tag{6}$$

where Δx_j and A_j indicate the length and internal cross-sectional area of the *j*-th sub-segment, respectively. As shown in Equation (2), the pressure loss, ΔP_r, representing hydraulic resistance and the dynamic pressure difference, Δp_d, should be separated from the pressure difference measured between the pipeline measurement cross-sections, Δp. In total, the integral expression of Equation (2) defines the pressure difference resulting from the inertia force of the mass of liquid retained in the pipeline measuring section (segment). The values of ΔP_r and Δp_d can be calculated with good accuracy using their dependence on the square of the flow rate in the forms written in Equation (4) and (5).

Measurements made using the pressure-time method, as was the case concerning the volumetric gauging method, were carried out for both flow directions through a reversible machine equipped with Francis type runner. Measuring flow rate in the pump direction requires appropriate modifications of the pressure-time method to the calculation procedures described in the standards, which were postulated by the authors in earlier publications [11,22,23] and which resulted with formula in Equation (5) (introducing term $Q|Q|$ instead of Q^2).

A comprehensive discussion of some problems related to the computational procedures in the pressure-time method is provided in standards [4,6] as well as in monograph [11]. A description of some important problems related to the use of the pressure-time method for measuring flow rate in hydropower plants can also be found in publications [22–29]. Calculation of friction losses according to the quasi-stationary hypothesis is consistent with the conclusions presented in [30]. It was proved that the modelling of unsteady friction losses has little effect on the course of water hammer in its initial time-phase that is taken into account in the pressure-time method. Nevertheless, it should be emphasized that including the transient nature of friction losses into the calculation method, under certain circumstances, may improve predictions of the pressure-time method as described in [27–29].

Several variants of the pressure-time method are used in practice. They differ mainly in methods of measuring the pressure differences between pipeline measurement cross-sections. In the considered case, the pressure-time method was used in the variant based on measuring the pressure changes at the cross-section of the pump-turbine spiral case outlet/inlet and relating these changes to the pressure exerted by the water column from the head water reservoir. This variant requires the determination of the geometric factor *F* accounting the entire penstock of the tested machine, starting from the inlet section and ending with the outlet/inlet cross-section of the spiral case.

The recommendations of the standards [4–6] allow the use of the *F* factor for straight-axis measuring pipelines of variable diameter (according to the Formula (6), taking into account their geometry). However, in the case of more complex changes in the geometry occurring in the measuring section of the pipeline (changes in the shape of the flow section, changes in the direction of the pipeline axis or branches), there is a need to take into account the influence of these changes on the flow conditions.

Irregular parts (components) of the penstock cause flow disturbances in the form of non-uniform water velocity distribution. This should be taken into account in order to ensure better accuracy of discharge measurement. In the considered case, except for the straight pipe sections with constant internal diameters, the penstock has three elbows (two vertical and one horizontal), a number of short conical sections connecting pipes of different diameters, and two short branches, where one branch remained closed during the tests. In addition, the square cross-section as well as transition section from square to the circular cross-section in the highest part of the penstock had to be taken into consideration. In the previously published work [24], authors presented the procedure, based on CFD, used for correction of *F*-factor calculated in case of penstocks with elbows. The assumption of equal kinetic energy resulting from the simulated and the uniform water flow velocity distributions in the same flow parts of the penstock was the main, except mass conservation law, theoretical basis for this procedure. In this work, using CFD, an extended procedure was developed and applied to correct the value of the *F*-factor for the above-mentioned irregular components of the penstock under consideration. The procedure is presented in detail in Appendix A. The selected results of CFD calculations and the *F*-factor correction for the studied case are presented later in this paper.

2.3.2. CFD Based Correction of Penstock Geometrical Factor

The *NUMECA/Hexpress* commercial software [31] was used for generating the computational grid representing the penstock geometry (Figure 5). The unstructured grids consisted of hexahedral elements.

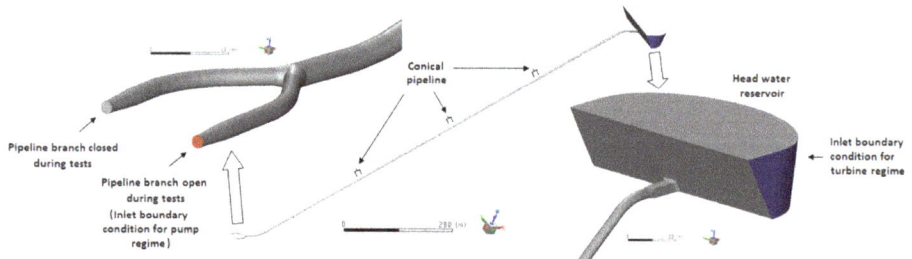

Figure 5. Geometry of hydraulic system (calculation domain): head water reservoir (hydraulic diameter of virtual half-cylindrical inlet 30 m) → square pipeline (4.3 × 4.3 m) → cylindrical pipe (4.3 m) → conical pipe (4.3/3.9 m) → cylindrical pipe (3.9 m) → conical pipe (3.9/3.6 m) → cylindrical pipe (3.6 m) → conical pipe (3.6/3.2 m) → cylindrical pipe (3.2 m) → pipe branch for two pump-turbines (2.276 m) → conical pipe (2.276/1.654 m) → outlet cylindrical pipe (1.654 m)).

For flow calculations, *ANSYS/Fluent* commercial software was used [32]. The flow was simulated by solving the steady-state Reynolds Average Navier-Stokes (RANS) equations with the k-ω SST turbulence model. Many studies demonstrate the great usefulness of this turbulence model in the calculation of industrial flow systems [33,34]. It's commonly known that the k-ω SST model integrates advantages of both k- turbulence model and standard k-ω turbulence model [35].

The second-order upwind discretization was used with the SIMPLE scheme of pressure-velocity coupling. Non-dimensional distance from wall Y^+ was assumed to be in range 1 to 5 according to the used turbulence model. Initialization of calculation was done from all zones limiting the computational domain. The calculations were conducted until all of the residuals (continuity residual, velocity components, turbulent kinetic energy, and specific rate of dissipation) reached values less than 0.001. The parameters for a closure of turbulence model were hydraulic diameter and turbulence intensity. First of them was calculated using formula: $D_h = 4A/P$ [m], in which A is the area and P is the perimeter (hydraulic diameter was 1.654 m at inlet/outlet of lower part the penstock and 30 m at inlet/outlet of upper part of the penstock). The second parameter was calculated using the formula [32]: $I = 0.16\,Re^{(-1/8)}$ in which Re is Reynolds number at inlet or outlet cross-section. At the outlet of the measuring section, constant static pressure was assumed for all calculation cases. The free surface of the reservoir was assumed as a no-slip boundary condition.

The CFD calculations were conducted for four discharge values (20, 25, 30, and 35 m^3/s) in the turbine operation modes and for two discharge values (26 and 28 m^3/s) in the pump operation modes. The sample of calculation results in the form of water velocity distributions in cross-sections for three chosen flow parts of the penstock were presented in Figures 6–8 for both flow directions, for analyzed discharge of 35 m^3/s in turbine regime, and 28 m^3/s in pump regime.

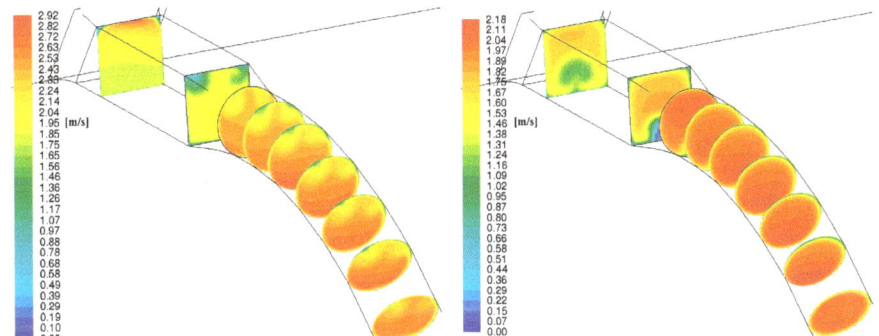

Figure 6. The water velocity contours in the penstock inlet part with first elbow for discharge of $Q = 35$ m^3/s in turbine regime (left view) and for discharge of $Q = 28$ m^3/s in pump regime (right view).

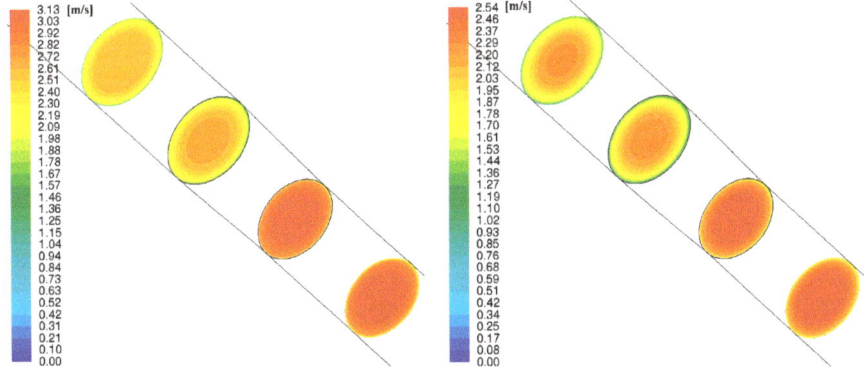

Figure 7. The water velocity contours in the penstock part containing the cone pipe for discharge of $Q = 35$ m^3/s in turbine regime (left view) and for discharge of $Q = 28$ m^3/s in pump regime (right view).

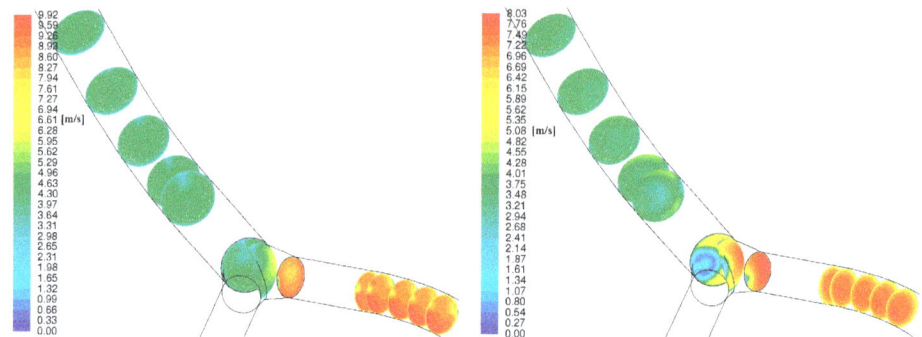

Figure 8. The water velocity contours in the penstock part containing the pipe branch for discharge of $Q = 35$ m^3/s in turbine regime (left view) and for discharge of $Q = 28$ m^3/s in pump regime (right view).

The CFD simulation results received for the analyzed penstock flow parts (Figures 6–8) can be characterized as follows:

- The water velocity distributions inside the area of the penstock inflow/outflow (in the cross-sections near the head water reservoir) are different for the turbine and pump operation modes.
- The largest irregular flow occurs in the penstock branch and despite the fact that it only affects the velocity distribution locally, the propagation of these irregularities in the direction of the water flow is clearly more visible than in the opposite direction. The intensity of the flow disturbance decreases rapidly with distance. On the other hand, the smallest flow irregularities in the penstock are induced by the existing short tapered pipe sections.
- The velocity distributions in the elbows also differ depending on the direction of flow, which is quite obvious—the elbows induce disturbances in the flow pattern, which propagate to the next penstock components with decreasing intensity. For example, for the turbine operation mode the flow achieving the elbow #2 is almost uniform because of the long straight section of pipe before this elbow (looking in turbine flow direction), while in pump operation mode, a similar effect takes place in elbow #1.

The CFD results taking account flow irregularities induced in the penstock were used to calculate the equivalent factor F_e according to the original procedure presented in Appendix A.

The deviation factor, Δf, representing a relative difference between the equivalent penstock factor, F_e, (obtained using CFD calculations) and the penstock geometrical factor, F, was included in discharge determination according to the pressure-time method. This factor is calculated as follows:

$$\Delta f = \frac{F_e - F}{F} \qquad (7)$$

The values of quantity, Δf, determined for chosen discharge values for both flow directions are presented in Table 1. It can be stated that Δf is kept almost constant for both flow directions separately. However, it presents different level for both turbine and pump operational modes: the average value of Δf is about +0.13% and about +0.77% for turbine and pump modes of operation, respectively. These values were used as correction quantities of the geometrical factor F calculated based only on the geometry of the entire penstock.

Table 1. The relative differences of F-factor, Δf, determined for the entire penstock for the assumed discharge values in the both machine operation modes.

Machine Operation Mode	Discharge, Q_0	Relative Difference of F-Factor, Δf
-	m^3/s	%
Turbine operation mode	20	0.15
	25	0.14
	30	0.13
	35	0.11
Pump operation mode	26	0.77
	28	0.77

2.3.3. Flow Rate Measurement, Uncertainty

The values of flow rate (discharge) were calculated based on the difference of pressures measured between the inlet/outlet cross-section of the tested pump-turbine (cross-section (B-B)) and the reservoir (cross-section (A-A)) and accounting for F_e factor obtained using CFD. Calculations were carried out using the computer program *GIB-ADAM* that has been tested and successfully verified on many occasions related to the implementation of laboratory tests as well as e.g., efficiency tests in hydropower plants [11]. Examples of the results measured or calculated for both modes of operation of the pump-turbine under investigation are shown in Figure 9. Measurements begin ca. 30–40 s before shut-off device start closing and end about 30–60 s after its complete closure or after extinction of the free pressure oscillation remaining in the flow system after the flow cut off. The time of closing the wicket gates of the tested machine was about 25 s and 20 s during turbine and pumping mode of operation, respectively. These time intervals were (8–10) times longer than the pipeline pressure wave period of about 2.5 s. Closing of the wicket gates was carried out in two stages in both modes—the faster stage followed by slower one. The reason for this common method of closing the wicket gates is to maintain the safety of the hydraulic system by preventing excessive pressure oscillations caused by too rapid shut-off of the flow, especially in the final phase of wicket gates closing.

The analysis of the influence of the above-mentioned and other parameters on the uncertainty of the results of the flow rate measurement with the applied method is presented in Appendix C.

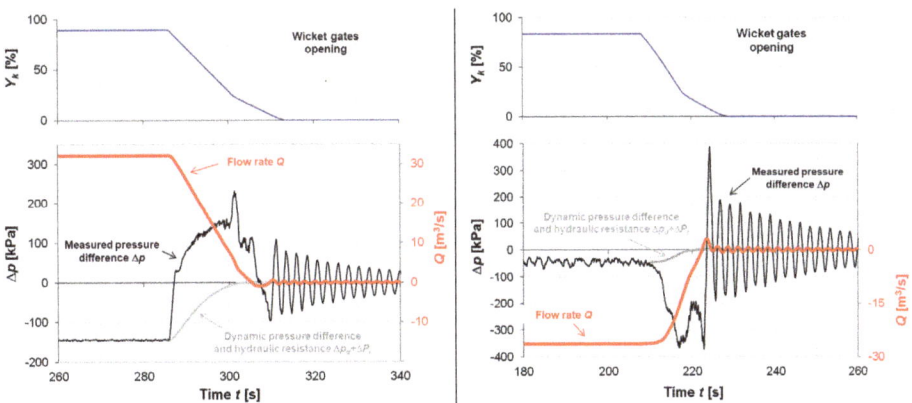

Figure 9. Examples of measured values of wicket gates opening and pressure difference and discharge through the machine calculated using the pressure time method. Left view: turbine operation mode, right view: pump operation mode.

3. Results and Discussion

The volumetric gauging method of flow measurement, due to the high requirements that must be met, is difficult to apply when testing real objects. For this reason, the examples of its practical application are quite rarely published. More valuable are the results presented in this paper, which were obtained for a pumped-storage power plant equipped with an artificial head water reservoir with known geometric characteristics. This made it possible to use the volumetric gauging method to measure the flow rate through the tested reversible hydrounit. The required narrow uncertainty band was obtained by supplementing the method with a special solution for accurate measurement of the water level change in the reservoir that also allowed including the impact of waves, as well as the amount of rainfall and leaks during measurements. It should be emphasized that measuring the upper water level in a standard way usually cannot ensure sufficient accuracy of the volumetric gauging method used for measuring flow in hydroelectric power plants.

The application of the pressure-time method to measure the flow rate in a real flow system with complex geometry additionally requires the use of an innovative calculation methodology to determine the F-factor—one of the critical parameters for maintaining a sufficiently narrow measurement uncertainty band. Owing to this factor, the geometrical characteristics of a pipeline measuring segment and impact of its flow elements on flow irregularities are taken into account. Disregarding changes in flow velocity profiles resulting from the variable shapes of pipeline elements leads to an increase in the inaccuracy of measurement using the pressure-time method, which cannot be corrected only by improving the modeling of friction losses in these elements, as discussed in [27–29] or by improving the computational model [22,28]. In addition, increasing the accuracy of estimation of the leakage rate through closed-flow shut-off devices is not enough [26]. In order to take into account changes in liquid velocity profiles in pipeline bends, the authors proposed a special calculation procedure (described in [24]) using CFD analysis for correction of the F factor. Verification of this procedure based on the analyzed examples confirmed that its application significantly increases the measurement accuracy of the pressure-time method. In this paper, the procedure based on CFD has been extended and used for piping systems with complex geometry (including curves, branches, conical elements, and inlets with changes in the shape of the flow section). In contrast to such a solution, the standard application of the pressure-time method does not provide the required uncertainty of flow rate measurement results. This innovative procedure provides the basis for using the pressure-time method in case of geometrically complex pipelines, and not only in turbine mode of operation, but also in the pump flow conditions of the tested reversible machine.

The uncertainties (standard and expanded) of the flow rate measurement results using both methods under consideration were as follows:

- Volumetric gauging method: standard and extended uncertainties were not greater than +/−0.38% and +/−0.76%, respectively, for all measured flow rates—Appendix B;
- Pressure-time method: standard and extended uncertainties were not greater than +/−1.0% and +/−1.1%, respectively, for all measured flow rates—Appendix C.

3.1. Turbine Operation Mode

Because it was not possible to measure water discharge through the tested machine using both methods (volumetric gauging and pressure-time methods) simultaneously, the comparison of the results measured for the turbine operation mode was performed using the Winter–Kennedy method. According to this method, the measurement of discharge is based on the relationship between the discharge, Q, and the difference of pressures, Δp_{wk}, between the outer and the inner side of a spiral case of the machine under test:

$$Q = k \Delta p_{wk}^n \tag{8}$$

where k and n are constant coefficients experimentally determined during the calibration process. A value of the exponent, n, was assumed from the theory as equal to 0.5. Such assumption insignificantly influenced the measuring results as was proven in [17] and it is negligible for purposes of comparison presented in this paper. For the tested machine, the values of k coefficient were determined independently on the basis of discharge measurement conducted using the volumetric gauging and the pressure-time methods—in Figure 10. The difference between k coefficient values obtained using these two different methods is very small, only about 0.2%. It should be emphasized that for the penstock geometric factor, F, used in the pressure-time method without the Δf correction, the difference in the value of the k coefficient is slightly larger and amounts to approximately 0.33%. Although in the case under consideration the difference is not large, taking into account the various pipeline geometries that encounter in practice, it is recommended to support the pressure-time method by means of CFD analysis in the case of measuring sections of pipelines with irregular elements causing disturbances in the flow.

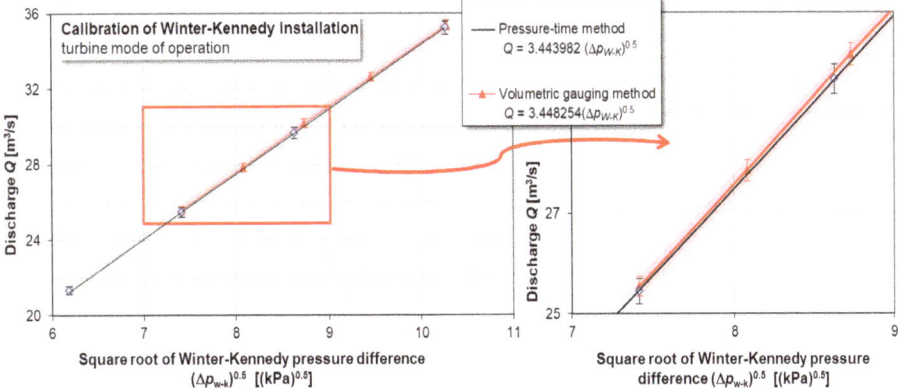

Figure 10. Turbine operation mode of the tested hydrounit: Comparison of the volumetric measurement method and the pressure-time method based on the results of calibration of the technical installation of the Winter–Kennedy method, with which the tested pump-turbine was equipped.

3.2. Pumping Operation Mode

The use of the Winter–Kennedy method for measuring flow rate in the pump mode of operation of hydraulic machines is not recommended by the standards [4–6]. This made it impossible to compare the pressure-time and volumetric gauging methods in a manner analogous to that used for turbine mode of operation, i.e., based on the results of simultaneous flow measurements. The comparison of results obtained using the analyzed methods was made by referring them to the head of the plant—Figure 11. The analysis also covered the impact of the penstock geometry irregularities on the results obtained using the pressure-time method. The differences between the discharge results obtained from the volumetric gauging method and pressure-time method were from −0.16% to +0.58% for lower (426 m) and higher head (439 m), respectively. Without correction of F geometrical factors, the differences were much greater—their values were +0.6% and +1.35%, correspondingly.

The comparison shows that the differences between the results obtained using the analyzed methods are much larger for pump mode of operation than for turbine mode of operation. At this stage of research, the causes of such observations cannot be clearly explained. Measurement of the hydraulic machine discharge using the pressure-time method is much more difficult to perform in pump operation than in turbine operation. This fact may suggest the reasons for this comparison results. This may also be the main reason why current standards do not recommend using this method in pump mode of operation of tested machines. However, it should be emphasized that the differences obtained in the analyzed case are still within the range of the measurement uncertainty characterizing the compared methods.

In addition, it should be emphasized that between the pump and turbine modes, in addition to obvious differences, there are those that can significantly affect the results obtained using the pressure-time method:

- Shutoff during pumping is characterized by much more irregular pressure changes than when cutting off flow during turbine mode of operation. This is related to the fact that during turbine operation, the flow was cut off while maintaining the generator connected to the network, while in pump operation, complete flow cut-off with the motor connected to the network was unacceptable.
- At the final stage of closing the machine's wicket gates, during pump operation, there is a short change in the direction of fluid flow—from the pump to the turbine direction;
- Due to the direction of flow, it should be noted that the pump operation mode, in contrast to the turbine operation mode, induces pressure pulsations with a much higher level, which propagate along the pipeline and have a direct impact on the measured pressure difference.
- The flow in the pump direction takes place along the expanding flow elements of the pipeline (diffusers), which is the reason for greater hydraulic losses (pressure losses occur due to local losses caused by greater turbulence in the boundary layers) and as a result requires greater correction of the F geometrical factor compared to turbine flow (and flow through the confusors).

Precise identification of how these differences may affect the final accuracy of flow measurement results obtained with the pressure-time method in the pump mode of operation of the hydraulic machines requires thorough professional testing and analysis. Currently, there is insufficient data on this topic, which hinders the extension of the applicability of this method and can also lead to excessive simplifications resulting in increased measurement uncertainty.

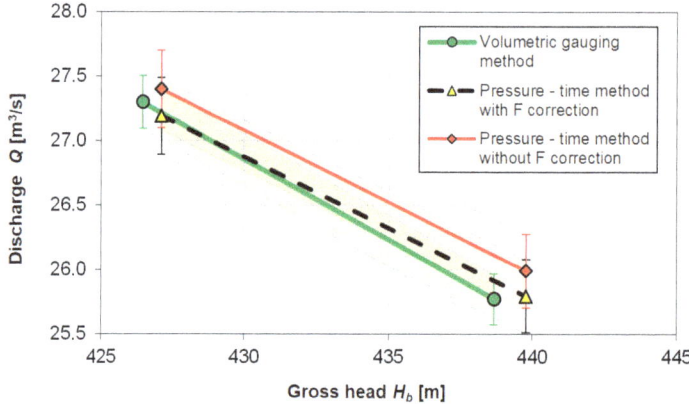

Figure 11. Pump operation mode of the tested hydrounit: Comparison of the discharges measured by the volumetric gauging method and the pressure-time method.

4. Conclusions

The paper presents experiences concerning the use of the volumetric gauging method and the pressure-time method for measuring the water discharge through a reversible hydraulic machine at a pumped storage power plant. Research using these methods concerned both turbine and pump mode of operation of the tested machine. As part of the research, new original procedures have been used aimed at significant reduction of the measurement uncertainty.

In the case analyzed in the article by appropriate treatment consisting of the use of high-quality transducers, with the use of appropriate measurement techniques and procedures supporting the measurements of the flow rate with the use of both methods, a satisfactorily low measurement uncertainty was achieved.

The use of a high-class transducer measuring the pressure difference between the upper reservoir and the auxiliary tank in the volumetric gauging method, as well as the original method of analysis of the measured pressure difference, allowed to increase the accuracy of measuring the change in water volume over time significantly, and also allowed us to take into account water waving, which, when ignored, can meaningly distort measurements.

The pressure-time method, which required taking into account the complex geometry of the pipeline connected to the tested hydrounit, was supported by CFD analysis of flow in the area of geometric irregularities (inlet, diameter changes, elbows, changes in cross-sectional shape). The original procedure using the results of this analysis provided the information necessary to introduce appropriate adjustments (correction) to the geometric factor F, which in turn, contributed to a significant reduction in the flow rate measurement uncertainty.

In contrast to the very good compliance of the results of discharge measurements obtained with the analyzed methods for the turbine operation of the tested machine (differences in the range of ±0.2%), in the case of pump operation, larger differences between the results were observed; however, they were still in the uncertainty band for measuring each of these methods independently (differences from −0.16% to +0.58%). At this stage, it is difficult to clearly explain these observations. The authors point out the differences in the course of flow phenomena during shut-off in turbine and pumping operation carried out as part of tests executed using the pressure-time method. There is a need for further research to explain the reasons of the obtained differences and their influence on the accuracy of discharge measurement using the pressure-time method in pump operation mode.

It is worth emphasizing the positive effect achieved by using the CFD procedure to support the pressure-time method. A measure of this effect is the reduction of the differences between the measurement results obtained using the volumetric gauging method and the pressure-time method. In the turbine operation mode, the CFD-based correction of the F factor resulted in a 1.5-fold increase in the convergence of the compared results. In the case of pumping mode of operation, the convergence has improved several times (more than 2- to almost 5-fold, depending on the point of operation). This result proves the correctness of the assumptions made when using the CFD procedure and using its results for the pressure-time method of measuring the flow.

Particularly noteworthy are the results obtained for the pumping mode of operation, for which the use of the pressure-time method is not recommended by the standards. The comparison and consistency of these results with the results obtained with the volumetric gauging method confirmed the correctness of the assumptions underlying the proposed and applied modifications to the calculation procedure of the pressure-time method. This includes also the correct consideration of the temporary change in the flow direction occurring during its cutting off in the pumping mode of operation. Such experience from using this method in practice can help working out the relevant changes in the standards leading to the recommendation of the pressure-time method also for the pumping mode of reversible hydraulic machine operation.

Author Contributions: Conceptualization, A.A.; Data curation, W.J. and M.L.; Formal analysis, A.A.; Investigation, W.J. and M.L.; Methodology, W.J.; Software, W.J.; Supervision, A.A.; Validation, W.J. and M.L.; Visualization, M.L.; Writing—original draft, W.J. and M.L.; Writing—review & editing, A.A. All authors have read and agreed to the published version of the manuscript.

Funding: This research was financed from the statutory funds of The Szewalski Institute of Fluid Flow Machinery.

Conflicts of Interest: The authors declare no conflict of interest.

Nomenclature

A	area; [m^2],
D	internal diameter of a pipeline; [m],
e_k	kinetic energy per unit of mass (specific kinetic energy); [J/kg],
F	geometrical factor of a pipeline; [m^{-1}],
L, l	pipeline length; [m],

$\dot{m}$	mass flow rate; [kg/s],
p	pressure; [Pa],
Q	volumetric flow rate; [m³/s],
t	time; [s],
u	absolute standard uncertainty,
V	water volume [m³] or water flow velocity; [m/s],
x	distance along pipeline axis; [m],
x, y, z	coordinates; [m],
Y	turbine guide vane opening; [%],
Δf	relative deviation factor of F factor; [%],
ρ	liquid density; [kg/m³],
δ	relative standard uncertainty [%].

Indexes

d	dynamic pressure value,
e	equivalent value,
f	final value
I	total number of numerical cross-sections in a considered pipeline; [-],
J	total number of sub-segments with different dimensions (geometry) in a considered pipeline; [-],
m	average (mean) value,
r	hydraulic resistance
0	initial value.

Appendix A. Procedure for Calculating Equivalent Geometrical F Factor in The Pressure-Time Method for Pipelines with Irregular Shape Sections of the on the Basis of CFD Analysis

The determination of the geometrical F-factor from Equation (3) is fully acceptable for straight measuring sections of pipelines where there are no flow irregularities. This equation does not take into account changes in the flow velocity profiles in irregularly shaped pipeline elements, such as elbows, bifurcations, cones, pipe inlets, etc. Therefore, the authors of this paper recommend a special calculation procedure to consider the effect of these irregular shaped flow elements on the pressure-time measurement results.

The procedure shown below is an extension of the procedure for the curved pipe sections published in [24].

Step 1: Determination of the geometry of the considered pipeline flow system, discharge Q_j, etc., and the computational control flow space—Figure A1.

Step 2: Division of the computational control flow space into I numerical elements using cross-sections normal to the axis of the considered i-th ($i = 1, 2, ..., I$) pipe elements.

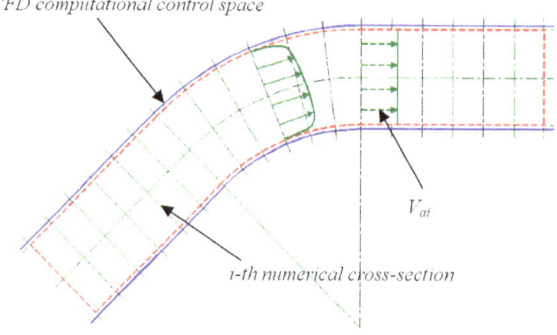

Figure A1. A pipe elbow with marked computational space.

Step 3: Simulation of velocity field $V(x,y,z)$ in the flow elements of the considered pipeline within the frame of the computational control space using CFD computer software.

Step 4: Computation of mean flow velocity, V_{ai}, for each i-th numerical cross-section from the previously derived *CFD* results (step 3), and assumption of equal kinetic energy resulting from the simulated and the uniform flow velocity distributions:

$$e_{kCFDi} = e_{kai}; \quad \rho = const \tag{A1}$$

$$e_{kCFDi} = \frac{1}{\dot{m}} \iint_{A_i} \frac{1}{2} V_i^2 [\rho V_i dA] = \frac{\rho}{2\dot{m}} \iint_{A_i} V_i^3 dA; \quad \dot{m} = \rho V_{ai} A_i \tag{A2}$$

$$e_{kai} = \frac{1}{2} V_{ai}^2 = \frac{1}{2\dot{m}} \rho A_i V_{ai}^3 \tag{A3}$$

$$V_{ai} = \left[\frac{\iint_{A_i} (V_i^3 dA)}{A_i} \right]^{1/3} \tag{A4}$$

where V_i is the flow velocity axial component—the component perpendicular to the i-th numerical cross-section.

Step 5: Computation of the equivalent cross-sectional area, A_{ei}, for each numerical cross-section ($i = 1, 2, ..., I$) using the continuity equation $Q_j = V_{ai} A_{ei} = const$:

$$A_{ei} = \frac{Q_j}{V_{ai}} \tag{A5}$$

Step 6 Computation of coordinates of flow velocity centers in each i-th numerical cross-section, $i = 1, 2, ..., I$:

$$x_{Ci} = \frac{\iint_{A_i} xV(x,y,z)dA}{V_{ai}A_{ei}}; \quad y_{Ci} = \frac{\iint_{A_i} yV(x,y,z)dA}{V_{ai}A_{ei}}; \quad z_{Ci} = \frac{\iint_{A_i} zV(x,y,z)dA}{V_{ai}A_{ei}} \tag{A6}$$

Step 7: For the considered flow rate Q_j through the analyzed pipe element, computing the equivalent factor F_{eQj} from the formula:

$$F_{eQj} = \sum_{i=1}^{I-1} \frac{l_{i \to i+1}}{0.5(A_{ei} + A_{ei+1})} \tag{A7}$$

where $l_{i \to i+1}$ denotes the distance between the resultant velocity centers for computational sections i and $i + 1$, A_{ei} and $A_{e\,i+1}$—equivalent areas of computational cross-sections i and $I + 1$, respectively.

The above computation should be performed for several discharge values (Q_j, $j = 1, 2, ..., m$) from the whole scope of its variation ($Q_{min} < Q_j \leq Q_{max}$). The average value of equivalent factor, F_e, can be calculated from the relationship:

$$F_e = \frac{1}{m} \sum_{i=1}^{m} F_{eQj} \tag{A8}$$

In the above procedure, it was assumed that the changes in velocity profiles are the same under steady and transient flow conditions. This assumption is correct for cases where the flow shut devices are not closed very quickly when using the pressure-time method. Practically, such cases occur in all hydraulic machines, due to the need to protect their flow systems against the destructive effects of the water hammer phenomenon.

Taking the equivalent value of F_e instead of the value F calculated directly from the geometry of pipeline sections it is possible to increase the pressure-time method accuracy in cases when pipelines have irregular flow elements.

Appendix B. Analysis of the Uncertainty of Measuring the Flow Rate by the Volumetric Gauging Method

The estimation of uncertainty of measuring the flow rate by the volumetric gauging method takes into account the following factors influencing the measured flow rate, both of a systematic and random nature:

1. Accuracy of geodetic measurements of the geometry of the head water reservoir of the power plant in order to determine the volume of water contained in it as a function of the water level
2. Accuracy class of the differential transducer used
3. The accuracy of the measurement data acquisition system used
4. Sampling frequencies of the differential transducer and accuracy of measuring the time interval in which the measurement took place
5. Selection of the time interval from t_0 to t_f, used to calculate the change in the volume of water in the reservoir taking into account waves on water surface

The uncertainty of measurement of the water level change resulting from rainfall while it was occurring was disregarded as irrelevant. It was also assumed that uncertainties resulting from water evaporation and leaks through the concrete embankments of the reservoir and steel pipelines connected to it are negligible.

The uncertainty of determining gravitational acceleration and water density in the studied conditions was neglected as practically irrelevant in measuring the change in water level with a differential transducer, and, as follows from further considerations, very small uncertainties of time registration and water level changes related to the resolution of the applied data acquisition system were not taken into account.

The relative accuracy of determining the volume of the reservoir was determined at $\delta \Delta V = 0.4\%$, which resulted from the available documentation of the geodetic measurements of the reservoir, made more than 30 years ago after the completion of its construction. According to the principles, the relative standard uncertainty type B associated with it was determined as:

$$\delta_B(\Delta V) = \frac{\delta \Delta V}{\sqrt{3}} = \sim 0.23\% \tag{A9}$$

The pressure difference transducer with the measuring range set at range Δz_{range} = 5 m of water column and accuracy class K_z = 0.075% was used to measure the water level change in the reservoir Δz. The standard uncertainty of type B concerning measurement of this quantity was calculated from the formula:

$$u_B(\Delta z) = \frac{K_z \cdot \Delta z_{range}}{\sqrt{3}} = \sim 0.0022 \text{ m w.c.} \tag{A10}$$

Due to the fact that flow rate values were measured for the water level in the reservoir changing by at least 1 m, the relative standard uncertainty type B resulting from the measurement of this changes was not worse than:

$$\delta_B(\Delta z) \cong 0.22\% \tag{A11}$$

For registering Δz, a computer data acquisition system with a measurement card of an absolute accuracy of Δ_{DAQ} = 0.55 mV was used. In order to determine the measurement uncertainty of the water level resulting from using such a measurement card, the scaling of the water level transducer should be taken into account (in the considered case the full measuring range of the transducer corresponded to the voltage change $U_{\Delta z\text{-}range} = 3.5$ V). The standard uncertainty of water level measurement resulting from that can be determined using formula:

$$u_B(\Delta z_{DAQ}) = \frac{1}{\sqrt{3}} \frac{\Delta_{DAQ} \cdot \Delta z_{range}}{U_{\Delta z_{range}}} \cong \frac{1}{\sqrt{3}} \frac{0.00055 \cdot 5}{3.5} \cong 4.5 \cdot 10^{-4} \text{ m} \qquad (A12)$$

After referring this uncertainty to the maintained minimum change of the water level in the reservoir (1 m of water), the relative standard uncertainty was not worse than:

$$\delta_B(r_{\Delta z}) \cong 0.05\% \qquad (A13)$$

Type B standard uncertainty regarding the measurement of the time range from t_0 to t_f and resulting from the accuracy and time resolution of a digital recorder (computerized data acquisition system) can be determined from the formula:

$$u_B(\Delta t) = \frac{\Delta_{tDAQ}(t_f - t_0)}{\sqrt{3}} \cong 0.1 \text{ s} \qquad (A14)$$

where $\Delta_{tDAQ} = 50 \times 10^{-6}$ is the time accuracy of the measuring card used in the data acquisition system, including its resolution.

Given the measurement time of each flow rate value that was not less than 1 h, the relative standard uncertainty of type B achieves negligible small value $\delta_B(\Delta t) \cong 0\%$.

The last of the above factors had random character and the standard uncertainty of type A that results was determined by statistical means. The recorded measurement signal of the water level change in the reservoir was characterized not only by changes resulting from waves on water surface, but also by random changes. The uncertainty arising from such nature of water changes was taken into account when calculating the Q_V value as described below. The calculations were started with the selection of the first time limits t_0 and t_f corresponding to the intersection of the trend line with the recorded signal $\Delta z(t)$—Figure 3. Then, the t_0 limit was shifted to the left to the next intersection of the trend line and the next Q_{Vi} value was calculated while maintaining the t_f limit. Then, the next Q_{Vi} calculations were made by shifting the t_0 limit to the right from the original value to the intersection of the trend line with the signal $\Delta z(t)$. Similar calculations were carried out for the t_{ki} time limit shifted in a similar way. The obtained Q_{Vi} calculation results were then subjected to statistical analysis, i.e., the average Q_{Vm} value and standard uncertainty type A were calculated from the formula:

$$Q_{Vm} = \frac{1}{n} \sum_{i=1}^{n} Q_{Vi} \qquad (A15)$$

$$u_A(Q_V) = k \sqrt{\frac{1}{n(n-1)} \sum_{i=1}^{n} (Q_{Vi} - Q_{Vm})^2} \qquad (A16)$$

where k is the extension coefficients calculated for the Student's t-distribution at a confidence level of 68.2% and the number of degrees of freedom $(n-1)$, n—the number of Q_{Vi} values calculated.

The Q_{Vm} value was treated as the flow rate value measured by the method discussed. The uncertainty calculated according to the above procedure took different values depending on the measured case, but in none of the examined cases in relation to the measured flow rate was not greater than:

$$\delta_A(Q_V) = 0.2\% \qquad (A17)$$

Finally, using the law of uncertainty propagation, the total relative standard uncertainty was determined from the formula:

$$\delta_c(Q_V) = \sqrt{\delta_A^2(Q_V) + \delta_B^2(\Delta V) + \delta_B^2(\Delta z) + \delta_B^2(r_z) + \delta_B^2(\Delta t)} \tag{A18}$$

This value of this uncertainty is as follows:

$$\delta_c(Q_V) = \pm 0.38\%. \tag{A19}$$

It should be emphasized that the above-estimated standard uncertainty relates to a confidence level of about 68% and by using a coverage factor of $k = 2$, we obtain expanded uncertainty for measuring the flow rate by volumetric gauging method with a confidence level of about 95% of:

$$\delta(Q_V) = k \cdot \delta_c(Q_V) = \pm 0.76\%. \tag{A20}$$

A summary of the estimated uncertainty of measuring Q by the volumetric method is presented in Table A1.

Table A1. The results of calculations of uncertainty of the flow rate measurement results obtained using the volumetric gauging method.

Name	Designation	Value	Unit
relative uncertainty in determining the reservoir volume	$\delta(\Delta V)$	0.4000	%
relative standard uncertainty in determining the reservoir volume	$\delta_B(\Delta V)$	0.2309	%
standard uncertainty of water level measurement	$u_B(\Delta z)$	0.0022	m
relative standard uncertainty of measurement of water level related to a change in level of 1 m	$\delta_B(\Delta z)$	0.2165	%
standard uncertainty of water level measurement resulting from the measurement card used	$u_B(\Delta z_{DAQ})$	0.0005	m
relative standard uncertainty of water level measurement resulting from the measurement card used	$\delta_B(\Delta z_{DAQ})$	0.0454	%
standard uncertainty of time interval measurement	$u_B(\Delta t)$	0.1000	s
relative standard uncertainty of a time interval measurement	$\delta_B(\Delta t)$	0.0028	%
relative standard uncertainty due to the nature of the changes in the measured change in water level	$\delta_A(Q_v)$	0.2000	%
total standard uncertainty of flow rate measurement	$\delta_c(Q_v)$	0.3772	%
expanded uncertainty of flow rate measurement ($k = 2$)	$\delta(Q_v)_{k=2}$	0.7544	%

Appendix C. Uncertainty Analysis of Flow Rate Measurements by Means of the Pressure-Time Method

Standards [4,6] specify the requirements that must be met so that the uncertainty of the flow rate measurement obtained using the pressure-time method is in the range of ±1.5% (2.3%) according to [4] and ±1.0% according to [6]. However, a way to calculate this uncertainty is not provided. The algorithm for estimating this uncertainty was the subject of only few available papers [36,37] but the presented algorithms do not comply with the applicable principles of expressing measurement uncertainty, presented in [19].

Below is a method for estimating the uncertainty of flow rate measurement under the considered conditions. The method is currently used by the authors of this contribution and complies with the recommendations presented in [19]. To present it, a simplified formulation of Equation (2) is introduced in the following form:

$$Q_0 = \frac{1}{\rho F}(\Delta p_m + \Delta p_{dm} + P_{rm})(t_f - t_0) + Q_f \tag{A21}$$

where Δp_m, Δp_{dm}, and P_{rm} are the values of Δp, Δp_d and P_r, respectively, after averaging over the time interval from t_0 to t_f.

Treating all the constituent quantities (components) in the above dependence as uncorrelated with each other, the value of the relative standard total uncertainty $\delta_c(Q_0)$ can be calculated from the formula resulting from the law of uncertainty propagation:

$$\delta_c(Q_0) = \sqrt{\delta^2(\rho) + \delta^2(F) + \delta^2(\Delta p_m) + \delta^2(\Delta p_{dm}) + \delta^2(P_{rm}) + \delta^2(t_f - t_0) + \delta^2(Q_f)} \quad (A22)$$

The largest uncertainty component is related to the measurement and recording of the pressure difference. In the measurement procedure used by the authors of this work, the initially recorded pressure difference signal $\Delta p(t_i)$ is numerically corrected taking into account characteristic of signal between limits t_f and t_{ff} as well as the flow rate at final conditions (Q_f) and the C_r coefficient of frictional resistance characterizing the pipeline between measuring cross-sections. All measurement results of differential pressure values $\Delta p(t_i)$ are corrected according to the formula:

$$\Delta p(t_i)_{correction} = \Delta p(t_i) - \left(\frac{1}{N_f}\sum_{t_f}^{t_{ff}}\Delta p(t_i) - C_r Q_f |Q_f| - \Delta p_{df}\right) \quad (A23)$$

where the second component on the right is the average value calculated from the recorded signal $\Delta p(t_i)$ in the time interval (t_f, t_{ff}), i.e., in the phase of suppression of free pressure oscillations after the flow is cut off, N_f is the number of recorded values of $\Delta p(t_i)$ in the time interval (t_f, t_{ff}), and Δp_{df} means the difference of dynamic pressures in the final steady state conditions (the method of calculating the difference of dynamic pressures is analogous to the calculation of the average difference of dynamic pressures—see the further part of the Appendix).

The C_r factor is determined from the formula (A23) on the basis of the measured pressure difference $\Delta p_{0correction} = P_{r0} + \Delta p_{d0}$ caused by friction losses in the pipeline measuring section and dynamic pressure difference in the initial steady flow conditions, i.e., immediately before the closing of the flow shutoff device. Thus, the value of P_{r0} is calculated as the average of the measured pressure difference (after correction) in the time interval (t_{00}, t_0):

$$P_{r0} = \Delta p_0 - \Delta p_{d0} = \frac{1}{N_0}\sum_{t_{00}}^{t_0}\Delta p(t_i)_{correction} - \Delta p_{d0} \quad (A24)$$

where N_0 is the number of recorded values of $\Delta p(t_i)$ in the time interval from $t_i = t_{00}$ to $t_i = t_0$, and Δp_{d0} means the difference of dynamic pressures in the initial steady.

The method of correction according to formula (A23) allows us to get rid of the most important part of uncertainty arising from the exact determination of the "zero" pressure differential transducer. The residual uncertainty associated with it is estimated when analyzing the effect of t_f limit on the uncertainty value. It should be emphasized that the correction applied takes place in the iterative process of calculating the Q_0 value.

Therefore, the mean pressure difference Δp_m is calculated from the measured and corrected values of $\Delta p(t)_{correction}$ using the formula:

$$\Delta p_m = \frac{1}{N}\sum_{t_0}^{t_f}\Delta p(t_i)_{correction} \quad (A25)$$

where N is the number of recorded values of $\Delta p(t_i)$ in the time interval from $t_i = t_0$ to $t_i = t_f$.

The absolute standard uncertainty of type B measurement of pressure difference Δp, resulting from the classes of transducers used, was determined as follows:

$$u_{kB}(\Delta p_m) = \frac{K_{\Delta p} \cdot \Delta p_{range}}{\sqrt{3}} \tag{A26}$$

After considering the pressure difference transducer class $K_{\Delta p} = 0.075\%$ and its range $\Delta p_{range} = \pm 500$ kPa (1 MPa), this uncertainty was: $u_{kB}(\Delta p_m) = 0.43$ kPa.

To record Δp_m, a computer data acquisition system with a measurement card with an absolute accuracy of 0.55 mV was used. In order to determine the measurement uncertainty of the water level resulting from the used measurement card, the scaling of the level transducer should be taken into account (in the case under consideration the full width of the transducer measuring range corresponded to a 3.5 V voltage change). The resulting standard uncertainty of level measurement can be determined by the formula:

$$u_{rB}(\Delta p_m) = \frac{\Delta_{DAQ} \cdot \Delta p_{m-range}}{\sqrt{3}} \frac{1}{U_{\Delta p_{m-range}}} \cong \frac{0.00055 \cdot 1000}{\sqrt{3} \cdot 3.5} \cong 0.09 \text{ kPa} \tag{A27}$$

In connection with the above, the total standard uncertainty $u(\Delta p_m)$, calculated from the formula:

$$u(\Delta p_m) = \sqrt{u_{kB}^2(\Delta p_m) + u_{rB}^2(\Delta p_m)} \tag{A28}$$

was not worse than:

$$u(\Delta p_m) = 0.44 \text{ kPa}$$

After referring these uncertainty values to the average pressure difference increases caused by the inertia forces after flow cut-off during the measurement, i.e.,

$$\Delta p_{m-inertia} = (\Delta p_m + \Delta p_{dm} + P_{rm}) \tag{A29}$$

the relative standard uncertainty $\delta(\Delta p_m)$ is determined, which, together with other uncertainty components, has been presented in the uncertainty balance table Table A2. This uncertainty is approximately 0.36% and 0.43% for turbine and pump mode of operation, respectively.

In addition to the P_{r0} value resulting from the measurement and calculations, the values of friction pressure drop P_r during flow cut off are calculated according to the relationship (A24) in the time interval (t_0, t_f). For this range, the average pressure drop P_{rm} can be calculated from the formula:

$$P_{rm} = \frac{C_r}{N_0} \sum_{t_0}^{t_f} Q(t_i) |Q(t_i)| - C_r Q_f |Q_f| - \Delta p_{df} \tag{A30}$$

where N is the number of calculated $Q(t_i)$ values in the range (t_0, t_f). The values of the second and third components to the right of the above dependence are negligibly small, so it can be neglected when estimating their uncertainty.

The standard uncertainty type B resulting from the calculation of the P_{rm} value was estimated from the formula:

$$u_B(P_{rm}) = u(P_{rm}) = \frac{\delta_{P_{rm}} P_{rm}}{\sqrt{3}} \tag{A31}$$

where δ_{Prm} is the average, relative difference in friction losses calculated using the quasi-stationary model (friction coefficient depending on the Re number) and the stationary model (constant friction coefficient)—the δ_{Prm} value was adopted according to approximately parabolic dependence of this difference on the flow rate proposed in monograph [11]: $\delta_{Prm} = \delta_{Prmax}/3 = \sim 0.025/3 = 0.0083$. It is worth emphasizing here that for calculating the flow rate, δ_{Prm} value was not used to correct friction loss calculations, i.e., the calculations were carried out assuming a constant C_r factor, not dependent on Re.

The effect of other factors on uncertainty $u(P_{rm})$, e.g., unsteadiness of flow, was omitted as irrelevant from the practical point of view. References [38,39] indicate that dissipation of mechanical energy during flow deceleration (taking place when the pressure-time method is applied) is only slightly less than that obtained from the quasi-steady hypothesis. It is the opposite to accelerating flow where energy dissipation is much larger than according the quasi-steady modeling. Some unsteady friction loss models in the closed conduits use these features [40]. These models have been confirmed experimentally—there is a high conformity between experimental and numerical results of the water hammer course [30]. With reference to the pressure-time method, the above assessment is confirmed by [27–29].

Finally, after the referring the $u(P_{rm})$ to the value of $\Delta p_{m\text{-}inertia}$, the relative standard uncertainty associated with the calculation of P_r, for the highest value of flow rate measured is presented in the uncertainty balance table Table A2.

The uncertainty of calculating the dynamic pressure difference between the pipeline measuring cross-sections, $u(\Delta p_{dm})$ was estimated as follows. The average dynamic pressure difference, Δp_{dm}, in the time interval (t_0, t_f) was calculated from the formula:

$$\Delta p_{dm} = \frac{1}{2}\left(\frac{\alpha_B \rho}{A_B^2} - \frac{\alpha_A \rho}{A_A^2}\right)\frac{1}{N}\sum_{t_0}^{t_f}[Q(t_i)]^2 \tag{A32}$$

in which N denotes the number of calculated $Q(t_i)$ values in the interval (t_0, t_f), and A_A with A_B are the cross-sectional areas of the upper and lower pipeline measuring cross-sections, and α_A and α_B—Coriolis coefficients.

In the considered case, it was assumed that $A_A = \infty$ and the effect of calculating Δp_m on the uncertainty of flow measurement results from changes in the Coriolis coefficient in the lower measuring cross-section of the pipeline. In calculations $\alpha_B = 1.05$ was taken as the average value of the Coriolis coefficient for fully developed turbulent flow in the pipeline determined within the limits from 1.04 to 1.06 [23]. On this basis, the standard uncertainty type B resulting from the calculation of the Δp_{dm} value was calculated using the following formula:

$$u_B(\Delta p_{dm}) = \frac{0.01 \Delta p_{dm}}{\sqrt{3}} \tag{A33}$$

For the cases with the highest values of measured flow rates, the values of standard uncertainty $u(\Delta p_{dm})$ determined in this way was 0.21 kPa and 0.16 kPa for turbine and pump mode of operation, respectively.

Table A2 of the uncertainty balance lists the relative standard uncertainty associated with the calculation of Δp_{dm}, after relating $u(\Delta p_{dm})$ to the value of $\Delta p_{m\text{-}inertia}$ for the highest values of measured flow rates in the turbine and pump mode of operation of the tested machine.

The time accuracy of the computer acquisition system measuring the pressure difference signal $p(t_i)$ was omitted as having no impact on the standard uncertainty type B regarding the measurement of the time interval from t_0 to t_f. It can be calculated using the following formula:

$$u_B(\Delta t) = u_B(t_f - t_0) = \frac{\Delta_{tDAQ}(t_f - t_0)}{\sqrt{3}} \tag{A34}$$

where $\Delta_{tDAQ} = 50 \times 10^{-6}$ is the time accuracy of measurement card used in the data acquisition system including its resolution.

The value of $u_B(t)$ is about 0.0007 s and 0.0005 s for turbine and pump mode of operation, respectively.

For the flow rate measurements, the time interval (t_0, t_f) during turbine mode of operation was not longer than $T = \sim 25$ s, and during pump mode of operation $T = \sim 20$ s, using a sampling frequency of 200 Hz. Table A2 of the uncertainty balance lists the relative standard uncertainty associated with the measurement of the time interval (t_0, t_f).

The method of determining the t_f time limit, i.e., the upper limit of integration in the pressure-time method, was presented in [21]—an earlier author's publication. This method significantly influences the uncertainty of measuring Q_0 in cases where the free pressure oscillations after the closing of the shut-off device have relatively high amplitudes compared to the average Δp_m values. The value of t_f should be selected at the top of the peak or the bottom of the valley of free oscillations of pressure differences, with its exact determination taking place in the calculation program. It is recommended to choose the limit t_f from the first clear peak or valley of free oscillations in order to minimize the impact of these oscillations on the measurement result Q_0. Pulsations superimposed on these oscillations, which are random in nature, have been included in the estimation of uncertainty type A. For this reason, a series of calculations of Q_{0i} values for several values of time t_{fi}, selected in close proximity of the original value of t_f selected in accordance with the above principle, was carried out in the range covering only one valley and one peak visible in the measured quick-change pressure difference signal (pressure difference pulsation). It should be emphasized that it is not advisable to significantly shift the t_{fi} value from the tops of peaks and bottom of valleys of free differential pressure oscillations. The obtained Q_{0i} calculation results were subjected to statistical analysis, i.e., the average Q_{0m} value and standard uncertainty were calculated using the formula:

$$u_{tfA}(Q_0) = k \sqrt{\frac{1}{n(n-1)} \sum_{i=1}^{n} (Q_{0i} - Q_{0m})^2} \tag{A35}$$

where k is the extension coefficients calculated from the Student's t-distribution for the confidence level $p = 68.2\%$ and the number of degrees of freedom $(n-1)$, n—number of calculated Q_{0i} values.

After relating the $u_{tfA}(Q_0)$ values determined in the above described manner to the measured flow rate Q_0, the relative standard uncertainties δ_{tfA} did not exceed $\delta_{tfA}(Q_0) = 0.08\%$ for turbine mode of operation and $\delta_{tfA}(Q_0) = 0.1\%$ for pump mode of operation.

The uncertainty $\delta(\rho)$ results from the variability of water density with pressure change and from the accuracy of its determination for given temperature and average absolute pressure in the pipeline occurring during tests. This uncertainty is very small; therefore, it was omitted in calculating the uncertainty of flow rate measurement.

The standard uncertainty $\delta(F)$ for determining the geometric factor F results from the accuracy of measuring the length of individual pipeline segments (L_i) and the area of their internal cross-sections (A_i) and from the accuracy of the correction of the F factor using CFD calculations. The uncertainty of determining the F factor based on the available post-completion documentation of the pipeline, positively verified by direct measurement of L_i and A_i, was not worse than:

$$\delta(F_{geom}) = 0.15\% \tag{A36}$$

Due to the fact that the uncertainty of the F factor correction introduced reaches about 0.75%, the uncertainty of this correction based on CFD calculations is of the same order assuming even 20% accuracy of CFD calculations, and as a result we get standard uncertainty:

$$\delta(F) = \sqrt{\delta^2(F_{geom}) + \delta^2(F_{CFD})} \cong 0.21\% \tag{A37}$$

The flow rate under final conditions, being that the leakage through the closed wicket gates of the pump-turbine, Q_f, was measured in a separate way. For this purpose, under closed wicket gate conditions, pressure changes in the pipeline were recorded when closing the shut-off valve characterizing with very high tightness. On this basis, also using the pressure-time method, Q_f values were determined. For turbine mode of operation, it was equal $Q_f = \sim 0.14$ m^3/s, while for pump mode of operation $Q_f = \sim 0.18$ m^3/s, which is about 0.7% in relation to the minimum flow rate values for turbine and about 0.65% for pump flow direction. No detailed analysis of the Q_f uncertainty was carried out, but it was assumed with a large excess that it is not worse than 10%, which gives uncertainty:

- $\delta(Q_f)$ = ~0.07% for turbine mode of operation,
- $\delta(Q_f)$ = ~0.065% for pump mode of operation.

The uncertainty resulting from the iterative algorithm for calculating the flow rate is $\delta(Q_{0iter})$ = 0.1%. This is due to the condition used for ending the calculations, which assumes that the calculations are finished when two subsequent values $Q_{0iter-1}$ and Q_{0iter} do not differ by more than 0.1%.

The balance of the estimated uncertainty of Q measurement using the pressure-time method is presented in Table A2.

Table A2. Summary results of calculations of uncertainty of flow rate results measured using the pressure-time method.

Name	Symbol	Value Turbine	Value Pump	Unit
standard uncertainty of pressure measurement resulting from the applied differential pressure transducer	$u_{kB}(\Delta p_m)$	0.4330		kPa
standard uncertainty of pressure measurement resulting from the measurement card used	$u_{rB}(\Delta p_m)$	0.0907		kPa
total standard uncertainty of pressure measurement	$u(\Delta p_m)$	0.4424		kPa
relative standard uncertainty of pressure measurement related to the average differential pressure increase	$\delta(\Delta p_m)$	0.3600	0.4300	%
standard uncertainty of calculating friction losses	$u_B(P_{rm})$	0.0555	0.1458	kPa
relative standard uncertainty of calculating friction losses	$\delta_B(P_{rm})$	0.0584	0.1487	%
standard uncertainty of calculating the dynamic pressure difference	$u_B(\Delta p_{dm})$	0.2100	0.1600	kPa
relative standard uncertainty of calculating the dynamic pressure difference	$\delta(\Delta p_{dm})$	0.2211	0.1633	%
standard uncertainty of time interval measurement	$u_B(\Delta t)$	0.0007	0.0005	s
relative standard uncertainty of time measurement	$\delta_B(\Delta t)$	0.0029	0.0029	%
standard uncertainty resulting from setting the upper limit of integration	$u_{tfA}(Q_0)$	0.0270	0.0280	m^3/s
relative uncertainty resulting from setting the upper limit of integration	$\delta_{tfA}(Q_0)$	0.0800	0.1000	%
standard uncertainty of determining the geometrical factor	$\delta(F_{geom})$	0.1500		%
standard uncertainty of CFD calculations	$\delta(F_{CFD})$	0.1500		%
total standard uncertainty of determining the geometric factor	$\delta(F)$	0.2100		%
uncertainty of determining the flow rate at final conditions	$\delta(Q_f)$	0.0700	0.0650	%
uncertainty resulting from iterative calculation of the flow rate	$\delta(Q_{iter})$	0.1000		%
relative total standard uncertainty	$\delta_c(Q_0)$	0.4973	0.5496	%
relative expanded uncertainty (k = 2)	$\delta(Q_0)_{k=2}$	0.9946	1.0991	%

References

1. Merzkirch, W. *Fluid Mechanics of Flow Metering*; Merzkirch, W., Ed.; Springer: Berlin/Heidelberg, Germany; New York, NY, USA, 2005; ISBN 3-540-22242-1.
2. Miller, R.W. *Flow Measurement Engineering Handbook*, 3rd ed.; McGraw-Hill Book Company: New York, NY, USA, 1996.

3. Urquiza, G.; Basurto, M.A.; Castro, L.; Adamkowski, A.; Janicki, W. Flow measurement methods applied to hydro power plants, Chapter 7. In *Flow Measurement*; Urquiza, G., Castro, L., Eds.; INTECH Open Access Publisher: Rijeka, Croatia, 2012; pp. 151–168.
4. *Field Acceptance Tests to Determine the Hydraulic Performance of Hydraulic Turbines, Storage Pumps and Pump-Turbines*; IEC 41:1991; European Equivalent: EN 60041:1999; International Electrotechnical Commision: Geneva, Switzerland, 1991.
5. *Hydraulic Machines—Acceptance Tests of Small Hydroelectric Installations*; IEC 62006:2010; European Equivalent: EN 62006:2011; International Electrotechnical Commision: Geneva, Switzerland, 2010.
6. *Hydraulic Turbines and Pump-Turbines. Performance Test Codes*; ASME PTC 18 Standard; The American Society of Mechanical Engineers: New York, NY, USA, 2011.
7. Gibson, N.R. The Gibson method and apparatus for measuring the flow of water in closed conduits. *ASME Power Div.* **1923**, *45*, 343–392.
8. Gibson, N.R. Experience in the use of the Gibson method of water measurement for efficiency tests of hydraulic turbines. *ASME J. Basic Eng.* **1959**, *81*, 455–487. [CrossRef]
9. Voser, A.; Bruttin, C.; Prénat, J.-E.; Staubli, T. Improving acoustic flow measurement. *Water Power Dam Constr.* **1996**, *48*, 30–34.
10. Lüscher, B.; Staubli, T.; Tresch, T.; Gruber, P. Accuracy analysis of the acoustic discharge measurement using analytical, spatial velocity profiles. In Proceedings of the Hydro 2007, Granada, Spain, 15–17 October 2007. Paper 17.05.
11. Adamkowski, A. Discharge measurement techniques in hydropower systems with emphasis on the pressure-time method. Chapter 5. In *Hydropower–Practice and Application*; Hossein, S.-B., Ed.; INTECH Open Access Publisher: London, UK, 2012; pp. 83–114.
12. Doering, J.C.; Hans, P.D. Turbine discharge measurement by the velocity-area method. *J. Hydraul. Eng.* **2001**, *127*, 747–752. [CrossRef]
13. Gandhi, B.K.; Verma, H.K. Simultaneous multi-point velocity measurement using propeller current meters for discharge evaluation in small hydropower stations. In Proceedings of the International Conference on Small Hydropower Hydro Sri Lanka, Kandy, Sri Lanka, 22–24 October 2007.
14. Proulx, G.; Cloutier, E.; Bouhadji, L.; Lemon, D. Comparison of discharge measurement by current meter and acoustic scintillation methods at La Grande-1. In Proceedings of the IGHEM, Luzern, Swiss, 14–16 July 2004.
15. Llobet, J.V.; Lemon, D.D.; Buermans, J.; Billenness, D. Union Fenosa Generación's field experience with Acoustic Scintillation Flow Measurement. In Proceedings of the IGHEM, Milan, Italy, 3–6 September 2008.
16. Adamkowski, A.; Janicki, W.; Krzemianowski, Z.; Lewandowski, M. Volumetric gauging method vs Gibson method—Comparative analysis of the measurement results of discharge through pomp-turbine in both operation modes. In Proceedings of the IGHEM 2016, Linz, Austria, 24–26 August 2016; p. 567.
17. Adamkowski, A.; Lewandowski, M. Some experiences with flow measurement in bulb turbines using the differential pressure method. *IOP Conf. Ser. Earth Environ. Sci.* **2012**, *15*, 062045. [CrossRef]
18. Adamkowski, A.; Lewandowski, M.; Lewandowski, S.; Cicholski, W. Calculation of the cycle efficiency coefficient of pumped-storage power plant units basing on measurements of water level in the head (tail) water reservoir. In Proceedings of the 13th International Seminar on Hydropower Plants, Vienna, Austria, 24–26 November 2004.
19. *Uncertainty of Measurement—Part 3: Guide to the Expression of Uncertainty in Measurement*; (GUM: 1995), ISO/IEC GUIDE 98-3:2008; International Organization for Standarization: Geneva, Switzerland, 2008.
20. Çengel, Y.A.; Cimbala, J.M. *Fluid Mechanics. Fundamentals and Applications*; McGraw-Hill Book Company: New York, NY, USA, 2006.
21. White, F.M. *Fluid Mechanics*; WCB/McGraw-Hill: Boston, MA, USA, 1999.
22. Adamkowski, A.; Janicki, W. Elastic water-hammer theory–based approach to discharge calculation in the pressure-time Method. *J. Hydraul. Eng.* **2017**, *143*, 06017002. [CrossRef]
23. Adamkowski, A.; Janicki, W.; Krzemianowski, Z.; Lewandowski, M. Flow rate measurements in hydropower plants using the pressure-time method—Experiences and improvements. *Flow Meas. Instrum.* **2019**, *68*, 101584. [CrossRef]
24. Adamkowski, A.; Krzemianowski, Z.; Janicki, W. Improved Discharge Measurement Using the Pressure-Time Method in a Hydropower Plant Curved Penstock. *ASME J. Eng. Gas Turbines Power* **2009**, *131*, 053003. [CrossRef]

25. Adamkowski, A.; Janicki, W. Selected problems in calculation procedures for the Gibson discharge measurement method. In Proceedings of the IGHEM, Roorkee, India, 21–23 October 2010; pp. 73–80.
26. Bortoni, E.C. New developments in Gibson's method for flow measurement in hydro power plants. *Flow Meas. Instrum.* **2008**, *19*, 385–390. [CrossRef]
27. Jonsson, P.P.; Ramdal, J.; Cervantes, M.J. Development of the Gibson method—Unsteady friction. *Flow Meas. Instrum.* **2012**, *23*, 19–25. [CrossRef]
28. Dunca, G.; Iovănel, R.G.; Bucur, D.M.; Cervantes, M.J. On the Use of the Water Hammer Equations with Time Dependent Friction during a Valve Closure, for Discharge Estimation. *J. Appl. Fluid Mech.* **2016**, *9*, 2427–2434. [CrossRef]
29. Sundstrom, L.R.J.; Saemi, S.; Raisee, M.; Cervantes, M.J. Improved frictional modeling for the pressure-time method. *Flow Meas. Instrum.* **2019**, *69*, 101604. [CrossRef]
30. Adamkowski, A.; Lewandowski, M. Experimental Examination of Unsteady Friction Models for Transient Pipe Flow Simulation. *ASME J. Fluids Eng.* **2006**, *128*, 1351–1363. [CrossRef]
31. NUMECA International—Computational Fluid Dynamics Software and Consulting Service. Available online: https://www.numeca.com (accessed on 15 August 2020).
32. ANSYS Inc. *ANSYS Fluent User's Guide 18*; Release 18; ANSYS Inc.: Canonsburg, PA, USA, 2017.
33. Menter, F.R. Two-equation eddy-viscosity turbulence models for engineering applications. *AIAA J.* **1994**, *32*, 269–289. [CrossRef]
34. Wilcox, D.C. *Turbulence Modeling for CFD*; DCW Industries, Inc.: La Canada, CA, USA, 1993.
35. Hellsten, A.; Laine, S. *Extension of the k-ω-SST Turbulence Models for Flows over Rough Surfaces*; AIAA Paper; AIAA-97-3577; AIAA: Reston, VA, USA, 1997. [CrossRef]
36. Ramdal, J.; Jonsson, P.P.; Dahlhaug, O.G.; Nielsen, T.K.; Cervantes, M. Uncertainties for pressure-time efficiency measurements. In Proceedings of the IGHEM 2010, Roorkee, India, 21–23 October 2010; pp. 64–72.
37. Hulås, H.; Dahlhaug, O.G. Uncertainty analysis of Pressure-Time measurements. In Proceedings of the IGHEM 2006, Portland, OR, USA, 30 July–1 August 2006; pp. 1–13.
38. Brunone, B.; Golia, U.M.; Greco, M. Some Remarks on the Momentum Equations for Fast Transients. In Proceedings of the 9th Round Table, IAHR, International Meeting on Hydraulic Transients with Column Separation, Valencia, Spain, 4–6 September 1991; pp. 201–209.
39. Bughazem, M.B.; Anderson, A. Problems with Simple Models for Damping in Unsteady Flow. In Proceedings of the International Conference on Pressure Surges and Fluid Transients, BHR Group, Harrogate, UK, 16–18 April 1994; pp. 537–548.
40. Vitkovsky, J.P.; Lambert, M.F.; Simpson, A.R.; Bergant, A. Advances in Unsteady Friction Modeling in Transient Pipe Flow. In Proceedings of the 8th International Conference on Pressure Surges, The Hague, The Netherlands, 12–14 April 2000; pp. 471–482.

© 2020 by the authors. Licensee MDPI, Basel, Switzerland. This article is an open access article distributed under the terms and conditions of the Creative Commons Attribution (CC BY) license (http://creativecommons.org/licenses/by/4.0/).

Article

Differences of Flow Patterns and Pressure Pulsations in Four Prototype Pump-Turbines during Runaway Transient Processes

Zhiyan Yang [1], Zirui Liu [1], Yongguang Cheng [1,*], Xiaoxi Zhang [2], Ke Liu [1] and Linsheng Xia [3]

1. State Key Laboratory of Water Resources and Hydropower Engineering Science, Wuhan University, Wuhan 430072, China; mry@whu.edu.cn (Z.Y.); liuzr97@whu.edu.cn (Z.L.); liukeyf@whu.edu.cn (K.L.)
2. School of Environmental Science and Engineering, Xiamen University of Technology, Xiamen 361024, China; zhangxiaoxi@xmut.edu.cn
3. China Ship Development and Design Center, Wuhan 430064, China; xialinsheng@whu.edu.cn
* Correspondence: ygcheng@whu.edu.cn

Received: 24 August 2020; Accepted: 5 October 2020; Published: 11 October 2020

Abstract: Frequent working condition conversions in pumped-storage power stations often induce stability problems, especially when the operating point enters the S-shaped region, during which flow transitions and pressure fluctuations are serious. The pump-turbines with different specific speed values show different characteristics, but their differences in stability features are still not clear. In this study, four different pump-turbines were selected to simulate the runaway processes from turbine modes. The similarities and differences of flow patterns and pressure fluctuations were analyzed. For the similarities, pressure pulsations increase gradually and fluctuate suddenly once the backflows occur at the runner inlets. For the differences, the evolutions of backflows and pressure pulsations are related to specific speeds and runner shapes. Firstly, it is easier for the lower specific speed turbines to enter the reverse pump mode. Secondly, the blade lean angle influences the position where backflows occur, because it determines the pressure gradient at the runner inlets. Thirdly, the runner inlet height influences pressure pulsations in the vaneless space, because the relative range of backflow transitions will be enlarged with the decrease of specific speed. Overall, investigating the mechanisms of flow pattern transitions and pressure variations is important for runner design and transient process control.

Keywords: pump-turbine; flow patterns; pressure pulsations; similarities; differences; S-shaped characteristics; runaway transient process

1. Introduction

With the substantial increase of electricity consumption and the rapid development of green sustainable energies, pumped-storage power undertakes the functions of peak load regulation, valley filling, frequency modulation, phase modulation, and emergency standby in the power grids [1,2]. Its match-up with nuclear power and complement with wind and solar powers make it an indispensable tool to ensure safety, stability, and efficiency of clean energies [3–5]. To undertake these important functions, the stability and safety of pumped-storage power systems are essential. However, some stability problems in operating pumped-storage power stations, such as violent vibration of pump-turbine units [6], grid connection failure [7,8], runner lifting-up [9], and rotor-stator crashing [10], were frequently reported. These problems were generally attributed to the frequent conversions of operating conditions, especially when the working points pass through the so-called S- and hump-shaped characteristics regions, in which intense flow and pressure fluctuations occur. To know the mechanism, solve the stability problems, and predict working conditions, many studies on the transient processes of pump-turbine generator units were conducted in recent years [11].

Among many transient processes, the runaway process is the most dangerous one. Even if this scenario, it is rarely seen in practical operation, predicting the risk in the design phase is always required. The runaway process happens if the generator is cut from the power grid but the guide-vanes fail to close. Without retarding torque, the runner will be driven only by the unceasing water power, and the unit will be accelerated to the runaway speed. During this process, the working point slides rapidly through the S-shaped characteristic region that is comprised of the high-speed turbine, turbine braking and reverse pump modes, and violent vibrations in the unit happen due to quick flow pattern transitions and strong pressure pulsations [1]. Therefore, it is very important to ensure the safety and stability of the unit by analyzing the laws of flow pattern transitions and pressure pulsation changes, and revealing the interrelations of these key factors.

The existing studies about the runaway instability of pump-turbines mainly focused on unsteady flow patterns and pressure pulsations in the runner and vaneless space [12,13]. Two main situations [11,12], working at a runaway point and running away from a turbine working point, were both investigated. They concluded that strong backflows and vortices in the runner and the vaneless space lead to large pressure pulsations, channel blockage, discharge decrease, and pressure increase [12]. As for the simulations about static working at a runaway point, Gentner et al. [14] found toroid-like vortex structures around the vaneless space, and claimed that the secondary vortex in each runner channel can cause negative head gradient and pressure rise. Wang et al. [15] captured the obviously detached vortexes on the pressure sides of blades near the crown and pointed out that they may be the very reason for huge pressure fluctuations. Widmer et al. [16] showed the flow separation, recirculation, and vortex formation in every runner channels of a pump-turbine operating at the speed-no-load conition, and observed the obvious backflows and pressure fluctuations. Hasmatuchi et al. [17] investigated the flow distribution near the runaway point through experiments and found that the low-frequency pressure components can be captured in the spiral-casing and the guide-vanes channel. Jacquet et al. [18] pointed out that the position of backflows at the runner inlet depended on the operating point, and the accompanying pressure fluctuations can reach the maximum at the speed-no-load condition.

As for transient process studies, Trivedi et al. [19–22] concluded that the highest amplitudes of pressure fluctuations in pump-turbine were under the running away condition, according to the measurement of pressure fluctuations in the speed-no-load, running away, total load rejection, start-up, and shut-down conditions. Yin et al. [23] showed that the vortex formation at the runner inlet severely blocks the runner passages periodically, inducing torque and rotational speed fluctuations. Zhang et al. [24] also simulated the runaway process by computational fluid dynamics (CFD) and found that the successive features of transient flow patterns may induce pressure differences between the similar dynamic operating points in different moving directions. Xia et al. [1] conducted simulations of runaway processes of a model pump-turbine with different guide-vane openings (GVOs), and found that the backflows at the runner inlet can lead to quite different pressure fluctuations. Other research investigating the runaway instability by specifying discharge oscillating boundary condition at the turbine inlet or draft-tube outlet were also conducted. For example, Widmer et al. [16] decreased the discharge at the boundary starting from the runaway point, and found that the pressure pulsations can generate abnormal low-frequency signals with the number of stalled channels increased, which was similar to those in the runaway process.

The research discussed above shows that whether at the runaway point or during runaway process, flow blockages and severe pressure fluctuations are strong in the runner and vaneless space, which are the common features in pump-turbines. However, in much reported research, the problems encountered by different pump-turbines are mostly different. For example, a runner lifting-up happened in Tianhuangping power station during a load increase process [9], many grid connecting failures occurred in Baoquan power station under low head conditions [8], and a rotor-stator collision happened in Huizhou power station during a load rejection process [25]. Besides these accidents, there are still many other accidents that need to be paid attention to. Although these accidents are related to many factors, it is undeniable that the characteristics of the pump-turbine itself have a great influence on them. Most obviously, different pump-turbines have different S-characteristics because of their rated output, head, discharge, rotational speed, along with their runner shapes being different. Therefore, the flow patterns and pressure pulsations may not be similar in local and detailed perspectives, which may be related to the different problems mentioned above. For example, the conclusions in Hasmatuchi [17] and Jacquet [18] are different. In Hasmatuchi's paper, the low-frequency component will further increase in amplitude as the zero-discharge condition is approached, while those in Jacquet's paper reach at the maximum at the no-load conditions. In addition, Zhou et al. [26] optimized the blade inlet and showed the different developing trends of flow patterns and pressure fluctuations of two turbines during the runaway processes, though other geometry features of turbines were kept unchanged.

Therefore, we should not only focus on the common phenomena, but also the differences in different pump-turbines, in order to better understand the mechanism and solve the problems. As a common convention, the characteristics of pump-turbines are always labelled by their specific speeds. However, no research shows whether runaway process characteristics are related to the specific speed. These characteristics include the attenuation of runaway, the transition of flow patterns, the fluctuations of pressure pulsations, and runner forces. In order to answer these questions, we selected four prototype pump-turbines with different water heads, and simulated their runaway transient processes from the turbine mode. The evolutions of pressure pulsations and flow patterns were analyzed, their similarities and differences were discussed, and the mechanism was revealed. The paper will be arranged as follows: the Section 2 describes the basic simulation model and parameters; the Section 3 shows the resulting histories of macro parameters, and the evolutions of flow structures and pressure pulsations, along with their relations with specific speeds; the Section 4 explains the influences of runner shapes for the differences in the evolutions of flow structures and pressure pulsations; and conclusions are drawn in the Section 5.

2. Three-Dimensional CFD Setups

Software for simulation: Three-dimensional (3D) CFD simulations were carried out by using commercial software ANSYS FLUENT 17.0 (ANSYS, Canonsburg, PA, USA).

Computational domain: four pump-turbines with different specific speeds were selected. Because of their main parameters, such as head, discharge, output, and layout out of water conveyance systems are different, it is difficult to ensure that all the settings in the simulations are the same, which is also unrealistic. Therefore, in order to fully reflect the characteristics of the pump-turbines during the transient process, the actual water conveyance systems were removed in the simulations to eliminate the impact of flow inertia in water conveyance systems [1]. This removal will affect the variation period and maximum value of macro parameters due to the flow inertia in pipelines, but we mainly focused on the evolutions of flow patterns and pressure pulsations, which are more affected by the pump-turbine unit. In addition, two extended tubes were added to the inlets of spiral-casings and the outlets of draft-tubes for setting boundary conditions at the locations with smooth flow patterns. Also, a conventional hydraulic turbine was chosen to compare with the above four pump-turbines. The 3D computational domains and monitoring points of the five turbines are shown in Figure 1, and the main parameters are listed in Table 1. The specific speed is defined by $n_s = n_r \sqrt{Nr}/Hr^{1.25}$, in which n_r, Nr, and Hr are the rated rotational speed, output, and head, respectively. The flow patterns have a certain regularity in n_{11}-Q_{11} plane under large guide vane opening conditions, especially at the runner inlets (in one pump-turbine) [1]. Therefore, the runaway processes of the four pump-turbines are all started near their corresponding rated turbine working conditions, while that of the conventional hydraulic turbine is started from a large guide vane opening condition, in which the runaway characteristics are similar to those in the rated one.

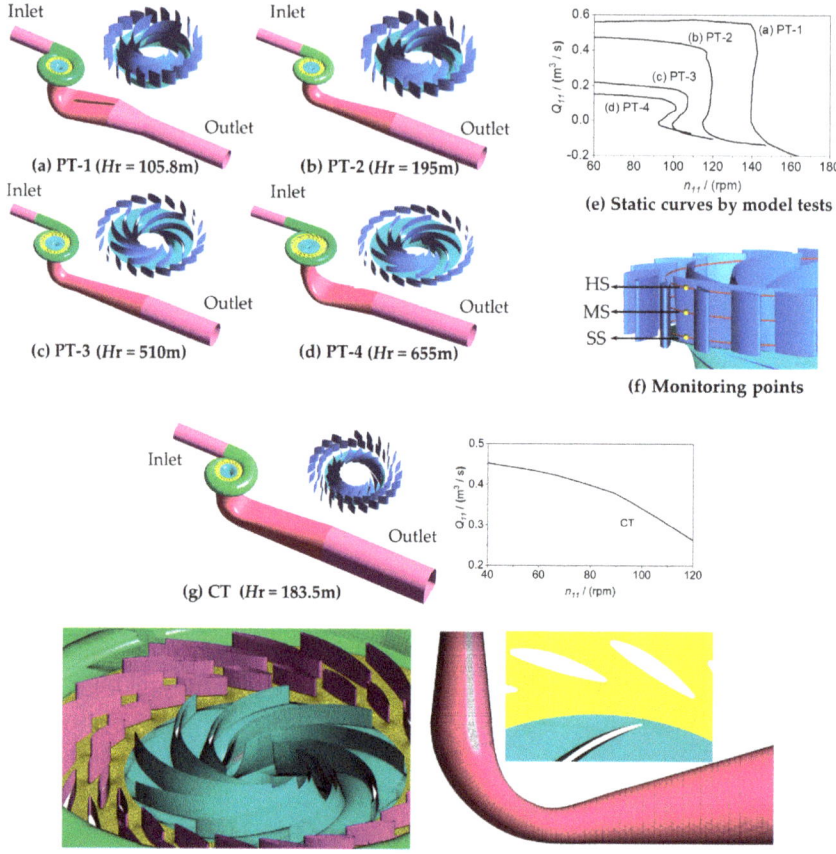

Figure 1. Computational domains of the pump-turbines (PT) and conventional turbine (CT), the schematic of monitoring points, and mesh information.

Table 1. Main parameters of the four pump-turbines and a turbine.

-	Specific-Speed n_s (m·kW)	Rated Head Hr (m)	Rated Output Nr (MW)	Diameter of Runner Inlet D (m)	Height of Runner Inlet b_0 (m)	Relative Runner Inlet b_0/D (-)	Number of Runner Blades (-)	Inertia of Rotating Parts GD^2 ($\times 10^7$ kg·m^2)
PT-1	219.8	105.8	139	5.23	1.12	0.214	7	1.092
PT-2	189.8	195.0	306	5.26	0.79	0.150	9	1.092
PT-3	114.1	510.0	306	3.82	0.34	0.089	9	1.092
PT-4	90.2	655.0	357	4.23	0.30	0.071	9	1.092
CT	148.4	183.5	466	6.0	1.08	0.180	16	1.092

Mesh Generation: The upstream and downstream extended tubes, spiral-casings, runners, and draft-tubes were discretized by hexahedral structure grids, while the vane regions were discretized by wedge grids. Also, the areas near the blades and guide-vanes were locally refined. Grid refinement evaluations were performed for each pump-turbine and we found that when the grid number is more than 5.0 million, the relative differences in resulting macro parameters under steady conditions are negligible. Therefore, the cell numbers of the five turbines are 5.42 million, 5.58 million, 5.76 million, 5.97 million, and 5.54 million, respectively.

Numerical Scheme: After many comparisons, considering the calculation time and accuracy at the same time, we selected the timesteps for the five turbines as 0.00125, 0.001, 0.001, 0.001, and 0.00166667 s, corresponding to the times needed for the runner to rotate 1.5, 1.5, 3.0, 3.0, and 1.5 degrees, respectively. The SST-based scale-adaptive simulation model (SAS-SST) turbulence model [1] was adopted, and all the convergence criteria of residuals at each timestep were set to 1.0×10^{-4}, including continuity, x-velocity, y-velocity, z-velocity, k, and omega. For both steady and unsteady simulations, the SIMPLEC algorithm was chosen to achieve the coupling solution of the velocity and pressure equations [1].

Boundary Conditions: The total pressure was defined at the inlet of the extended pipe of the spiral-casing, and the static pressure was defined at the outlet of the extended pipe of the draft-tube. The remaining solid walls were imposed with the no-slip wall condition.

3. Results of the Runaway Transient Processes

3.1. Macro Parameters Histories

The runaway dynamic characteristics of the four pump-turbines are shown in n_{11}-Q_{11} plane in Figure 2, in which the unit parameters are defined as $n_{11} = nD_1/\sqrt{H}$ and $Q_{11} = Q/(D_1^2\sqrt{H})$, where H = $E1$–$E2$, with $E1$ and $E2$ the total energy values at the spiral-casing inlet and runner outlet, respectively. Comparing the computed results (red lines) of the four pump-turbines, we know that the dynamic trajectories of PT-1 and PT-2 have very high amplitudes in high frequency pulsation signals in the n_{11}-Q_{11} plane, while those of PT-3 and PT-4 are relatively smaller and become obvious only near the runaway points. In addition, the low-pass filtered curves (green lines) of the original data do not go along the static characteristic curves (black lines) obtained from the model tests, however, they have good agreements before entering the S-shaped region. Once entering the S-shaped region, the dynamic curves deviate from the measured static ones. These deviations have been analyzed in [27], in which the influences of the sections for head definition, the water inertia in pipes and the rotational inertia of unit on the dynamic trajectory were discussed. In this paper, due to neglecting water inertia in pipes and choosing the same rotational inertias, the deviations are different. In fact, the simulating rotational inertia is based on the actual value of PT-1, therefore, the actual rotational inertia of PT-2 is much larger, and those of PT-3 and PT-4 are much smaller. For PT-2, small simulating rotational inertia will lead to large speed increasing rate, then the dynamic trajectory is on the right side of the static curve obviously, which is opposite to the phenomenon in PT-3 and PT-4. To verify the rationality of the above settings and results, we take reference [28] as an example, in which the influence of the inertia of rotating part has been well explained, and it shows that the dynamic trajectories affected by different rotating part inertia in n_{11}-Q_{11} plane are very similar with those in this paper. In addition, there is no very large deviation in the dynamic trajectories, though the pulsations in the n_{11}-Q_{11} plane and variation period of rotational speed are different. From the above analysis, we know that the results of transient process are quite different from the static ones and it is necessary to consider the dynamic effect in transient simulations.

The time histories of the main macro parameters during the runaway processes are also shown in Figure 2. Generally speaking, the dynamic histories of PT-1 and PT-2 show damped oscillations, while those of PT-3 and PT-4 demonstrate undamped oscillations. The working points of PT-1 and PT-2 go through the turbine (T) and turbine braking (TB) modes, but do not enter the reverse pump (RP) mode, and the macro parameters fluctuate in the T and TB regions with gradually decreasing amplitudes. On the other hand, the working points of PT-3 and PT-4 not only go across the T and TB modes, but also go down to the RP mode, and fluctuate periodically in these three modes. Overall, the fluctuation periods of the macro variables of the four pump-turbines are about 11.5, 10, 14.4, and 9.6 s, respectively, though the inertia values of rotating parts are the same (Table 1) in the simulations. The periods are also influenced by the rated rotating speed, discharge, and output. In addition, the maximum rotational speeds are heavily affected by the above factors [27,28], and can reach more than 1.4 times that of the initial value in PT-1 but less than 1.2 times in PT-4.

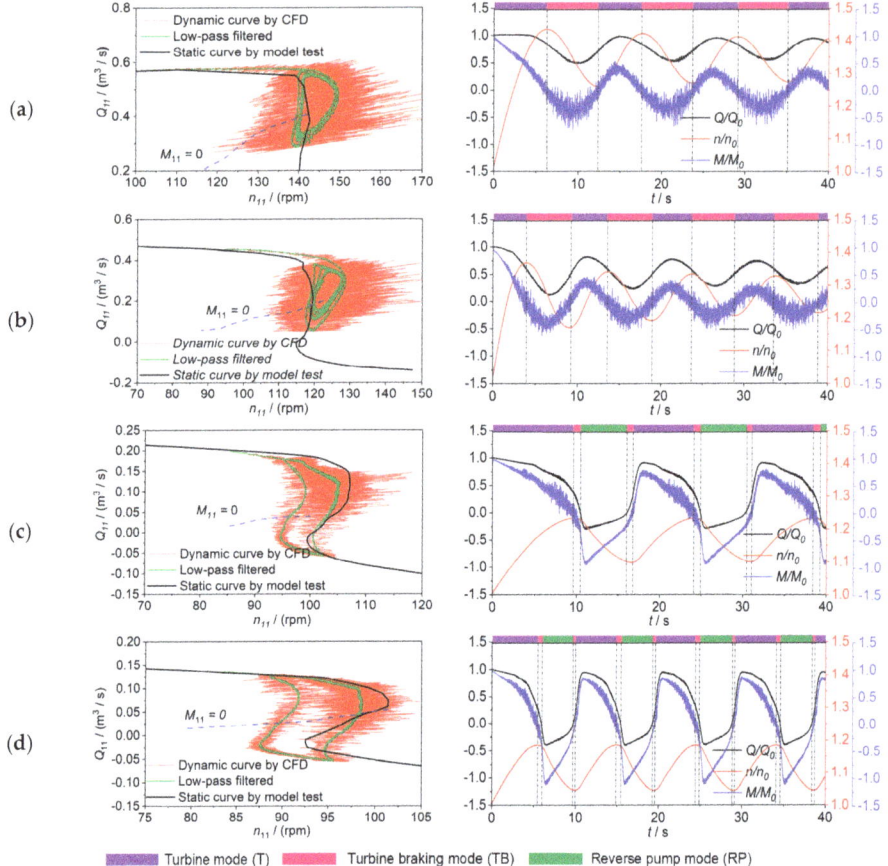

Figure 2. Working point trajectories and parameter histories of the four pump-turbines: (**a**) PT-1, (**b**) PT-2, (**c**) PT-3, (**d**) PT-4.

3.2. Radial Velocity Variations and Backflow Transitions at the Runner Inlets

The aforementioned fluctuations of dynamic trajectories are closely related to the unstable flow patterns near the runner inlets and outlets [29]. The variations of flow velocity at the runner inlet can reasonably demonstrate the characteristics of flow evolutions during the runaway processes. Figure 3 show the variations of normalized radial velocity v_r at the three monitoring points (HS, MS, and SS shown in Figure 1f, namely hub side, mid span and shroud side, respectively) in the four runners. The normalized velocities were defined by:

$$v_r = \frac{60 U_r}{\pi n_1 D_1} \qquad (1)$$

where U_r is the instantaneous radial velocity, n_1 is the initial rotational speed, and D_1 is the runner inlet diameter. Here, positive values of v_r are defined as the direction of water flowing into the runner passages, while negative values of v_r mean the backflows from the runner passages to the vaneless space. In addition, v_r (O) and v_r (L), in Figure 3, are the original and low-pass filtered data, respectively, and the upper frequency limit of low-pass filtered data is 2 Hz.

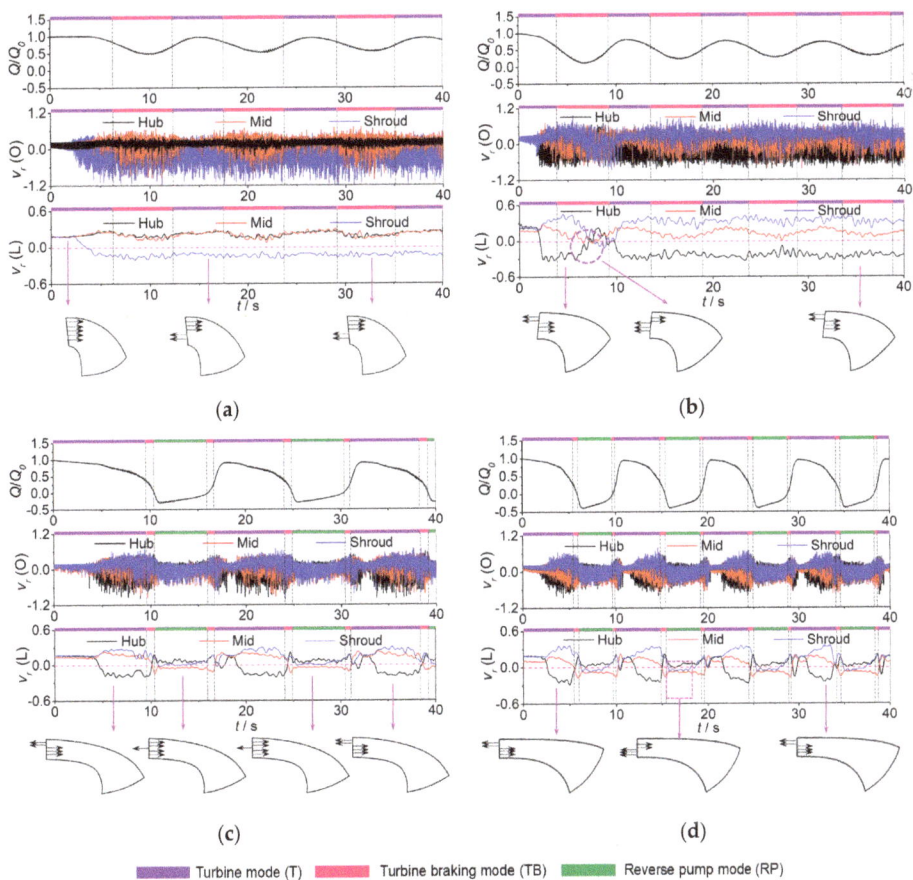

Figure 3. Variations of the normalized radial velocity v_r at the three monitor points: (**a**) PT-1, (**b**) PT-2, (**c**) PT-3, (**d**) PT-4.

In general, during the beginning period of the runaway process, the rotational speed increases, the inflow attack angle decreases, and the velocity pulsations increase due to the growing impact at the runner inlet. When the backflows occur at the runner inlet (the reverse direction of v_r), the velocity pulsations suddenly increase. Also, the velocity pulsations are almost the largest near this critical time. The lower the specific speed, the smaller the differences of velocity pulsations in different monitoring points. Consistent with the features in Figure 2, the velocity pulsations in PT-1 and PT-2 are the largest, and those in PT-4 is the smallest. In addition, though the discharge varies periodically, the variations of radial velocity in PT-1 and PT-2 are not obviously, especially at the location where the backflows occur, which are affected by the absence of flow transitions. But for PT-3 and PT-4, the variation period of radial velocity is corresponding to that of discharge. Overall, with the changes of flow rate, there are significant differences in flow features at the runner inlets.

1. PT-1: The dynamic trajectory of PT-1 only goes through the turbine (T) and turbine braking (TB) modes, and the macro parameters only fluctuate in relatively small amplitudes, therefore, the radial velocity (low-pass filtered data) cannot vary violently. At around $t = 3.6$ s (in the T mode), the radial velocity direction at the shroud side alters, indicating the appearance of backflows. At the same time, the velocity fluctuations increase significantly, namely the flow instability is intensified. However, the radial velocity directions on the hub side and mid span keep unchanged, and the increased

values (high-frequency data) indicate that the water flow can rush into the blade passages more easily. Although the rotational speed and flow rate fluctuate greatly, the radial velocity direction at the runner inlet remains unchanged after t = 3.6 s (Figure 3a).

2. PT-2: Though the working modes experienced are the same as those of PT-1, the developments of backflows show different characteristics because the backflows start from the hub side (t = 2.1 s) in the turbine mode and have transitions. At the early stage of backflow generations, the radial velocity at the mid span increases briefly and then decreases gradually, while that on the shroud side increases rapidly. At about t = 8–10 s (in the TB mode), there are significant transitions of radial velocity directions, namely the backflows occur suddenly at the mid span and shroud side at the same time, while those at the hub side disappear for a short time. After a short stay, backflows return to the hub side again. Similar to the phenomenon in PT-1, although the speed and discharge still fluctuate afterward, backflows keep staying at one location, and there is no transition (Figure 3b).

3. PT-3 and PT-4: Besides the turbine and turbine modes, the dynamic trajectories of these two pump-turbines also go through the reverse pump mode and the backflow transitions are basically similar. All of them generate from the hub side (in the T mode), then turn to the mid span and shroud side (in the TB mode). However, the only difference is that when the working point enters the reverse pump mode, the backflows in PT-3 mainly alternate between the hub side and mid span, while those in PT-4 also spread to the shroud side (Figure 3c,d).

In order to further explore the flow patterns at the runner inlets, Figures 4–7 show backflows at typical times in a single passage. Generally speaking, when the working points leave from the optimal ones, the water will impact on the blades and form backflows, making some water returning to the vaneless space and some water jumping over and impacting the next blade.

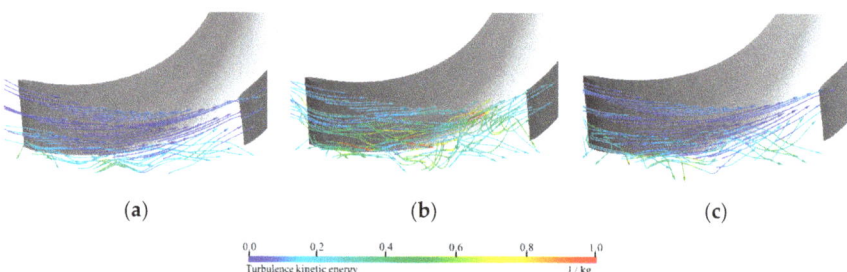

Figure 4. Flow patterns at the runner inlet in PT-1: (**a**) t = 3.6 s (turbine (T)), (**b**) t = 10.0 s (turbine braking (TB)), and (**c**) t = 15.0 s (T).

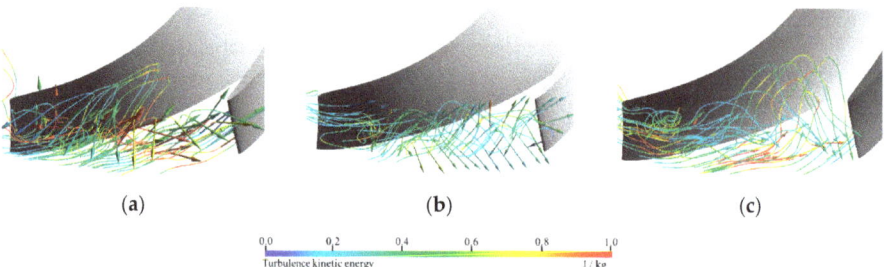

Figure 5. Flow patterns at the runner inlet in PT-2: (**a**) t = 5.0 s (TB), (**b**) t = 8.0 s (TB), and (**c**) t = 15.0 s (TB).

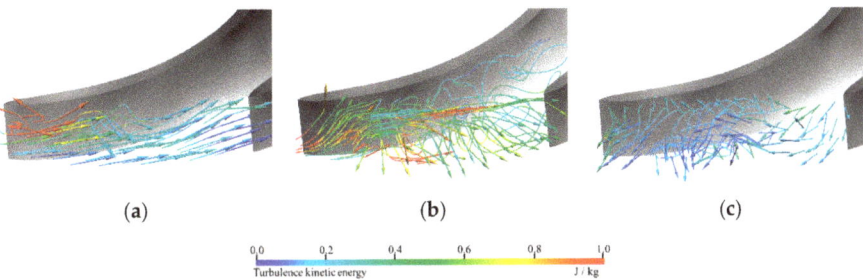

Figure 6. Flow patterns at the runner inlet in PT-3: (**a**) t = 8.0 s (T), (**b**) t = 10.0 s (TB), (**c**) t = 13.0 s (reverse pump (RP)).

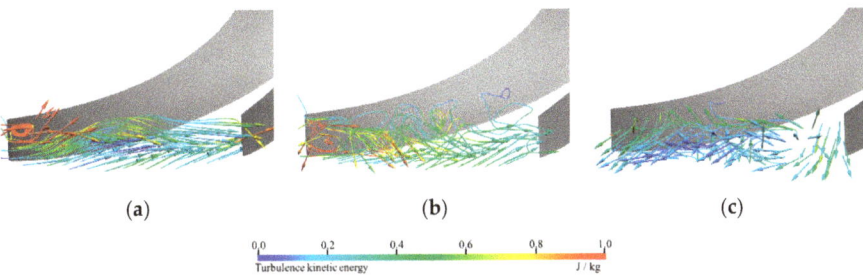

Figure 7. Flow patterns at the runner inlet in PT-4: (**a**) t = 4.0 s (T), (**b**) t = 5.8 s (TB), (**c**) t = 7.4 s (RP).

1. PT-1: The backflows generate from the shroud side, while the water flows into the blade passage easily on the hub side. Because the inlet height of PT-1 is relatively large, the backflows are mainly maintained near the shroud over the entire runaway process, and just influence the normal inflow at the mid span (Figure 4a).

2. PT-2: Backflows generate from the hub side and gradually evaluate to other locations. Compared with those in PT-1, the inlet height of PT-2 is smaller, and the backflows are easy to expand to the whole inlet. There is an obvious transition in the flow patterns, and the backflows suddenly occur on the shroud side and at the mid span (Figure 5b, t = 8.0 s), which is consistent with the transition of v_r in Figure 3b. But with the speed and discharge tending to steady, the backflows keep stay on the hub side.

3. PT-3 and PT-4: The inflow attacks on the blades at the mid span, leading to the upward deviation of the normal inflow on the hub side, then backflows generate and evaluate to other locations. Once entering the reverse pump mode, the backflows at the mid span in PT-3 have less influence to the hub and shroud sides, while those in PT-4 affect the shroud side obviously (Figure 7c).

3.3. Pressure Fluctuations in the Time Domain at the Runner Inlets

The dimensionless pressure fluctuations at each monitoring point in the vaneless space are analyzed by comparing with the pressures at the initial time. The normalized pressure was calculated by equation:

$$C_p = \frac{p - p_{initial}}{0.5 \rho u_1^2} \quad (2)$$

where p is the instantaneous pressure signals, $p_{initial}$ is mean initial pressure values at the initial time, ρ is the water density, and u_1 is the tip velocity of the runner blade leading edge. In addition, C_p (O) and C_p (L) in Figure 8 are the original and low-pass filtered data, respectively, and the upper frequency limit of the low-pass filtered data is 2 Hz.

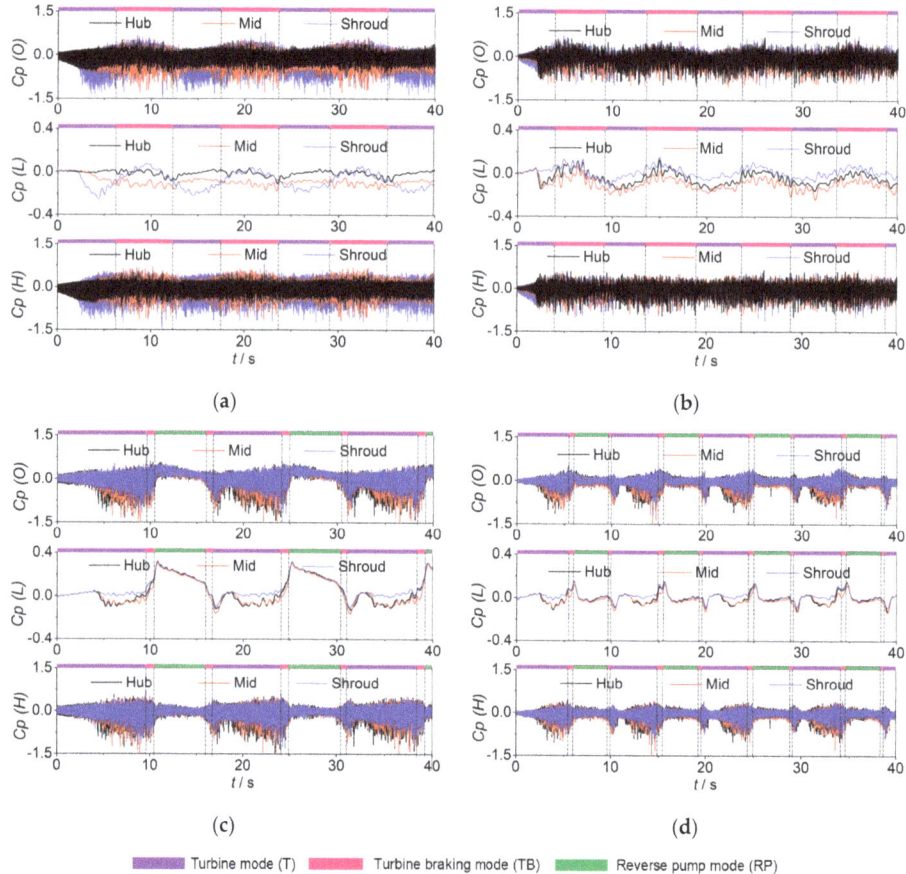

Figure 8. Variations of normalized pressure C_p at the three monitoring points of runner inlet: (**a**) PT-1, (**b**) PT-2, (**c**) PT-3, (**d**) PT-4.

Previous research has shown that after runaway, backflows will enhance the rotor–stator interactions and greatly increase the amplitudes of pressure pulsations [1]. Figure 8 shows the pressure pulsations in the time domain at the runner inlets of the four pump-turbines. On the whole, under the same total rotational inertia of runner and generator, the amplitudes in PT-1 and PT-3 are relatively large, while those in PT-2 and PT-4 are relatively small. It is found that the longer fluctuation periods of PT-1 and PT-3 mean the longer residence time in the S-shaped region and larger pressure pulsations. In addition, with the variations of rotational speed and discharge, the pressure pulsations present regular changes, with the amplitudes reach the maximum near the runaway point. Due to the different working conditions, there are obvious different characteristics of pressure pulsations.

1. PT-1 and PT-2: The working points only go through the T and TB modes, and the filtered data only slightly vary with the changes of rotational speed and discharge, while the amplitudes of high-frequency signals have no obvious change.

2. PT-3 and PT-4: The trends of pressure pulsations in these two pump-turbines are basically the same, and before the RP mode, they are all similar to those in PT-1 and PT-2 because the low-pass filtered pressure has a shut down when the backflow occurs. However, with the conversion from the TB mode to the RP mode, the low-frequency signals have a significant increase. And when the reverse discharge increases to the maximum value, the low-frequency signals also reach at the maximum.

This is because the rotating energy of the runner and rotor is converted to the water head of the pump-turbine. In addition, the pressure variations in PT-3 and PT-4 in the RP mode are still quite different. In particular, the low-frequency signals decrease slowly in PT-3, while those in PT-4 decrease rapidly. The reason is that the backflows at the runner inlet are quite different during this period. In PT-3, backflows are mainly at the mid span, contributing to poor flow capacity to get water out of the blade passages, forming flow blockage at the inlet and increasing pressure [1]. However, in PT-4, backflows occur at the mid span and on the shroud side at the same time, with strong flow capacity and rapid pressure reduction. For the high-frequency signals, the amplitudes of those in the T mode gradually increase, while those in the TB and RP modes decrease.

Compared with the velocity pulsations in Figure 3, it is found that when the working points of PT-3 and PT-4 enter the RP mode, the velocity pulsation always keeps high amplitude characteristics, while the amplitude of pressure pulsations decreases rapidly, which means the unsteady development of the flow patterns cannot accurately reflect the true values of the pressure pulsations. Figures 4–7 not only show the flow pattern development at the runner inlets, but also show the magnitude of turbulent kinetic energy. It can be seen that the turbulent kinetic energy at the runner inlet is relatively low after entering the RP mode, indicating that pressure pulsations will decrease rapidly when the turbulent kinetic energy becomes small.

3.4. Pressure Fluctuations in Time–Frequency Domain at the Runner Inlets

A time–frequency analysis of the transient pressure pulsations at the monitoring points was performed by using the Short Time Fourier Transform (STFT) method [30–32]. From Figures 9–12, at the beginning of the runaway process, the characteristics of pressure pulsations are mainly influenced by the runner. The dominant frequency in the spectrogram is the blade passing frequency (BPF) ($7f_0$ for PT-1; $9f_0$ for PT-2, PT-3, and PT-4, where f_0 is the rotating frequency of the runner rotation), and the rest high frequencies are the integer multiples of the BPF.

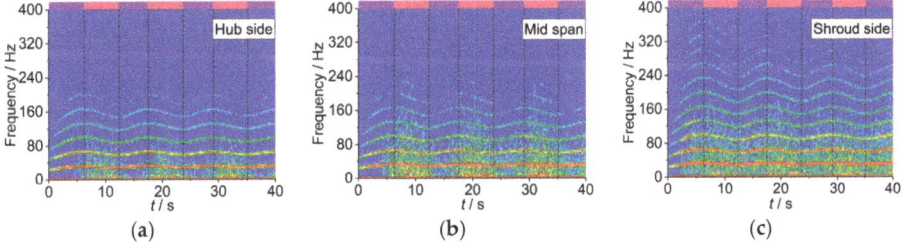

Figure 9. Frequency spectrums for pressures at the monitoring points of PT-1: (**a**) at hub side, (**b**) at mid span, (**c**) at shroud side.

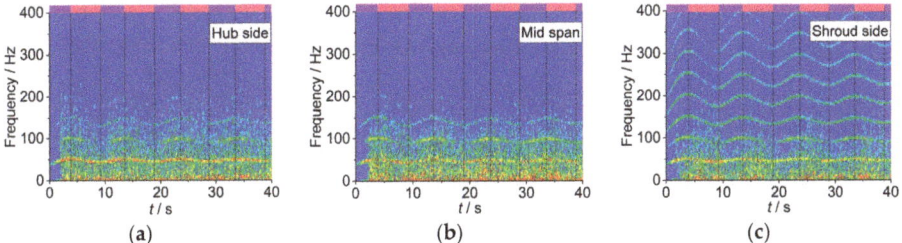

Figure 10. Frequency spectrums for pressures at the monitoring points of PT-2: (**a**) at hub side, (**b**) at mid span, (**c**) at shroud side.

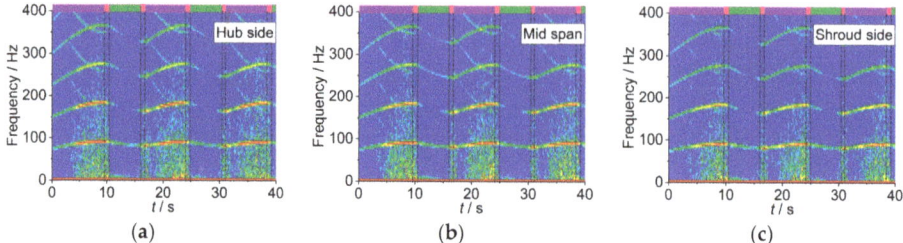

Figure 11. Frequency spectrums for pressures at the monitoring points of PT-3: (**a**) at hub side, (**b**) at mid span, (**c**) at shroud side.

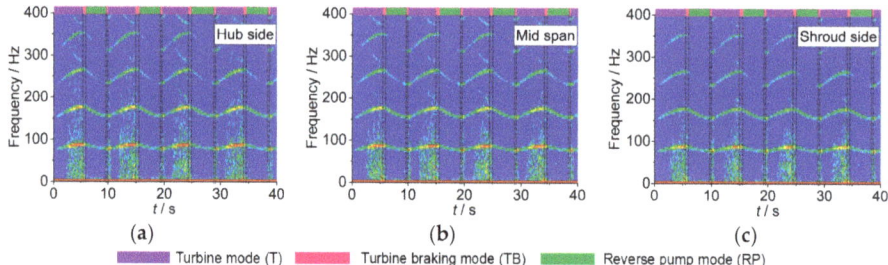

Figure 12. Frequency spectrums for pressures at the monitoring points of PT-4: (**a**) at hub side, (**b**) at mid span, (**c**) at shroud side.

In the runaway process, each outstanding frequency varies with the change of rotational speed. As a whole, the amplitude of each frequency increases obviously once the working point enters the S-shaped region, which is due to the enhancement of impact at the runner inlet and rotor-stator interaction. In addition, the high-amplitude low-frequency signals occur obviously, and their occurrence time is consistent with the reduction of inlet radial velocity. Once the backflows generate, the amplitude increases rapidly and reaches at the maximum near the runaway point. Previous studies shown that the high-amplitude low-frequency signals are mainly caused by rotating stalls [1].

In contrast, in PT-1 and PT-2, the durations of the maximum amplitude are mainly after the runaway point, while those in PT-3 and PT-4 are before the runaway point, indicating that the evolutions of unstable flow patterns are affected quite differently by the S-shaped characteristics. Because the working points of PT-3 and PT-4 have gone through the RP mode, the amplitudes suddenly decrease obviously at $t = 10$ s (PT-3) and $t = 5$ s (PT-4), and increase at $t = 16$ s (PT-3) and $t = 10$ s (PT-4), respectively. All of these phenomena are caused by the backflow transitions, consistent with the changes of pressure fluctuations in the time domain spectrum in Figure 8.

For each runner, the amplitudes of pressure pulsations in different locations at the runner inlet are also different. In PT-1 and PT-2, the differences of pressure pulsation characteristics at the three monitoring points Figure 8 are quite large, while those in PT-3 and PT-4 are smaller. Taking PT-1 as an example, with the runaway beginning, the radial velocity at the inlet decreases obviously, and the low-frequency signals gradually generate at each monitoring point. Once the backflows occur on the shroud side, the amplitudes increase rapidly. Compared with pressure fluctuations at the three locations, the duration of the low-frequency signals is the longest on the shroud side, and they exist in the whole S-shaped region, because the backflows keep staying at this location all of the time. However, the highest amplitudes of low-frequency signals are at the mid span, while the lowest ones are on the hub side, and there are only low-frequency signals at the runaway point. In PT-2, the same phenomenon as in PT-1 is that the location with the highest amplitudes is also at the mid span, though the backflows occur on the hub side. In PT-3 and PT-4, there are no significant differences in the frequency of pulsations in different locations.

From the analysis mentioned above, we know that the high-amplitude low-frequency signals will generate at the location where backflows occur, which is the most obvious in PT-1 because its inlet height is the largest. These phenomena also have the same laws in PT-3 and PT-4, but the difference is not obvious because their inlet heights are smaller. However, the pressure characteristics in PT-2 is an exception Figure 10, which will be discussed in the later chapter.

3.5. Flow Patterns in Blade Passage and Draft Tube

Even if the radial velocity at the runner outlet cannot be exactly monitored like that at the inlet, the outlet backflows can be observed clearly from the flow patterns in the draft-tube and near the blade suction side as seen in Figures 13–16. After the working point enters the S-shaped region, the streamlines in the blade channels are no longer as smooth as before. The main flow will enter the draft-tube along the side wall, or return to the runner from the draft-tube center, due to the changes in rotational speed and discharge [31]. As mentioned before, whether or not the working point enters the RP mode can lead to large differences in flow patterns, which has no exception at the runner outlet. For PT-1 and PT-2 (Figures 13 and 14), although the total flow rate is mainly in the turbine direction, the main stream water flow attacks the blade suction side from the draft-tube center, because of the increase of the pumping effect. Some water jumps into the nearby runner channel, and some go back to the draft-tube. Also, this phenomenon will be very obvious when the minimum discharge condition is approached. But in PT-3 and PT-4 Figures 15 and 16, the working points also enter the RP mode, and the flowing directions reverse to the pump direction. At this time, a part of water flow enters the upstream along the suction surface, and a part escapes to the next blade channel, and a little water returns to the draft-tube.

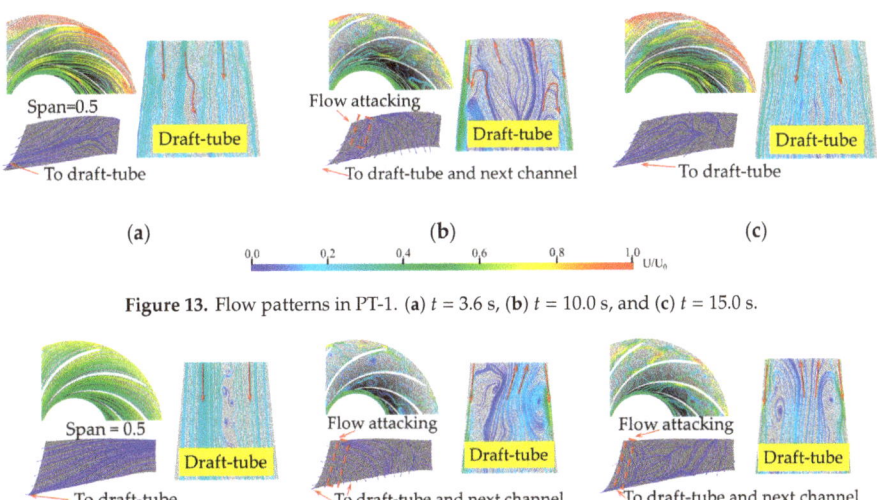

Figure 13. Flow patterns in PT-1. (**a**) $t = 3.6$ s, (**b**) $t = 10.0$ s, and (**c**) $t = 15.0$ s.

Figure 14. Flow patterns in PT-2. (**a**) $t = 0.1$ s, (**b**) $t = 7.0$ s, and (**c**) $t = 15.0$ s.

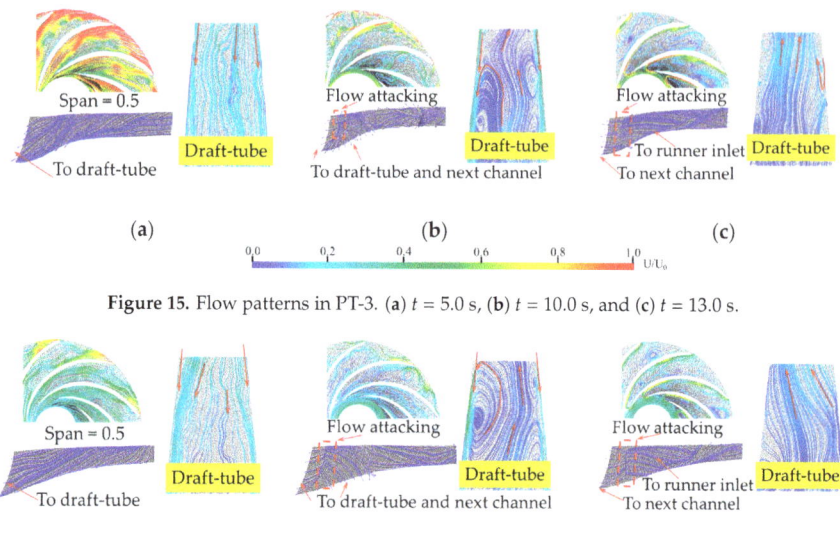

Figure 15. Flow patterns in PT-3. (**a**) $t = 5.0$ s, (**b**) $t = 10.0$ s, and (**c**) $t = 13.0$ s.

Figure 16. Flow patterns in PT-4. (**a**) $t = 4.0$ s, (**b**) $t = 5.8$ s, and (**c**) $t = 7.4$ s.

4. Discussions of Influences of Runner Shapes

It can be seen from the above analysis that the starting and staying locations of backflows at the runner inlets are different during the runaway processes in the pump-turbines with different specific speeds. Xia [33] pointed out that the backflow structures are mainly affected by the shape of the blade inlet and centrifugal force, which can change the pressure gradient. Similarly, the initial position of backflows is related to this factor. Figure 17 shows the different blade lean angles of the four pump-turbines, which mean the inclination angles of blade leading edges at the runner inlets. The blade lean angle of PT-1 is negative, and its backflows generate from the shroud side. The blade lean angle PT-2 is positive, and its backflows generate from the hub side. Interestingly, the inlets of PT-3 and PT-4 have no blade lean, but the backflows also generate from the hub side.

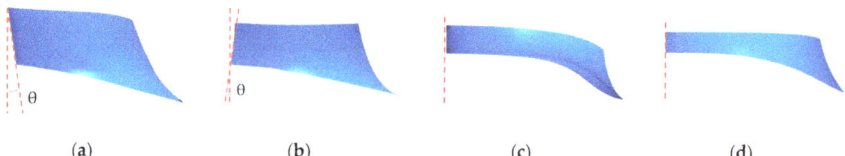

Figure 17. Lean angles of the blade leading edges of the four pump-turbines: (**a**) PT-1, negative lean angle, (**b**) PT-2, positive lean angle, (**c**) PT-3, no blade lean, (**d**) PT-4, No blade lean.

As shown in Figure 8, it can be seen from the filtered-data that in the early stage of runaway, the pressures at the monitoring points are approximately the same and there is no backflow. With the increase in rotating speed, the centrifugal force increases but the discharge decreases, then the pressure gradient between the hub and shroud sides becomes larger, resulting in water flows from the higher-pressure side to the lower one. Here, the blade lean angle affects the distribution of pressure gradient and leads to the different initial position of backflows. The negative lean angle of PT-1 forces the pressure to increase on the hub side, which makes the water turn from the hub side to middle and shroud ones, leading to backflows on the shroud side Figure 18a. On the contrary, the backflows in

PT-2 generate from the hub side due to the existence of a positive lean angle Figure 18b. Although there is no lean angle in PT-3 and PT-4, the pressure gradient distribution in them is consistent with that in PT-2, therefore the backflows all generate from the hub side Figure 18c.

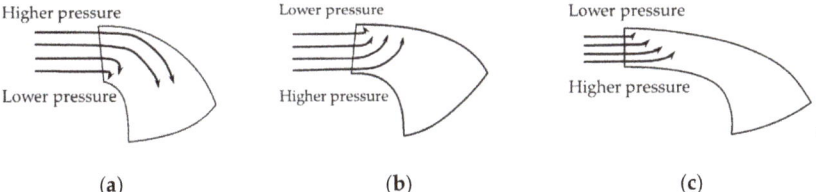

Figure 18. Diagram explaining the reason of backflows at runner inlet in four pump-turbines: (**a**) PT-1, (**b**) PT-2, (**c**) PT-3 and PT-4.

Secondly, the different heights of runner inlets affect the development of backflows. The smaller the height of runner inlet, the easier the backflows change location. The inlet height of PT-1 is the largest, therefore the backflows can only exist on the shroud side all the time, and the influence range of backflows is relatively small. Therefore, due to the lowest height of PT-4, in the RP mode, the relative backflow region can be larger than that in PT-3 Figure 3. Because of these differences in backflow transitions, pressure pulsation evolutions get large differences. With the decrease of the inlet height, the differences of the pressure fluctuations between three locations decrease. Hence, the difference of the pressure fluctuations at each location in PT-1 is the largest, while that in PT-4 is the smallest. In the above four runners, except for PT-2, the location where the backflows occur, the pressure amplitudes are the largest. As a special case, the blade inlet design of PT-2 is the main reason that the blade leading edge diameters at the three locations are quite different Figure 19b. Due to the difference of blade leading edge diameters at the three locations, the pressure characteristics in PT-2 is an exception. Therefore, besides the backflows, the size of the vaneless space and distance to the blade should be considered.

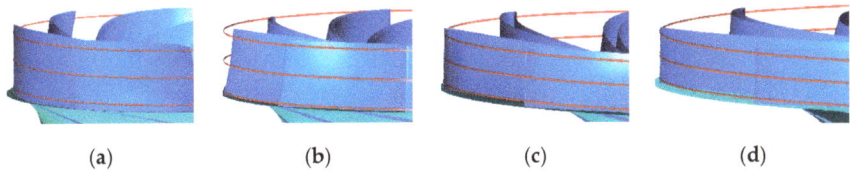

Figure 19. Differences of blade leading edge diameters of the four pump-turbines: (**a**) PT-1, (**b**) PT-2, (**c**) PT-3, (**d**) PT-4.

In order to further verify the analysis mentioned above, the runaway process of a conventional turbine was also simulated, and the detailed information including the lean angle of blade leading edge and inlet diameter was shown in Figure 20. Though the starting working condition of runaway is not the rated one, it is a large guide-vane opening case, which is near the rated working point and can reflect the main characteristics of backflows and pressure pulsations.

The results show that the macro parameters nearly maintain constant values after $t = 4$ s due to the absence of the S-shaped characteristics, and the period during this time is defined as the no-load mode (Figure 21). The radial velocity and flow patterns are selected (Figures 22 and 23), and it can be seen that the backflows only generate on the hub side, which is similar to those in PT-2 because these two turbines have the same blade lean angle (Figures 17b and 20a) and the same pressure gradient (Figure 18b). Also, the backflows keep staying on the hub side because the runner inlet height is relatively large, which is similar to those in PT-1.

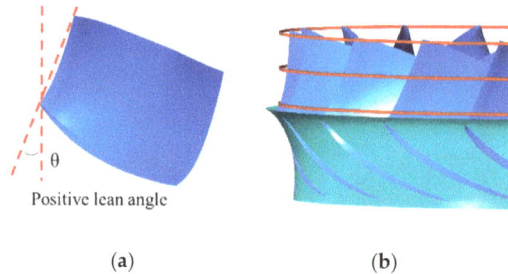

Figure 20. Lean angle of blade leading edge and inlet diameter of CT. (**a**) Inlet lean angle and (**b**) inlet diameter.

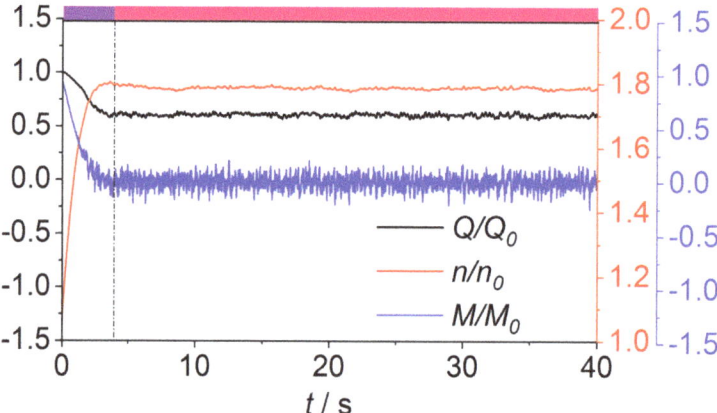

Figure 21. Histories of the macro parameters of CT during runaway processes.

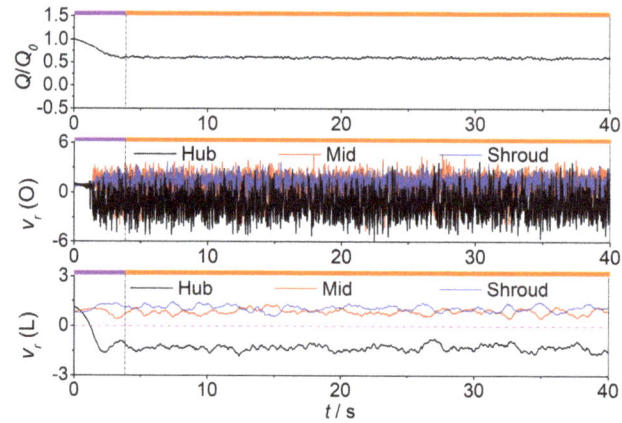

Figure 22. The variations of normalized radial velocity v_r of three monitor points in CT.

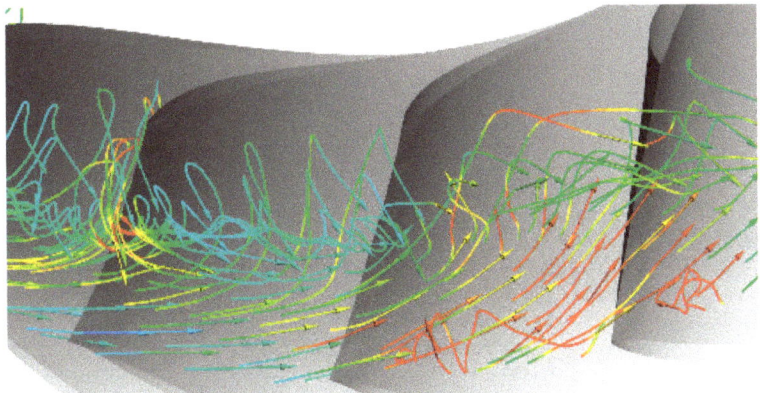

Figure 23. Flow patterns at the runner inlet of CT.

5. Conclusions

The transient processes of the four pump-turbines with different specific speeds from turbine mode were simulated, and the macro parameter variations, flow pattern evolutions, as well as pressure fluctuations were analyzed. The working conditions, the transitions of backflows at the runner inlet and outlet, and the pressure pulsations at different locations ware compared, and the following conclusions were drawn.

1. The lower specific speed of the pump-turbine, the easier the chance for pump-turbines to enter into the reverse pump mode, generating undamped runaway oscillations. During these runaway processes, backflows and violent pressure pulsations occur in all turbines, and similarities and differences are obvious.

2. The position where the backflows generate at the runner inlet is related to the blade lean angle, which can affect the distribution of pressure gradient. As a result, the water turns from the higher-pressure side to the lower one, then the backflows generate at the lower pressure side. In addition, because lower specific speed turbine has smaller inlet height, the backflows occupy relatively larger range at the runner inlet and are easier to have transitions.

3. The pressure pulsations at different locations are influenced by the relative runner inlet height, distance to runner blades and flow pattern transitions. The smaller the runner inlet height, the smaller the differences in the pressure signals at three locations. The smaller the distance to the runner blades, the larger the pressure pulsations. Furthermore, flow pattern transitions and the turbulent kinetic energy distribution are important and should be considered.

4. S-characteristics in different pump-turbines are quite different, therefore, besides the four pump-turbines in this paper, more pump-turbines should be chosen to investigate the evolutions of pressure pulsation and flow patterns during the runaway process. Also, more factors including water conveyance systems, inertia of rotating parts, and guide vane openings should be considered to study the flow patterns and pressure pulsations in practical power stations. In addition, control methods should be investigated in the design stage by 3D simulations of transient processes.

Author Contributions: Data curation, Z.L. and Z.Y.; formal analysis, Z.Y. and Z.L.; investigation, Z.Y. and L.X.; validation, X.Z.; writing—original draft, Z.Y. and Y.C.; writing—review & editing, K.L. and X.Z. All authors have read and agreed to the published version of the manuscript.

Funding: This work was supported by the National Natural Science Foundation of China (NSFC) (Grant Nos. 51839008 and 51579187), the Natural Science Foundation of Hubei Province (Grant No. 2018CFA010), the National Natural Science Foundation of China (Grant No. 51909226), and the Natural Science Foundation of Fujian Province, China (Grant No. 2018J01525).

Acknowledgments: The numerical simulations were conducted on the supercomputing system in the Supercomputing Center of Wuhan University.

Conflicts of Interest: The authors declare no conflict of interest.

Nomenclature

b_0	height of runner inlet (m)
C_p	normalized pressure at the runner inlets (-)
C_p (O)	original data of normalized pressure at the runner inlets (-)
C_p (L)	low-pass filtered data of normalized pressure at the runner inlets (-)
C_p (H)	C_p (O) − C_p (L), high frequency data of normalized pressure at the runner inlets (-)
D	diameter of the runner inlet (m)
E_1	total energy values at the spiral-casing inlet (m)
E_2	total energy values at the runner outlet (m)
GD^2	Inertia of rotating parts (10^7 kg·m^2)
Hr	rated head (m)
H	head during the runaway process (m)
M	moment during the runaway process (N·m)
M_0	moment at the initial time (N·m)
M_{11}	unit torque (N·m)
n	rotational speed during the runaway process (rpm)
n_0	rotational speed at the initial time (rpm)
n_1	rotational speed at the initial time (rad/s)
n_{11}	unit speed (rpm)
n_s	specific speed (m · kW)
n_r	rated rotational speed (rpm)
Nr	rated output (MW)
p	instantaneous pressure (Pa)
$p_{initial}$	mean initial pressure values at the initial time (Pa)
Q	discharge during the runaway process (m^3/s)
Q_0	discharge at the initial time (m^3/s)
Q_{11}	unit discharge (m^3/s)
t	times (s)
u_1	tip velocity of runner blade leading edge (m/s)
U_r	the instantaneous radial velocity (m/s)
v_r	normalized radial velocity at the runner inlets (-)
v_r (O)	original data of normalized radial velocity at the runner inlets (-)
v_r (L)	low-pass filtered data of normalized radial velocity at the runner inlets (-)
ρ	water density (kg/m^3)

References

1. Xia, L.; Cheng, Y.; Yang, Z.; You, J.; Yang, J.; Qian, Z. Evolutions of Pressure Fluctuations and Runner Loads during Runaway Processes of a Pump-Turbine. *J. Fluids Eng. Trans. ASME* **2017**, *139*, 091101. [CrossRef]
2. Fu, X.; Li, D.; Wang, H.; Zhang, G.; Li, Z.; Wei, X. Numerical simulation of the transient flow in a pump-turbine during load rejection process with special emphasis on hydraulic acoustic effect. *Renew. Energy* **2020**, *155*, 1127–1138. [CrossRef]
3. Li, D.; Wang, H.; Xiang, G.; Gong, R.; Wei, X.; Liu, Z. Unsteady simulation and analysis for hump characteristics of a pump turbine model. *Renew. Energy* **2015**, *77*, 32–42.
4. Barbour, E.; Wilson, I.; Radcliffe, J.; Ding, Y.; Li, Y. A review of pumped hydro energy storage development in significant international electricity markets. *Renew. Sustain. Energy Rev.* **2016**, *61*, 421–432. [CrossRef]
5. Durga Hari Kiran, B.; Sailaja Kumari, M. Demand response and pumped hydro storage scheduling for balancing wind power uncertainties: A probabilistic unit commitment approach. *Int. J. Electr. Power Energy Syst.* **2016**, *81*, 114–122. [CrossRef]

6. Cai, J.; Zhou, X.; Deng, L. The research of the abnormal water hammer phenomenon based on the unit 3 over speed test of Jiangsu. *Water Power* **2009**, *35*, 87–90. (In Chinese)
7. Li, Q.; Li, J.; Hu, Q.; Yu, J. Site test on S-shape characteristics of large-sized mixed flow reversible turbine-generator unit. *Northwest Hydropower* **2012**, *S1*, 81–85. (In Chinese)
8. Ma, M. Analysis and solution of grid connection failure under low head condition. *Mech. Electr. Tech. Hydropower Stn.* **2002**, *2*, 37–39. (In Chinese)
9. Le, Z.; Kong, L. Cause analysis on rotating part lifting of unit 2 in Tianhuangping pumped storage plant. *Mech. Electr. Tech. Hydropower Stn.* **2005**, *28*, 11–13. (In Chinese)
10. Yang, Z.; Cheng, Y.; Xia, L.; Meng, W.; Gao, L.; Dai, X. Evolutions of guide vane moment of a pump-turbine during runaway transient process after pump trip. *IOP Conf. Ser. Earth Environ. Sci.* **2019**, *240*, 072033. [CrossRef]
11. Li, D.; Fu, X.; Zuo, Z.; Wang, H.; Li, Z.; Liu, S.; Wei, X. Investigation methods for analysis of transient phenomena concerning design and operation of hydraulic-machine systems—A review. *Renew. Sustain. Energy Rev.* **2019**, *101*, 26–46. [CrossRef]
12. Zhang, Y.; Wu, Y. A review of rotating stall in reversible pump turbine. *Proc. Inst. Mech. Eng. Part C J. Mech. Eng. Sci.* **2017**, *231*, 1181–1204. [CrossRef]
13. Zuo, Z.; Liu, S.; Sun, Y.; Wu, Y. Pressure fluctuations in the vaneless space of High-head pump-turbines—A review. *Renew. Sustain. Energy Rev.* **2015**, *41*, 965–974. [CrossRef]
14. Gentner, C.; Sallaberger, M.; Widmer, C.; Braun, O.; Staubli, T. Numerical and experimental analysis of instability phenomena in pump turbines. *IOP Conf. Ser. Earth Environ. Sci.* **2012**, *15*, 032042. [CrossRef]
15. Wang, L.; Yin, J.; Jiao, L.; Wu, D.; Qin, D. Numerical investigation on the "S" characteristics of a reduced pump turbine model. *Sci. China Technol. Sci.* **2011**, *54*, 1259–1266. [CrossRef]
16. Widmer, C.; Staubli, T.; Ledergerber, N. Unstable characteristics and rotating stall in turbine brake operation of pump-turbines. *J. Fluids Eng. Trans. ASME* **2011**, *133*, 1–9. [CrossRef]
17. Hasmatuchi, V.; Farhat, M.; Roth, S.; Botero, F.; Avellan, F. Experimental evidence of rotating stall in a pump-turbine at off-design conditions in generating mode. *J. Fluids Eng. Trans. ASME* **2011**, *133*, 1–8. [CrossRef]
18. Jacquet, C.; Fortes-Patella, R.; Balarac, L.; Houdeline, J.B. CFD investigation of complex phenomena in S-shape region of reversible pump-turbine. *IOP Conf. Ser. Earth Environ. Sci.* **2016**, *49*, 042010. [CrossRef]
19. Trivedi, C.; Cervantes, M.; Gandhi, B. Investigation of a high head Francis turbine at runaway operating conditions. *Energies* **2016**, *9*, 149. [CrossRef]
20. Trivedi, C.; Gandhi, B.; Cervantes, M.; Dahlhaug, O. Experimental investigations of a model Francis turbine during shutdown at synchronous speed. *Renew. Energy* **2015**, *83*, 828–836. [CrossRef]
21. Trivedi, C.; Cervantes, M.; Gandhi, B.; Dahlhaug, O. Transient pressure measurements on a high head model Francis turbine during emergency shutdown, total load rejection, and runaway. *J. Fluids Eng. Trans. ASME* **2014**, *136*, 121107. [CrossRef]
22. Trivedi, C.; Cervantes, M.; Dahlhaug, O.; Gandhi, B. Experimental investigation of a high head Francis turbine during spin-no-load operation. *J. Fluids Eng. Trans. ASME* **2015**, *137*, 061106. [CrossRef]
23. Yin, J.; Wang, D.; Walters, D.; Wei, X. Investigation of the unstable flow phenomenon in a pump turbine. *Sci. China Phys. Mech. Astron.* **2014**, *57*, 1119–1127. [CrossRef]
24. Zhang, X.; Cheng, Y.; Xia, L.; Yang, J.; Qian, Z. Looping dynamic characteristics of a pump-turbine in the s-shaped region during runaway. *J. Fluids Eng. Trans. ASME* **2016**, *138*, 1–10. [CrossRef]
25. Wei, B.; Ji, C. Study on rotor operation stability of high-speed large-capacity generator-motor: The Accident of Rotor Pole in Huizhou Pumped-Storage Power Station. *Water Power* **2010**, *36*, 57–60. (In Chinese)
26. Zhou, Q.; Xia, L.; Zhang, C. Internal mechanism and improvement criteria for the runaway oscillation stability of a pump-turbine. *Appl. Sci.* **2018**, *8*, 2193. [CrossRef]
27. Zhang, X. Three-Dimensional Transient Flow in Pumped-Storage Plant: Simulation and Analysis by Coupling One-Dimensional Water Conveyance System with Three-Dimensional Pump-Turbine. Ph.D. Thesis, Wuhan University, Wuhan, China, 2015.
28. Zhang, X.; Cheng, Y.; Yang, Z.; Chen, Q.; Liu, D. Influence of rotational inertia on the runner radial forces of a model pump-turbine running away through the S-shaped characteristic region. *IET Renew. Power Gener.* **2020**, *14*, 1883–1893. [CrossRef]

29. Xia, L.; Cheng, Y.; Yang, Z.; Yuan, Y.; Zhu, Z. Numerical investigations into the transient behaviour of a model pump-turbine during load rejection process. *IOP Conf. Ser. Earth Environ. Sci.* **2019**, *240*, 072040. [CrossRef]
30. Liu, Q.; Su, W.; Li, X.; Zhang, Y. Dynamic characteristics of load rejection process in a reversible pump-turbine. *Renew. Energy* **2020**, *146*, 1922–1931. [CrossRef]
31. Yang, Z.; Cheng, Y.; Xia, L.; Meng, W.; Liu, K.; Zhang, X. Evolutions of flow patterns and pressure fluctuations in a prototype pump-turbine during the runaway transient process after pump-trip. *Renew. Energy* **2020**, *152*, 1149–1159. [CrossRef]
32. Fu, X.; Li, D.; Wang, H.; Zhang, G.; Li, Z.; Wei, X. Dynamic instability of a pump-turbine in load rejection transient process. *Sci. China Technol. Sci.* **2018**, *61*, 1765–1775. [CrossRef]
33. Xia, L. Mechanism of the S-Shaped Characteristics and the Flow-Induced Dynamic Instability of Pump-Turbines. Ph.D. Thesis, Wuhan University, Wuhan, China, 2017.

© 2020 by the authors. Licensee MDPI, Basel, Switzerland. This article is an open access article distributed under the terms and conditions of the Creative Commons Attribution (CC BY) license (http://creativecommons.org/licenses/by/4.0/).

Article

Numerical Investigation of the Geometrical Effect on Flow-Induced Vibration Performance of Pivoted Bodies

Hamid Arionfard [1,*] and Sina Mohammadi [2]

1 Centre for Industrial Mechanics, Southern Denmark University, 6400 Sonderborg, Denmark
2 Schmid College of Science and Technology, Chapman University, Orange, CA 92866, USA; smohammadi@chapman.edu
* Correspondence: arionfard@sdu.dk; Tel.: +45-655-08287

Abstract: In this study, the Flow-Induced Vibration (FIV) of pivoted cylinders (at a distance) is numerically investigated as a potential source of energy harvesting. In particular, we investigate the effect of pivot point placement, arm length, and natural frequency on the FIV performance of six different cross sections in the Reynolds number of around 1000. All sections have similar mass, area, and moment of inertia to eliminate non-geometrical effects on the performance. Classical studies show that the synchronization phenomenon (lock-in) occurs when the vortex formation frequency is close enough to the body's natural frequency. Due to the configuration of the cylinder in this research (pivoted eccentrically), the natural frequency is also a function of the flow velocity as well as the geometrical specifications of the system. The simulation is done for the arm lengths between −3D and +3D for all cross sections. Results show that maximum output power is principally influenced more by the pivot location than the arm length. Although the box cross section has a higher amplitude of vibration, the circular cross section has the highest efficiency followed by the egg shape.

Keywords: VIV; FIV; renewable energy; pivoted cylinder; cross section; geometry

1. Introduction

In recent years, the development of flow-induced vibrations (FIV) energy harvesters has increased rapidly to offer a new source of energy. Due to the large strains and geometric deformations during FIV, they have traditionally been classified as a destructive phenomenon. One of the well-known examples of flutter-induced destruction is the Tacoma Narrows Bridge collapse in 1940, where torsional flutter at sufficiently large amplitudes caused catastrophic failure of the entire bridge. However, common and accessible FIV could be considered as a way to extract energy. Bernitsas et al. [1] have developed a device that uses the vortex induced vibration (VIV) phenomenon to generate electricity. Contrary to the VIV phenomenon, where significant oscillations develop in a small range of flow velocities and with limited oscillation amplitudes, other aeroelastic instabilities like flutter occur for an infinite range of flow velocities and without a self-limited response beyond the critical flow velocity which makes the flutter more promising for generating energy.

For instance, Hobbs and Hu [2] tested micro-watt energy harvesters inspired by tree trunks swaying in the wind. Their converter consists of four pivoted cylinders which affixed to the ground via a piezoelectric transducer. Yoshitake et al. [3] generated minuscule amounts of energy, using a device composed of Hula-Hoops and an electro magnetic transducer mechanism, in air flow. To study the aerodynamic efficiency of a drag assisted energy-harvesting device, Sung et al. [4] investigated the effects of the cylinder cross-sectional shape on the VIV. Their numerical simulations have demonstrated that an elliptical cylinder undergoes much larger displacements than a circular one. Nevertheless, their research mainly focuses on improving maximum displacement or amplitude rather than the angular velocity of the vibration.

In an attempt to study the performance of FIV, Arionfard and Nishi [5] carried out an experiment on a pivoted cylinder instead of a transitionally moving one. Being assisted by the drag force, the pivoting cylinder showed an increase in performance comparing to transitional VIV of a cylinder. As a result, different configurations with one and two cylinders were considered in the following researches to increase the performance by utilizing different mechanisms of vibrations [6–8]. However, an important way to improve the FIV performance is through the geometry of the bluff body and enhancement of the geometrical parameters is necessary in order to increase energy extraction performance. For several years great effort has been devoted to the study the effect of cross sections on FIV. However, common cross sections in aviation and civil engineering has attracted much more attention; Airfoil flutter [9], galloping of square, triangular, and semicircular sections [10], rectangular and D-sections[11,12] are some examples. However, to the author's best knowledge, very few publications are available in the literature that discuss the role of the geometrical parameters of the bluff body on the performance of the vibration. This paper reports geometrical effects on FIV performance of pivoted cylinders. Six cross section shapes are compared in which the circular cylinder is checked with our experimental data for validating the numerical simulation.

The present paper is organized as follows. The case is described in Section 2 followed by details of the numerical method, domains, and boundary conditions. Verification and validations is reported in Section 4, and the results are presented in in Section 5. We make conclusive remarks in Section 6.

2. Case Description

The cases considered in this study are based on water channel tests performed by Arionfard and Nishi [5]. The channel length is 1 meter with a test section's dimension of 30 cm wide by 30 cm deep. For the numerical simulation, the submerged bluff body is defined as a cylindrical solid sub-domain which is pivoted at a specific distance l, enabling rotation around the Z-axis, where X is the streamwise coordinate and Y is the cross-stream coordinate. The variation of the arm length l is considered by using twelve different values from $-3D$ to $+3D$, where D is the diameter of the cylinder, negative values of l represent a pivot on the downstream of the cylinder (like Figure 1) and positive values represent a pivot point on the upstream side of the cylinder. A torsional spring is defined at the pivot point shown in Figure 1 and provides a restoring moment during oscillation.

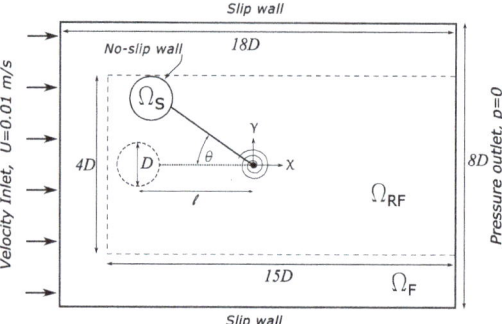

Figure 1. Schematic diagram of a typical computational domain and boundaries. Here, the pivot point is located at the downstream of the cylinder. The solid sub-domain is Ω_S, the fluid sub-domain is Ω_F, and Ω_{RF} is the refined part of the fluid sub-domain. The arm length l is the distance between the center of the bluff body and the pivot point

Six cross section shapes are chosen in this study as solid sub-domains. The area of all cross sections are equal and the height of sections (D) is as similar as possible to keep the

Reynolds number within the same range in all simulations. More details of the geometrical parameters of each cross-section is shown in Figure 2 and described in Table 1.

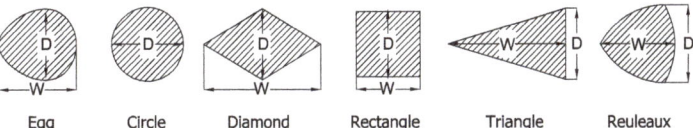

Egg   Circle   Diamond   Rectangle   Triangle   Reuleaux

Figure 2. Geometry of the bluff bodies. Dimensions are given in Table 1.

In all simulations, Reynolds number is calculated based on the uniform inlet velocity (0.01 m/s) and the vertical height of the cross section (D ≈ 10 cm).

Table 1. Geometric parameters of the cross sections.

Section	W (cm)	D (cm)	Area (cm^2)	Aspect Ratio	CG (cm)
CIR	10.36	10.36	84.35	1	5.18
BOX	9.18	9.18	84.35	1	4.59
DIA	16.87	10.00	84.35	1.68	8.43
TRI	16.87	10.00	84.35	1.68	11.25
REU	10.94	10.94	84.35	1	6.32
EGG	11.19	10.00	84.35	1.12	5.94

3. Numerical Method

3.1. Governing Equations

The unsteady flow field around the cylinder is numerically simulated by employing 3D Unsteady Reynolds-Averaged Navier–Stokes equations (URANS) in Cartesian coordinates. Although the average Reynolds number in this study is low (≈1000), the local Reynolds number increases in near wall boundaries. Therefore, a turbulent model is necessary to model the behavior of the vortexes on the wake side. There are many turbulence models available and the choice of model depends on many factors such as the physics of the problem, the accuracy required and the computational power available. The K-Omega-SST model is used in this study because it is favored for predicting the formation of the vortices and flow separation [13,14]. By applying Reynolds decomposition and taking the time-average of continuity and momentum equations yields the URANS equations for incompressible flows [15].

The equation of motion for a rigid body in the polar coordinate with linear torsional spring and damper is expressed as

$$I_t \ddot{\theta} + C_t \dot{\theta} + K\theta = M_{hf} \qquad (1)$$

where the dot symbol stands for differentiation with respect to time t, I_t is the moment of inertia of the moving cylinder and C_t is the total damping coefficient consist of the structural damping and equivalent generator damping. K represents the torsional stiffness of the spring and θ is the rotational displacement. M_{hf} is the hydrodynamic angular momentum applied on the cylinder about the CG (center of gravity) of the cylinder given by

$$M_{hf} = F_p r_p + F_v r_v \qquad (2)$$

where F_p and F_v are normal pressure and tangential viscous contributions. r_p and r_v are corresponding arm lengths from the center of the oscillating body (CG) to the center of rotation defined as

$$\begin{aligned} F_p &= \sum_i \rho_i s_{f,i}(p_i - p_{ref}) \\ F_v &= \sum_i s_{f,i}(\mu R_{DEV}) \end{aligned} \qquad (3)$$

where ρ is the density, $s_{f,i}$ the face area vector, p the pressure, μ the dynamic viscosity, and R_{DEV} the deviatoric stress tensor. The hydrodynamic force coefficients are calculated by using the built-in (forcecoeffs) function in OpenFoam given by

$$C_l = \frac{liftForce}{p_{Dyn}}$$
$$C_d = \frac{dragForce}{p_{Dyn}} \quad (4)$$
$$C_m = \frac{M_{hf}}{p_{Dyn}l}$$

where $p_{Dyn} = \frac{1}{2}\rho A U^2$, A is the cross section area (84.35 cm^2), l is the arm length, and lift and drag forces are calculated from the vertical and horizontal components of F_p and F_v given by Equation (3). The structural parameters used in this study are described in Table 2 (solid domain).

Equation (1) and URANS equations are strongly coupled with the following steps: First, based on initial and boundary conditions the pressure distribution is calculated. Second, the forces on the cylinder surface corresponding to the pressure are calculated. Third, the equation of motion is solved based on the acquired forces and the displacements are calculated, and finally the domain is re-meshed according to the new position of the cylinder. The algorithm used by solvers is discussed in more details in the following.

Table 2. Initial conditions for solid and fluid domain.

Solid Domain		Fluid Domain	
Angular displacement (Rad)	0.0	Inlet velocity (m/s)	0.01
Angular velocity (Rad/s)	0.0	Outlet pressure (Pa)	0.0
I_t (m^4)	0.056	κ (m^2/s^2)	0.00135
C_t (Nm.s/Rad)	0.1	ω (1/s)	33.4
K (Nm/Rad)	0.1	Max Courant number	1
Mass (Kg)	0.125	Pressure, velocity, κ and ω error tolerances	1×10^{-7}
Cell displacement error tolerance	1×10^{-5}		
Step size (s) 1×10^{-5} *			

* Automatically adjusted during the simulation base on the Courant number.

3.2. CFD Solver

The finite-volume-based open-source computational fluid dynamics library Open-FOAM is used to perform the numerical simulation of the flow field around the cylinder and solving the equation of motion. The governing equations were integrated over each control volume and the discrete values of the relevant quantities were determined at the center of the control volume. The diffusion term in the governing equations is discretized using second order central differencing scheme and for advection term, a second-order upwind scheme is utilized. To obtain a good resolution in time, time integration is performed by a second-order implicit scheme. Due to the unsteady nature of FIV, a PimpleDyM-Foam solver is used, which is a transient solver for turbulent incompressible flow on a moving mesh utilizing the PIMPLE (merged PISO-SIMPLE) algorithm. This solver is a modification of the pimpleFoam solver that supports meshes of class dynamicFvMesh. This class is a base class for meshes that can move and/or change topology. The built-in sixDoFRigidBodyMotion solver is utilized in the present study to model the rigid-body motion of the cylinder. One advantage of the sixDoFRigidBodyMotion is that the zone of dynamic mesh can be controlled with input parameters innerDistance and outerDistance, thus it is possible to fix the mesh near the cylinder wall. The fixed mesh moving with the cylinder ensures the large dynamical motion and computational accuracy of the flow near the cylinder wall. Otherwise, the finer mesh near the cylinder is vulnerable to be seriously distorted during the motion of the rigid body if the mesh near the cylinder wall is allowed to deform. Moreover, the fixed zone guarantees the accuracy of the outside boundary condition during the simulation.

3.3. Domain and Boundary Conditions

The mesh generation is performed by using the blockMesh and snappyHexMesh applications within the OpenFOAM package. A base hexahedral mesh is generated using blockMesh as a computational domain and the cylinder is snapped off the base mesh by using snappyHexMesh applications. Then, the remaining mesh is extruded to generate a 3D mesh.

The boundary condition on the cylinder is set to be a moving-wall, with no flux normal to the wall. The inlet boundary is defined as a velocity inlet with a uniform velocity of 0.01 m/s and zero pressure gradient was employed for the outlet. The top and bottom conditions defined as slip boundary while a no-slip condition is applied on the surfaces of the cylinder. The front and back walls are set to empty condition to simplify the simulation.

The initial conditions for the turbulence model were calculated from the inlet velocity and turbulence intensity at the inlet of the actual water channel, which was estimated by using PIV method. A summary of initial conditions is shown in Table 2.

4. Grid Independency and Validation

To reduce the computational cost and prevent mesh dependency, a preliminary study on necessary but sufficient resolution and domain size is done. To determine the domain size, six cases with different lengths and widths are simulated based on the CIR-3D conditions (CIR shape pivoted on the downstream with $l = -3D$). Then, the smallest size at which no further change is seen was selected. Similarly, the resolution of the background mesh (without refinement) is increased until the result did not change with increasing the mesh resolution. The most computationally efficient case is chosen based on the variation of C_l, C_d, and C_m. According to the results of the domain size and resolution study shown in Figures 3 and 4, a refined domain size of 4D by 30D, with a resolution of 7680 elements and total domain size of 8D by 18D is chosen which leads to a blockage ratio of 0.125. Being aware of the limitations of this numerical study, we anticipate that the blockage potentially effects the sections in a similar way allowing comparison based on the difference in motion and hydrodynamic forces. An example of the mesh is shown in Figure 5.

The numerical model used in this study has been validated against our previous experimental results of a pivoted circular cylinder described in [5,6]. In the actual experiment, the cylinder is pivoted at a distance by using a connector arm and the Reynolds number is in the range of $2880 \leq Re \leq 22,300$. A force moment sensor is used to measure the forces on the main shaft (at the pivot point) and then the measured forces and moments are used to calculate the hydrodynamic forces on the cylinder after dynamic and static tare. As the hydrodynamic forces are oscillating during the vibration, the corresponding amplitude to the peak frequency in the frequency domain is selected for evaluation after performing a Fast Fourier Transform (FFT). The numerical results are compared to the experiments done in the lowest Reynolds number in the experiment ($Re = 2880$). The numerical results are in good agreement with the experimental data according to Figure 6. Note that the experimental results are more accurate for *Arm length* ≈ 0 because for the smaller arm lengths the cylinder is more stationary and there is less turbulence induced noise on the cylinder as a result.

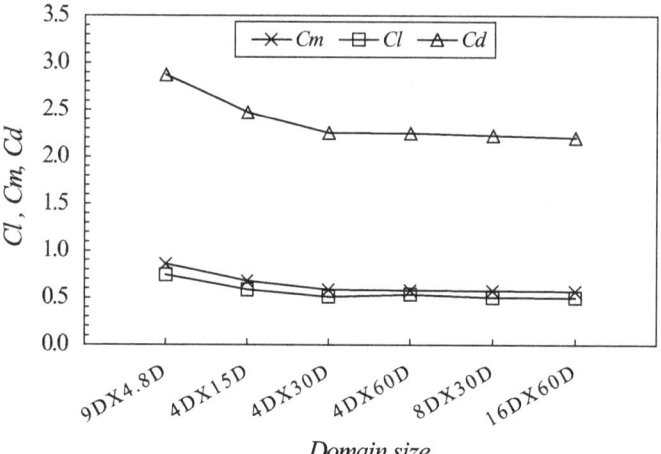

Figure 3. The variation of hydrodynamic coefficients with the domain size.

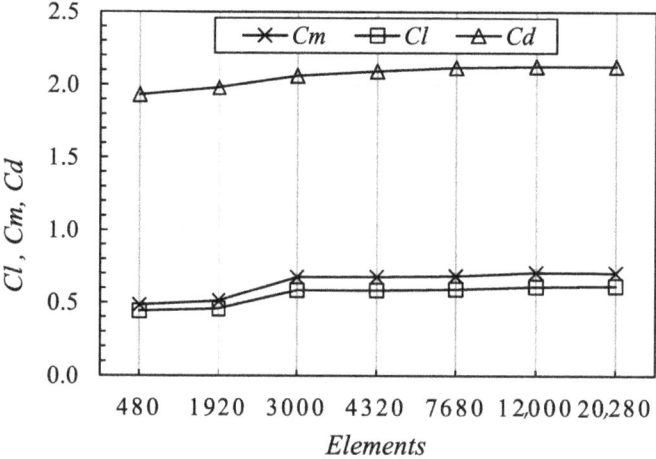

Figure 4. The variation of hydrodynamic coefficients with the mesh size.

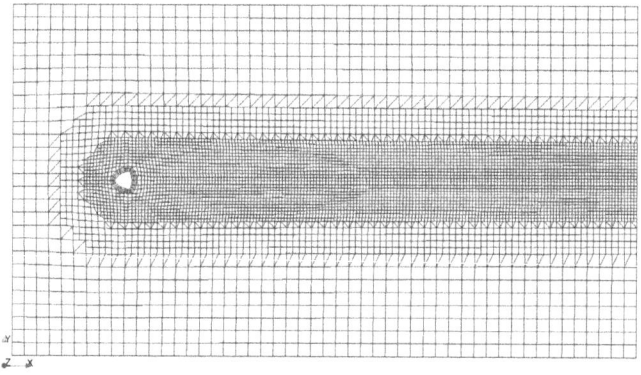

Figure 5. An example of the mesh with reuleaux shape snapped off of the grid.

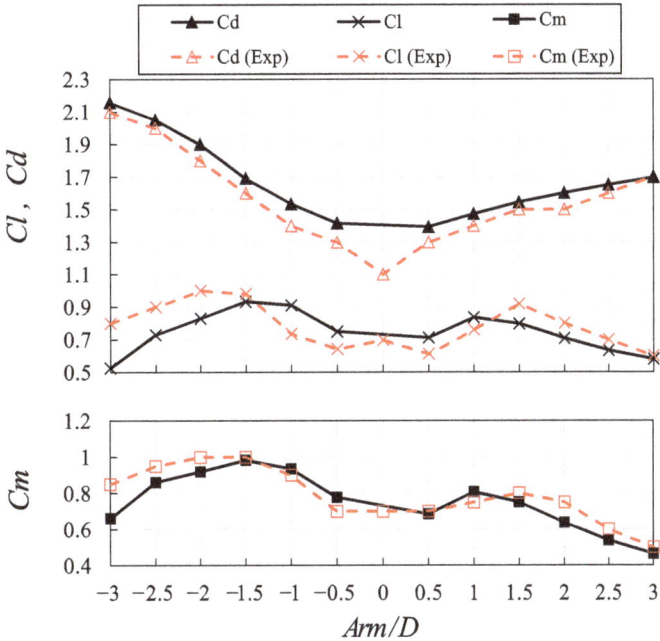

Figure 6. Comparison between the numerical results and experiment.

5. Results and Discussion

For simplicity, a Cartesian coordinate system is used for the discussion of results. The origin is the pivot point, and the X, Y, and Z axes are defined in the streamwise, transverse, and vertical direction, respectively. Figure 7 shows the maximum calculated power and the average amplitude of oscillation for each cross section including the corresponding arm ratio. The power spectrum density (PSD) of the angular velocity (which is widely being used for measuring the performance of random vibration converters) is used to calculate the power. The cumulative spectral power (CSP) of the PSD is then calculated by integrating over all frequencies base on the Parseval's theorem and used to estimate the dissipated power [16,17]

$$CSP = P = \frac{I_t}{Q} \int_0^\infty (PSD) df \quad (5)$$

where $Q = \sqrt{KI_t}/C_t$ is the quality factor and the PSD is calculated by using the fast Fourier transform of the angular velocity:

$$PSD = |FFT(\dot{\theta}(t))|^2 \quad (6)$$

where $\dot{\theta}(t)$ is the angular velocity of the vibration. By comparing the two charts, it is clear that the amplitude is not a proper performance metric even though it's been reported in many studies. For example, the highest power is achieved for the circular cross section while the box cross section oscillated with higher amplitude.

According to the results, the angular velocity is lower near the ends of oscillation for the non-circular cross sections when pivoted on the downstream. There are two possible reasons for lower angular velocity in a cross section: First is the higher drag force in a higher angle of attacks in non-circular cross sections [18]. Higher drag force changes the stiffness nonlinearly and shifts the natural frequency f_v out of the lock-in range based on the following equation derived from the equation of motion:

$$f_N = \frac{1}{2\pi}\sqrt{\frac{K \pm l\, A_{D0} U^2}{I_t}} \quad (7)$$

where $+l$ and $-l$ correspond to the location of the pivot point on the upstream side or downstream side, respectively. $A_{D0} = \frac{1}{2}\rho D H_w C_D U^2$ and $D H_w$ is the projected area of the cross section. For higher arm length, this increase in drag completely suppresses the vibration. The second reason is the lower spanwise correlation length. The first reason is discussed as vibration mechanism followed by a discussion over vorticity dynamic to understand the behavior of fluid around each section and its effect on correlation length.

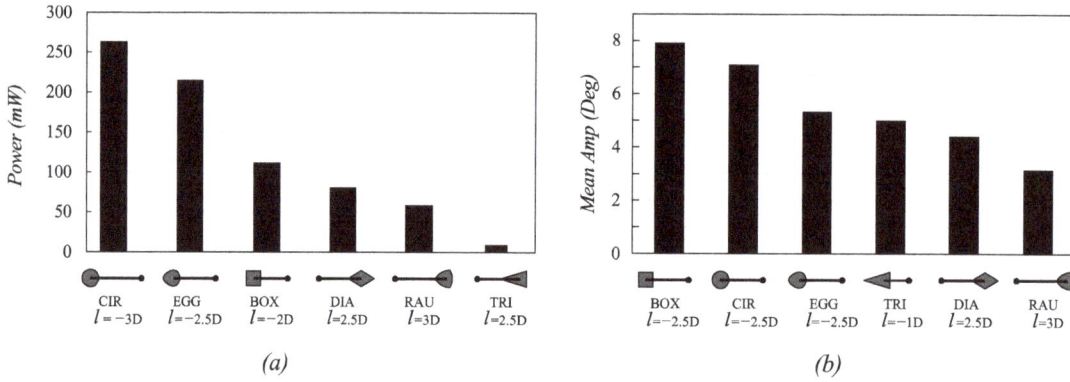

Figure 7. The maximum power output (**a**) and the mean amplitude (**b**) for each cross section.

5.1. Vibration Analysis

According to Figure 7, only the CIR and EGG cross sections produce reasonable power followed by BOX with a large difference (of around 50% lower power). The drag, lift, and moment ratio versus arm ratio are shown in Figure 8 for all sections along with the calculated power on a separate axis. These three sections show more power while the pivot is on the downstream side of the section as shown in Figure 8. However, the power is nearly zero for a BOX section pivoted on the upstream side ($l > 0$) regardless of the length of the arm. The opposite behavior is observed for DIA section: the power is nearly zero for a DIA section pivoted on the downstream side ($l < 0$) regardless of the length of the arm. The two remaining sections (RAU, TRI) show the lowest power with almost no effect of the arm length and the pivot location. The difference between the BOX and the rest of the sections is more clear by analyzing the vibration response shown in Figure 9. The vibration frequency (f_v) is far away from the natural frequency while the pivot is at the downstream of the section but it gradually goes up and close to the natural frequency. Even though aeroelastic instability is expected to be responsible for oscillation in this kind of cross section, the lock-in phenomena seem to improve the oscillation for sections with round edges. A similar change is seen for the Strouhal number St ($= f_s D/U$), where $= f_s$ is the predominant vortex shedding frequency), as shown in Figure 9. The Strouhal number is very low for the BOX section while pivoted on the downstream. It eventually increases by the arm length and converges to 0.13 but for the rest of the sections, the Strouhal number is close to 0.2 which is considered in the lock-in range.

The maximum power depends largely on the natural frequency of the system which is a function of the pivot location and spring stiffness in our setup. Arionfard and Nishi [5] found that for a circular cross section the drag force assists the motion by reducing the natural frequency when the pivot is located at the downstream side of the cylinder ($l < 0$)

based on Equation (7). As the moment of inertia (I_t), flow velocity (U), spring stiffness (K), and the projected area of the sections are constant, $l \, A_{D0} \propto l \, C_D$ is responsible for changes in the natural frequency.

Note that the mathematical analysis provided in [5] is only valid for round shapes where the drag and lift coefficients are not a function of the angle of attack. This is with agreement with the results shown in Figure 8: The calculated power changes with $l \, C_D$ for CIR, EGG, and RAU shape while the calculated power for BOX, DIA, and TRI shapes shows less dependency to the drag coefficient or arm length.

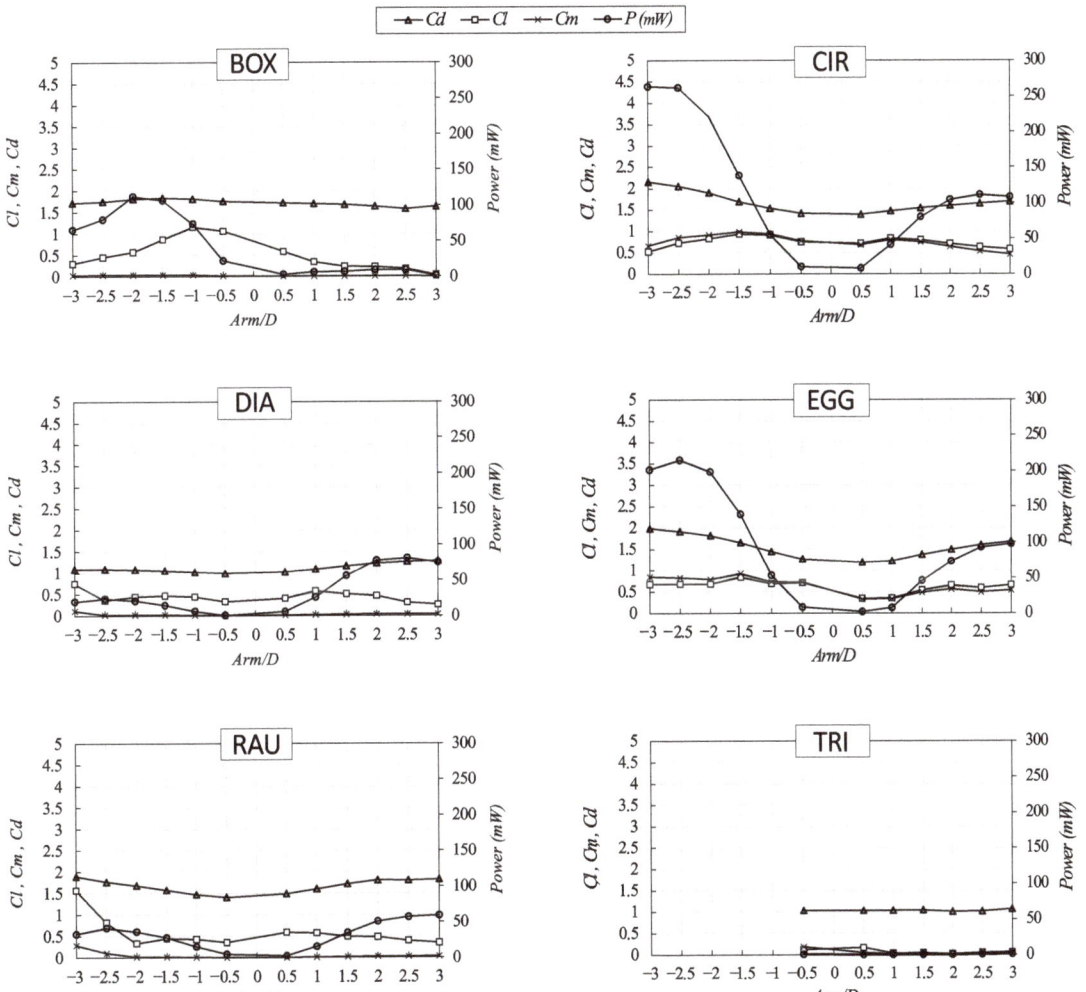

Figure 8. The calculated drag, lift, and moment ratios versus arm ratio for each cross-section. The calculated power is shown on a second Y-axis.

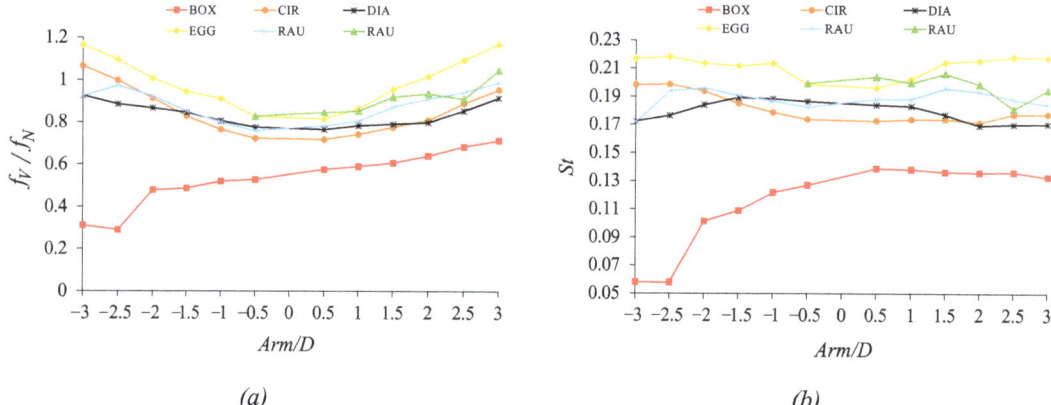

Figure 9. (a) The frequency ratio verses the arm ratio for each cross section. (b) The Strouhal number versus the arm ratio for each cross section. Here, negative Arm/D represents a pivot point at the downstream of the cross section and positive Arm/D represents a pivot point at the upstream side of the cross section

5.2. Vorticity Analysis

The steady-state vorticity field for the cases with the highest performance is shown in Figure 10. For sufficient oscillation amplitudes, symmetrical shedding with 2S mode is triggered in all cases as expected due to the low Reynolds number. The 2S mode is associated with the initial branch [19] where two single vortices shed per cycle, one by the top shear layer and another one by the bottom shear layer. The vorticity field animations can be found in the Supplementary Videos S1–S6.

To compare the correlation length (which is a measure of the span-wise length, that the vortices remain in phase) for each section, the three-dimensional state of the wake for each simulated case is visualized in Figures 11 and 12. The wakes are extracted by using a threshold filter the way that the pressure lies within 10 to 100 Pascal for all cases. A few factors influence the correlation length in FIV, including the amplitude of vibration, aspect ratio, surface roughness and the Reynolds number [15]. Here, the Reynolds number and surface roughness are similar for all cases while the amplitude of vibration and aspect ratio (which is a function of geometry) are changing.

The correlation length is higher when the pivot is at the upstream side ($l > 0$) for all sections except for the BOX. It is well known that body motion at a frequency close to that of the natural vortex shedding has a strong organizing effect on the shedding wake, which is manifested by a sharp increase in the spanwise correlation of the flow and forces on the body. However, the increase in three dimensionality of the flow behind the BOX section contradicts this pattern. A similar increase in three dimensionality is observed for the TRI section as well, but it is due to smaller vibration amplitude for all lengths in this section. The formation of the vortex line for the cross sections with the highest calculated power is more evident in the animations provided in the online Supplementary Videos V1–V6.

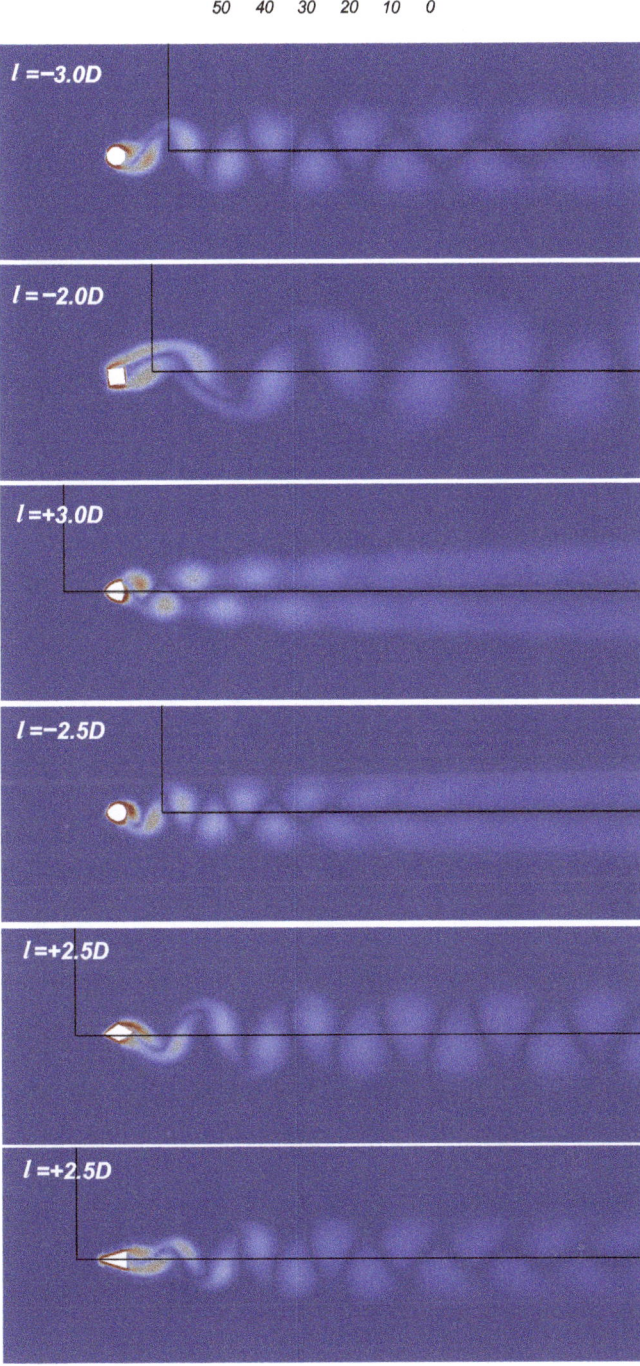

Figure 10. The steady state vorticity field for all cases with highest performance. The pivot is located at the origin of the black axes and the arm length is shown on top-left of each figure.

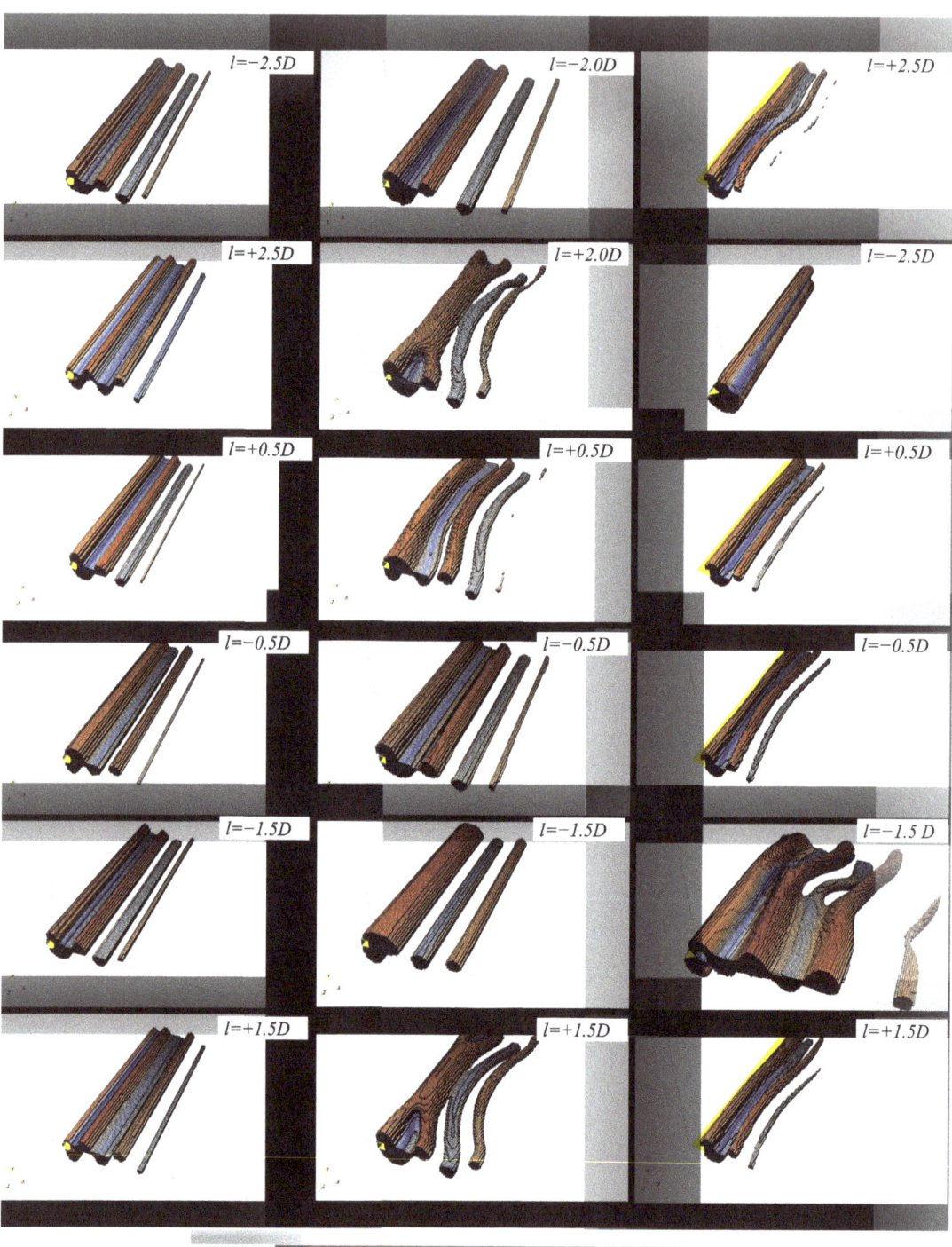

Figure 11. The velocity field on the wake side of the cylinders. The wakes are extracted by using a threshold filter on the pressure within 10 to 100 Pascal.

Figure 12. The velocity field on the wake side of the cylinders (continued).

6. Conclusions

3D numerical simulation of fluid-induced vibration has been reported for a series of cylinders with different cross sections including circular, rectangle, diamond, triangle, reuleaux, and egg shape. The cylinders are pivoted at distance from the centre to study the geometrical effect of the FIV performance and to compare the results with our previous experimental study. The cross-sectional area, moment of inertia, spring stiffness, inlet velocity, and damping coefficient are set to be similar for all cases to eliminate the effect of non-geometrical parameters. According to the results, the circular and egg shape cross sections are the most efficient shapes regardless of the pivot location followed by the box, diamond, reuleaux, and triangle shapes. The vorticity field shows that the 2S mode is triggered for all cases mainly due to the low Reynolds number; thus, the vibrations are expected to be in the initial branch. Moreover, 3D visualization of the wake for each section shows that the correlation length is higher for round shapes especially when the pivot is at the upstream side while for the shapes with sharp edges, the three-dimensionality of the wake is higher.

There are two major limitations in this study that could be addressed in future research. First, the domain size: even though a grid independency study is done for the circular cylinder and there is a good agreement with the experiment, similar results are not necessarily expected for other cross sections or arm lengths. This applies to the blockage ratio as well. It is assumed that the blockage has a similar effect on all cases if kept constant for all cross sections. Second, the Reynolds number: the results are compared to the experiments done with Reynolds number of around 2800 assuming both numerical and experimental tests are in the same flow regime ($1000 \geq Reynolds \geq 3000$). Moreover, the Reynolds number in this study is much smaller than that of actual operating conditions. Being aware of the limitations of this numerical study, we concluded that the hydrodynamic forces, displacement and calculated power of the cross sections are still comparable with each other if not to the experiment.

Supplementary Materials: The following are available online at https://www.mdpi.com/1996-1073/14/4/1128/s1, Video V1: The velocity field on the wake side of the BOX ($l = -2D$), Video V2: The velocity field on the wake side of the CIR ($l = -3D$), Video V3: The velocity field on the wake side of the DIA ($l = +2.5D$), Video V4: The velocity field on the wake side of the EGG ($l = -2.5D$), Video V5: The velocity field on the wake side of the RAU ($l = +3D$), Video V6: The velocity field on the wake side of the TRI ($l = +2.5D$), Video S1: The vorticity field for the CIR ($l = -3D$), Video S2: The vorticity field for the DIA ($l = +2.5D$), Video S3: The vorticity field for the EGG ($l = -2.5D$), Video S4: The vorticity field for the RAU ($l = +3D$), Video S5: The vorticity field for the TRI ($l = +2.5D$), Video S6: The vorticity field for the BOX ($l = -2D$).

Author Contributions: Formal analysis, S.M.; Investigation, H.A.; Visualization, H.A.; Writing—original draft, S.M. All authors have read and agreed to the published version of the manuscript.

Funding: This research received no external funding.

Acknowledgments: The authors wish to thank Fatemeh Talebi for her useful input and contribution. The calculations were carried out on supercomputer ABACUS 2.0 provided by the Southern Denmark University's eScience Center.

Conflicts of Interest: The authors declare no conflict of interest.

References

1. Bernitsas, M.M.; Raghavan, K.; Ben-Simon, Y.; Garcia, E.M.H. VIVACE (Vortex Induced Vibration Aquatic Clean Energy): A New Concept in Generation of Clean and Renewable Energy From Fluid Flow. *J. Offshore Mech. Arct. Eng.* **2008**, *130*, 1–15. [CrossRef]
2. Hobbs, W.B.; Hu, D.L. Tree-inspired piezoelectric energy harvesting. *J. Fluids Struct.* **2012**, *28*, 103–114. [CrossRef]
3. Yoshitake, Y.; Sueoka, A.; Yamasaki, M.; Sugimura, Y.; Ohishi, T. Quenching of vortex-induced vibrations of towering structure and generation of electricity using Hula-Hoops. *J. Sound Vib.* **2004**, *272*, 21–38. [CrossRef]
4. Sung, H.G.; Baek, H.; Hong, S.; Choi, J.S. Numerical study of vortex-induced vibration of pivoted cylinders. *Ocean Eng.* **2015**, *93*, 98–106. [CrossRef]

5. Arionfard, H.; Nishi, Y. Experimental investigation of a drag assisted vortex-induced vibration energy converter. *J. Fluids Struct.* **2017**, *68*, 48–57. [CrossRef]
6. Arionfard, H.; Nishi, Y. Flow-induced vibrations of two mechanically coupled pivoted circular cylinders: Characteristics of vibration. *J. Fluids Struct.* **2018**, *80*, 165–178. [CrossRef]
7. Arionfard, H.; Nishi, Y. Flow-induced vibration of two mechanically coupled pivoted circular cylinders: Vorticity dynamics. *J. Fluids Struct.* **2018**, *82*, 505–519. [CrossRef]
8. Arionfard, H.; Nishi, Y. Experimental investigation on the performance of a double-cylinder flow-induced vibration (FIV) energy converter. *Renew. Energy* **2019**, *134*, 267–275. [CrossRef]
9. Peng, Z.; Zhu, Q. Energy harvesting through flow-induced oscillations of a foil. *Phys. Fluids* **2009**, *21*, 123602. [CrossRef]
10. Ali, M.; Arafa, M.; Elaraby, M. Harvesting Energy from Galloping Oscillations. In Proceedings of the World Congress on Engineering, London, UK, 3–5 July 2013; Volume III.
11. Nakamura, Y.; Hirata, K. Critical geometry of oscillating bluff bodies. *J. Fluid Mech.* **1989**, *208*, 375–393. [CrossRef]
12. Al-Asmi, K.; Castro, I.P. Vortex shedding in oscillatory flow: Geometrical effects. *Flow Meas. Instrum.* **1992**, *3*, 187–202. [CrossRef]
13. Chowdhury, A.M.; Akimoto, H.; Hara, Y. Comparative CFD analysis of Vertical Axis Wind Turbine in upright and tilted configuration. *Renew. Energy* **2016**, *85*, 327–337. [CrossRef]
14. Pan, Z.Y.; Cui, W.C.; Miao, Q.M. Numerical simulation of vortex-induced vibration of a circular cylinder at low mass-damping using RANS code. *J. Fluids Struct.* **2007**, *23*, 23–37. [CrossRef]
15. A Rahman, M.; Rahman, M. Vortex-Induced Vibration of Cylindrical Structure with Different Aspect Ratio. Ph.D. Thesis, The University of Western Australia, Western Australia, Australia, 2015.
16. Ananthakrishnan, A.; Kozinsky, I.; Bargatin, I. Limits to inertial vibration power harvesting: power-spectral-density approach and its applications. *arXiv* **2014**, arXiv:1410.4734.
17. Peters, R.D. Tutorial on Power Spectral Density Calculations for Mechanical Oscillators. Available online: http://physics.mercer.edu/hpage/psd-tutorial/psd.html (accessed on 25 August 2020)
18. Matsumoto, M. Vortex shedding of bluff bodies: A review. *J. Fluids Struct.* **1999**, *13*, 791–811. [CrossRef]
19. Khalak, A.; Williamson, C.H.K. Motions, forces and mode transitions in Vortex-Induced Vibrations at low mass-damping. *J. Fluids Struct.* **1999**, *13*, 813–851. [CrossRef]

Article

Innovation of Pump as Turbine According to Calculation Model for Francis Turbine Design

Martin Polák

Faculty of Engineering, Czech University of Life Sciences Prague, Kamýcká 129, 16521 Praha 6, Czech Republic; karel@tf.czu.cz

Abstract: The effective utilization of micro hydropower sources is often realized through the use of pumps as turbines (PAT). The efficiency of PAT is about the same as that of the original pump. A further increase in efficiency and power output can be achieved by modifying the parts interacting with the flow, especially the impeller and the adjacent volute casing and draft tube. This paper presents a user-friendly calculation model of Francis turbine design and its application for PAT geometry modification. Two different modifications of a single-stage radial centrifugal pump were designed according to this model. The first modification (Turbine) consisted of a complete revision of the impeller geometry, volute casing and draft tube, which corresponded to a conventional Francis turbine. The second modification (Hybrid) was based on altered calculation model and consisted of a modification of only the impeller, which can be used in the original volute casing. Both modifications were tested on hydraulic test circuit at different heads. A comparison of the results of the Hybrid and the Turbine modification with the unmodified machine (Original) proved an increase in overall efficiency by 10%. Both modifications provided a higher flow rate and torque. This resulted in an overall power output increase—an increase of approximately 25% and 40% due to the Turbine and Hybrid modifications, respectively.

Keywords: pump as turbine (PAT); Francis turbine; calculation model; efficiency; hydropower

1. Introduction

The ability of pumps to operate efficiently in reverse mode as turbines was first established by Thoma [1] in 1931, while mapping the full operating characteristic of a centrifugal pump. In recent decades, there has been renewed interest in the use of pumps as turbines (PATs). It has been significantly used in power supply installations in remote areas, both on- and off-grid. A comprehensive overview of the current state of knowledge and experience in this area was provided by Carravetta et al. [2]. In addition to small hydropower plants, PAT is also used for energy recovery to cover the need for pressure reduction in water distribution networks (WDN) [3]. Besides power generation, PAT also acts as a throttle valve for flow control in this case. Experience with these applications was described by Venturini [4]. A case study of a specific installation (including an economic evaluation) was presented by Stefanizzi [5].

A pump design for turbine mode is a separate issue, which has been addressed many times. A chronological overview of the individual methods used for a solution was given by Ballaco [6]. An analysis of the models used for designing PAT and its experimental verification can be found in Stefanizzi [7], Derakhshan [8], and Barabareli [9]. It should be added that experimental investigations are still indispensable when an exact knowledge of turbine characteristics is required [10]. An example of a method used for determining such characteristics and their subsequent use for parameter conversion in the case of the hydrotechnical potential changing was given by Polák [11].

Various authors have provided several relatively simple modifications with positive results (such as modifications consisting of the impeller tip and hub/shroud rounding) in order to increase overall PAT efficiency. Specific example can be found in Singh [12,13], Doshi [14], and others. Capurso [15] dealt with the issue of the impact of blade geometry modification. More technically demanding modification of the pump (consisting of the installation of guide vanes in front of the impeller) was described by Giosio [16]. Some authors dealing with PAT design and modifications (such as Frosina [17]) followed the path of numerical flow modelling. However, such procedures already require specialized software, which is not available to a wide range of users. The aim of this study is to create a user-friendly design of a Francis turbine impeller and to experimentally verify its results as applied in the PAT modification.

2. Calculation Model

This section presents a calculation model, which was originally used to design the impellers of low specific speed Francis turbines; it is based on a method detailed in [18]. However, a modified model can also be used to great effect for the design of the geometry modification of an impeller for PAT. For experimental verification of the model results, the test impeller was manufactured according to the calculation model used for a particular PAT. The impeller was then tested on a hydraulic circuit. The test results are presented in the second part of the article. The model is designed as a mathematical algorithm, for which any software that has mathematical functions can be used. In this case, MS Excel software was used to ensure maximum clarity of the results and simple operation. The user then worked with the MS Excel calculation protocol. The input variables of the calculation model are the hydrotechnic potential of the turbine installation site and the size (diameter) of the impeller. The potential is given by the net head H (m) and the flow rate Q (m^3·s^{-1}). Based on these values, the specific speed of the turbine (with regard to the power Ns (min^{-1})) is estimated from the following equation:

$$Ns = N \cdot \sqrt{g} \cdot \frac{Q^{1/2}}{H^{3/4}} \tag{1}$$

where N (min^{-1}) is the assumed turbine shaft speed and g (m·s^{-2}) is the gravitational acceleration [19]. The value of Ns is entered into the green-coloured cell on the 1st line in the calculation protocol on page 6. The net head of the site H (m) is entered in line 8. Another necessary input value is the outer diameter of the impeller D_1 (m), which is entered in line 9. All key input variables are thus given.

To design the impeller, the calculation model uses the theory of hydraulic similarity, based on the geometric similarity of velocity triangles. Velocity triangles are related to performance parameters by means of Euler's equation [20]:

$$Y_T = u_1 \cdot c_{u1} - u_2 \cdot c_{u2} \tag{2}$$

or:

$$\eta_T \cdot \rho \cdot g \cdot Q \cdot H = \rho \cdot Q (u_1 \cdot c_{u1} - u_2 \cdot c_{u2}) \tag{3}$$

where Y_T (J·kg^{-1}) is the turbine specific energy, u_1, c_{u1} and u_2, c_{u2} (m·s^{-1}) are the velocity triangles vectors at the impeller inlet and outlet, respectively (see Figure 1), η_T (-) is the turbine efficiency, and ρ (kg·m^{-3}) is the fluid density.

The assumed total efficiency η_T is based on the size of the turbine here (i.e., on the outer diameter of the impeller D_1 according to Moody's relation [21]):

$$\eta_T = 1 - (1 - \eta_M) \sqrt[4]{\frac{D_M}{D_1}} \tag{4}$$

where η_M (1) is the efficiency of the corresponding turbine with the impeller diameter D_M (m).

The described calculation model allows for the designing of turbine impellers' geometry with specific speed values Ns = 80 min^{-1} and higher [18]. Figure 2 shows a diagram of the simplified overview of its algorithm. The background colours in the diagram correspond to the colours of the cells in the calculation protocol.

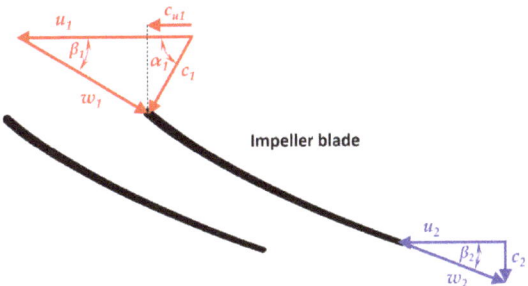

Figure 1. Velocity triangles at the inlet and outlet of the Francis impeller blade.

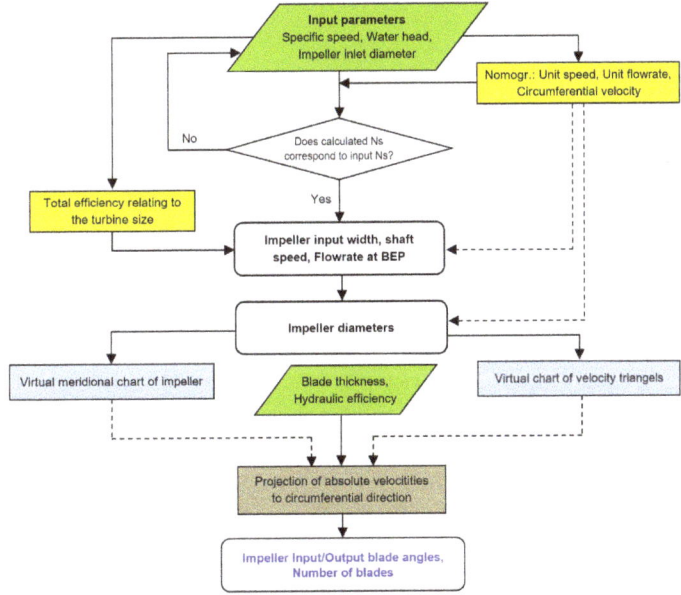

Figure 2. Algorithm of the impeller design in the calculation model.

The procedure stemming from the original design of the model required the entry of some dimensional characteristics directly from the drawing of the impeller meridional cross-section (see Figure 3). It had to be drawn at a certain stage of the impeller design. For greater user comfort, this phase was converted by the author into a calculation algorithm by means of mathematical functions, which is then used by the model for further designs. However, this "service" can be used only for limited range of specific speed Ns = 80 to 100 min^{-1}. The model can be also used for designing an impeller with a higher specific speed, but the required geometric characteristics need to be entered manually (lines 28, 29 and 31, 32) based on a self-made drawing. The procedure of this drawing is to divide the flow area of the impeller meridional cross-section into partial streams (two streams are sufficient in the case of a low specific speed narrow impeller, as shown in Figure 3). The border streamline is drawn at the inlet in the middle of the channel height. Inside the channel, the course of the streamlines is determined on the orthogonal trajectory using circles inscribed between the border streamline and the impeller contour (see Figure 3). At the same time, the multiplication of the diameters of these circles and the distances of their centres from the turbine axis must be approximately the same for all of them [18].

$$d_{AB} \cdot r_{AB} = d_{BC} \cdot r_{BC} = const. \tag{5}$$

Based on this requirement, the impeller flow area is divided and the values d_{AB}, r_{AB} and d_{BC}, r_{BC} gained from the drawing are entered into the above-mentioned lines.

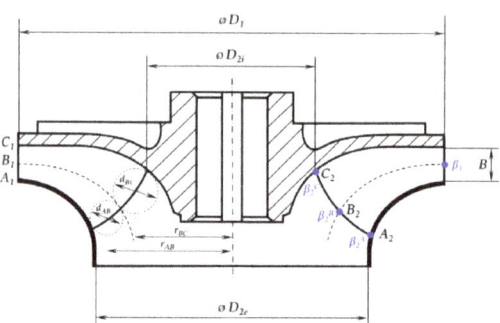

Figure 3. Meridional cross-section of the turbine impeller.

The values in the yellow-coloured cells in the calculation protocol are determined on the basis of mathematical functions, which the author created from the curves of the nomograms of the original Francis turbine design. To illustrate this, Figure 4 shows an example of the transformation of the curve $B/D_{1e} = f(Ns)$ from a nomogram to a mathematical function. The default original nomogram is at the bottom left, and a graphical representation of the transformation result can be seen at the top right. The black dashed line here corresponds to the original curve and the red line is calculated from the polynomial function shown below the graph. This equation is then used in the calculation model, namely in line 10.

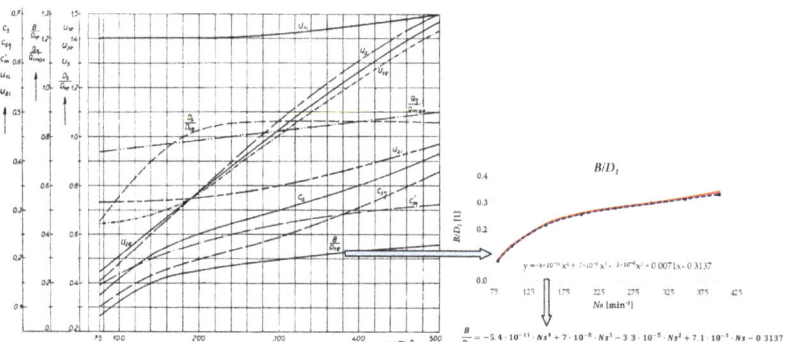

Figure 4. An example of transformation of curve from nomogram to mathematical function. Reproduced and modified from [18], SNTL Prague: 1962.

Some curves in the nomograms may differ according to different authors. The calculation model also takes this fact into account and allows a more experienced user to intervene in the calculation and change the values in the yellow cells as needed.

The next section of the impeller design (lines 35 to 39) is a combination of the previous results and the graphic construction of the velocity triangles. Again, in the original calculation design, making the drawing of triangles manual and measuring the values from the drawn construction for further calculation were required at this stage. Regarding maximum user comfort, these "manual" operations (presented in the diagram in Figure 2 by the dashed line) were transformed into mathematical functions and used by the calculation model in further operations.

The final outcomes of the model are the basic geometry characteristics for impeller construction, summarized in the form of the calculation protocol (see Figure 5). Besides the main impeller dimensions, the values of the angles (α_1, β_1) for the geometry of velocity triangles (or the blade at the inlet) are presented here. The shape of the blade at the outlet is determined by angles at three points—on the outer ($\beta_2{}^A$), mean ($\beta_2{}^B$), and inner streamline ($\beta_2{}^C$). The number of impeller blades z is presented at the very end of the protocol in line 48. In addition, the model also indicates the shaft speed N (line 12) and the flow rate Q_η (line 14) corresponding to the optimum operation (BEP) at a given net head H.

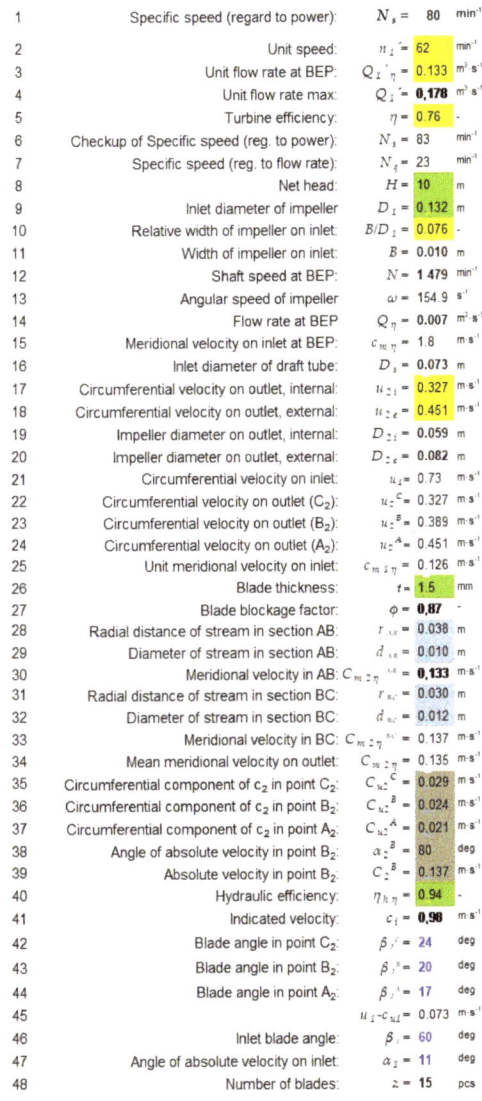

Figure 5. Calculation protocol of the Francis impeller design based on [18].

3. Experimental Verification of Proposed Modifications

For practical verification, the test impeller for this particular PAT was manufactured according to the design proposed by the calculation model. It was necessary to adapt the related flow parts at the same time (i.e., the volute casing and the draft tube). The fundamental change was to reduce the width of the impeller at the inlet from the original value of $B = 16$ mm to the width of $B = 10$ mm proposed by the model. The next change concerned the outlet cross section of the impeller. This was, on the contrary, necessary to increase the diameter ($D_2 = 65$ mm) for the original pump to the newly calculated value ($D_2 = 84$ mm). The impeller blades were also changed. A machine with completely new geometry was created, referred to as "Turbine" in the following text—see Figure 6 on the right. The original unmodified pump (META Plus 5 Czech Trade mark) is hereafter referred to as "Original" and is shown in Figure 6 on the left.

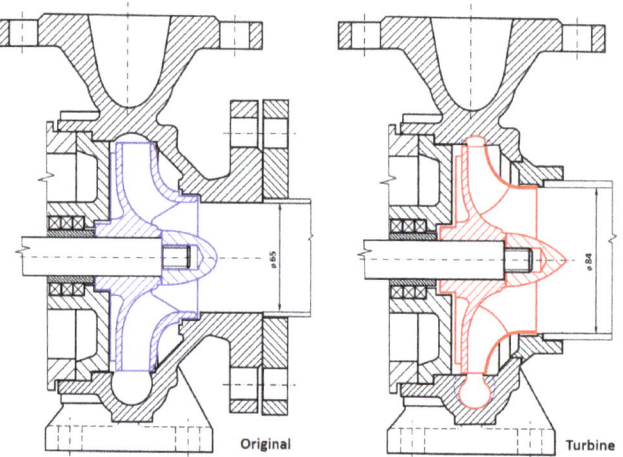

Figure 6. Cross-section of the Original PAT (**left**) and the Turbine after modification (**right**).

Photos of the impellers tested on the hydraulic circuit are shown in Figure 7. The unmodified original impeller on the left was made of cast iron in a sand mould. These types of impellers are used by the manufacturer as a standard for META Plus 5 pumps. The photo on the right is the impeller of the Turbine modification, with the geometry designed by the calculation model. To manufacture it, the hub and the rear shroud from the original impeller were used. The front shroud was made of copper sheet created by cold forming. All impeller blades were made from metal alloy by casting, and they were glued between the rear and the front shroud.

The numerical values of the geometry of both impeller variants are given in Table 1. The Turbine impeller has twice the number of blades compared to the Original. At the same time, the blades are almost half the length of the pump blades. This means a smaller wetted surface and, therefore, fewer hydraulic losses.

Table 1. Overview of the impellers' geometry.

Parameter		Original		Turbine	
		Inlet	Outlet	Inlet	Outlet
Diameter	D (mm)	132	65	132	84
Impeller width	B (mm)	16	-	10	-
Blade angle	β (mm)	24	18	60	20
Number of blades	z (-)	6		12	
Blade length	L (mm)	113		52	

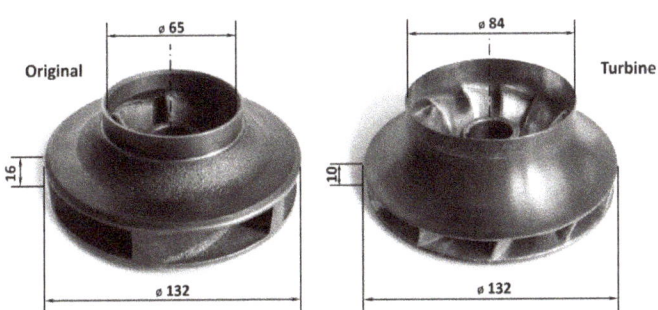

Figure 7. Impellers of tested variants—Original on the left, Turbine on the right.

An overview comparison of the geometry proposed by the calculation model with other Francis turbine impellers with corresponding specific speeds is given in Table 2. These are relative values related to the size of the impeller—outer diameter D_1. The results of the calculation model for the Turbine variant are shown in the left column of the table. The parameters of the test impeller of the Francis turbine F99 at NTNU Trondheim, Norway, are shown in the middle column [22]. The last column on the right presents the parameters of the Francis turbine impeller at Štěchovice hydroelectric power plant on the Vltava River, Czech Republic [18].

Table 2. Comparison of model results with the geometry of Francis turbines.

Parameter		Turbine, Model	F99, NTNU [22]	Štěchovice, CR [18]
Impeller diameter	D_1 (m)	0.132	0.622	2.47
Blade length	L/D_1 (-)	0.394	0.402	0.433
Impeller width	B/D_1 (-)	0.083	0.094	0.075
Outlet diameter	D_2/D_1 (-)	0.636	0.561	0.623
Blade angle—Inlet	β_1 (deg)	60	63	60
Blade angle—Outlet	β_2 (deg)	20	20	25

As the table above indicates, the basic geometric characteristics proposed by the calculation model correspond to the parameters of standard Francis turbines. Any differences may be caused by slightly different values of the specific speeds of individual types of impellers.

Hydraulic Test Circuit

Verification tests were conducted on an open hydraulic circuit in the laboratory of fluid mechanics at the Faculty of Engineering, Czech University of Life Sciences Prague. The circuit diagram is shown in Figure 8.

The test circuit consisted of a feeding pump, a reservoir with pipes, and control and measuring devices. With this setting, the feeding pump (FP) created the hydrotechnic potential for the tested PAT and the water flowed in the direction of the blue arrows. The generator with the momentum sensor (D) Magtrol TMB 307/41 (accuracy 0.1%) allowed for the continuous regulation of shaft speed via the frequency converter LSLV0055s100-4EOFNS. The water flow was measured using an electromagnetic flowmeter (Q) SITRANS FM MAG 5100 W (accuracy 0.5%). The pressures at p_p and p_s were measured by the pressure sensor HEIM 3340 (accuracy 0.5%), which was installed according to the first class accuracy requirements [23].

The hydraulic circuit described above was used for the testing of PAT variants with a head of 10 m, 20 m, and 30 m. The constant value of head was controlled by changing the speed of the feed pump by means of a frequency converter. Under these conditions, the basic parameters were measured, from which the performance characteristics were subsequently created.

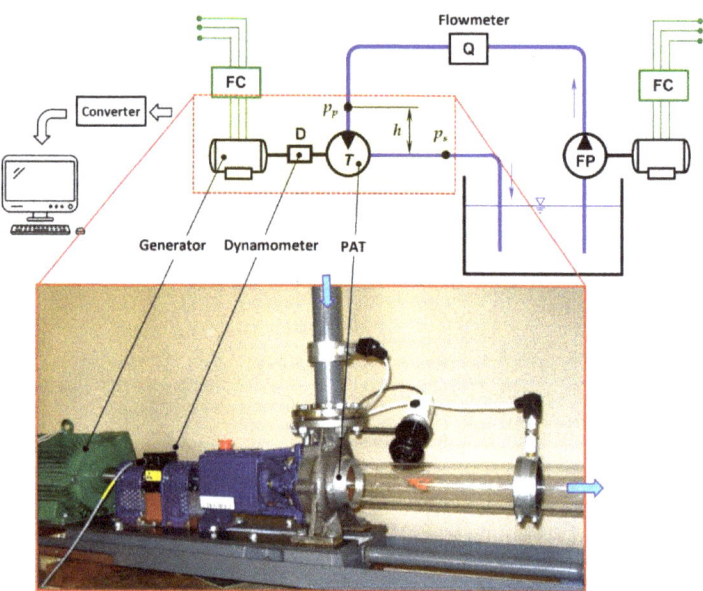

Figure 8. The hydraulic circuit scheme for testing PAT (Turbine variant shown in the photo): Q: flowmeter; FP: feed pump; PAT: pump as turbine; D: dynamometer; FC: frequency converter.

4. Results and Discussion

The partial results of the Original and the Turbine performance tests indicated the possibility of creating a new construction, which would be a combination of both variants. The aim was to maintain efficiency improvement while minimizing modifications to the pump. In accordance with these requirements, the calculation model was modified, and another variant of PAT was developed, which is referred to as "Hybrid" in the following text. The key outer dimensions of the Hybrid impeller remained the same in order to avoid volute casing modification. The purpose of this variant was to reduce the cost of the modification and, thus, the final price of PAT. The specific geometric parameters of the impeller are subject to the know-how of the author of the modification. It is the intellectual property of the university (CULS Prague) and can be provided on request. To manufacture this variant, the rear shroud of the original pump impeller was again used as a basis. Metal alloy blades were glued to the front shroud, and the entire product was glued to the rear shroud. The final appearance of PAT with this impeller visually corresponds to the variant in Figure 6 on the left.

The following charts indicate the performance characteristics of selected parameters depending on the shaft speed for all three variants of PAT—Original, Turbine, and Hybrid. The curves are created by mean values of three measurements at constant net head of 10 m, 20 m, and 30 m. There are also standard deviations marked on the curves. Values and curves corresponding to the unmodified Original variant are marked in blue. The characteristics of the Turbine and Hybrid variants are marked in red and green, respectively.

Figure 9 presents the first series of characteristics, which are the efficiency courses in dependence on the shaft speed. The increase in efficiency in both innovated variants is obvious. The absolute values of the efficiencies for BEP are summarized in Table 3. The relative increase regarding the Original is indicated in Table 4. The comparison at BEP also indicates a shift in the shaft speed to lower values, especially for the Hybrid variant.

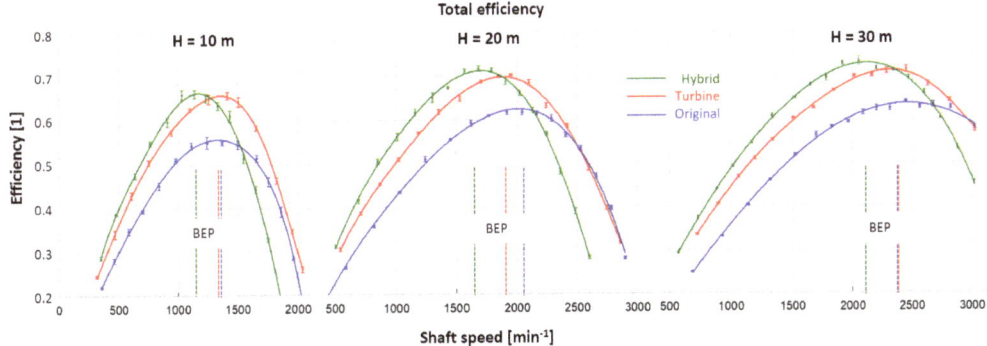

Figure 9. Efficiency in terms of dependence on shaft speed.

Figure 10 presents another series of characteristics—the dependence of torque on shaft speed. The comparison again indicates that the Turbine and the Hybrid variants prove higher torque, especially at lower speed.

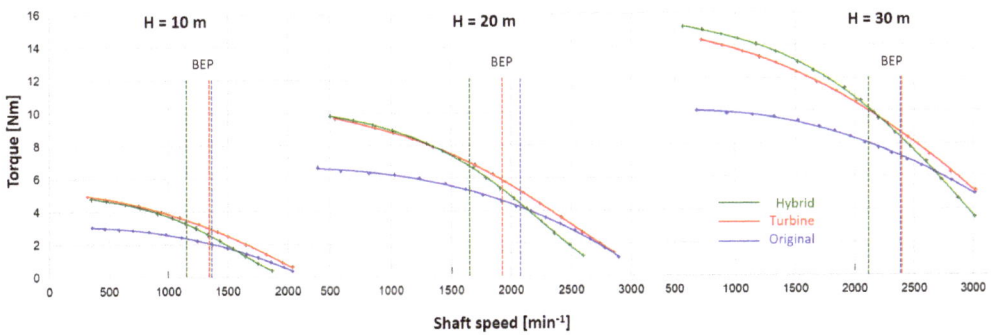

Figure 10. Torque in terms of dependence on shaft speed.

The mechanical power output courses (see Figure 11) basically copy the trends of the efficiency courses. The absolute values of the achieved power outputs obviously increase with increasing net head. The characteristics of the Turbine and the Hybrid also indicate a noticeably greater distance between the curves at higher net heads towards higher values. It is caused by a higher flow rate, as compared to that of the Original.

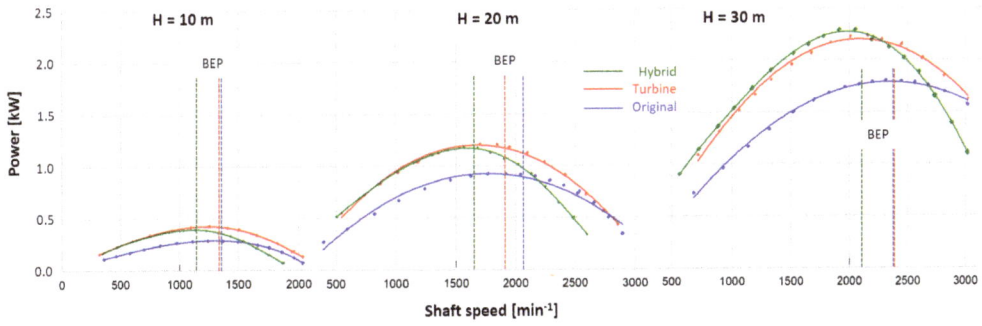

Figure 11. Courses of power output in terms of dependence on shaft speed.

The last series of characteristics represents courses of flow rate in terms of dependence on shaft speed (see Figure 12). The graphs of the flow rate courses indicate that the impeller´s flow rate decreases with increasing shaft speed. This characteristic also applies to Francis turbines with low specific speeds [20]. This is caused by the increasing centrifugal force, which acts against the centripetal direction of water flow.

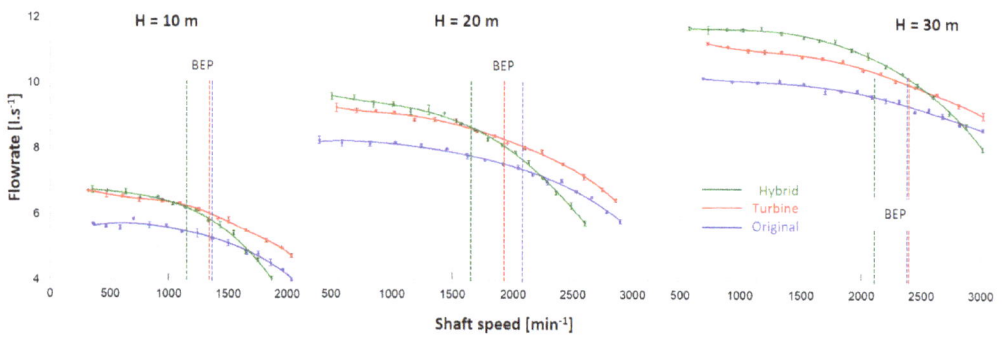

Figure 12. Courses of flow rate in terms of dependence on shaft speed.

Table 3. (a) Overview of absolute values of performance parameters achieved at BEP at net head of 10 and 20 m. (b) Overview of absolute values of performance parameters achieved at BEP at net head of 30 m.

(a)							
Parameter		10 m			20 m		
		Turbine	Hybrid	Original	Turbine	Hybrid	Original
Shaft speed	N (min^{-1})	1353 ± 1	1149 ± 1	1358 ± 2	1910 ± 3	1709 ± 1	2029 ± 1
Power	P (kW)	0.36 ± 0.001	0.41 ± 0.001	0.28 ± 0.001	1.1 ± 0.002	1.23 ± 0.002	0.90 ± 0.001
Flow rate	Q (L/s)	5.6 ± 0.01	6.3 ± 0.03	5.2 ± 0.04	8.0 ± 0.01	8.8 ± 0.04	7.4 ± 0.06
Head	H (m)	10 ± 0.13	10 ± 0.13	10 ± 0.09	20 ± 0.07	20 ± 0.16	20 ± 0.22
Efficiency	η (%)	66 ± 0.8	66 ± 0.9	55 ± 0.5	70 ± 0.3	72 ± 0.6	62 ± 0.7
Torque	T (Nm)	2.7 ± 0.01	3.3 ± 0.003	2.0 ± 0.002	5.6 ± 0.004	6.7 ± 0.01	4.2 ± 0.005
(b)							
Parameter		30 m					
		Turbine		Hybrid		Original	
Shaft speed	N (min^{-1})	2408 ± 3		2078 ± 3		2402 ± 2	
Power	P (kW)	2.05 ± 0.005		2.38 ± 0.004		1.70 ± 0.003	
Flow rate	Q (l/s)	9.8 ± 0.02		11.0 ± 0.11		9.0 ± 0.03	
Head	H (m)	30 ± 0.31		30 ± 0.36		30 ± 0.11	
Efficiency	η (%)	71 ± 0.7		73 ± 0.9		64 ± 0.2	
Torque	T (Nm)	8.2 ± 0.01		10.7 ± 0.01		6.9 ± 0.01	

Table 4. Relative increases of the performance parameters at BEP related to the Original.

Parameter		10 m		20 m		30 m	
		Turbine	Hybrid	Turbine	Hybrid	Turbine	Hybrid
Shaft speed	%N (min^{-1})	−0.3	−15.4	−5.9	−15.8	0.3	−13.5
Power	%P (kW)	28.8	44.5	23.0	37.2	20.6	39.7
Flow rate	%Q (L/s)	7.5	20.0	8.0	17.9	8.3	22.2
Efficiency	%η (%)	19.8	20.5	13.8	16.3	11.3	14.4
Torque	%T (Nm)	33.7	67.9	32.7	59.1	20.1	56.7

The variability of the flow rate can be used in cases where PAT functions as a replacement for the throttle valve in water distribution networks (WDN). In this case, PAT must be equipped with shaft speed control (e.g., by means of a frequency converter). The disadvantage of these applications is the resulting small range of flow control. Here, in the case of the Original variant, it is possible to regulate the flow rate by changing the shaft speed in the range of 33% of the nominal flow rate ($Q = 0.77 \div 1.1 \cdot Q_{BEP}$). The Turbine variant shows higher flow rate, but the regulation range is roughly the same (i.e., 33% again ($Q = 0.8 \div 1.13 \cdot Q_{BEP}$)). From this point of view, the most interesting is the Hybrid variant, where the steepest course of the flow rate was indicated—from the highest Turbine values to the lowest Original values. In absolute value, the Hybrid variant allows regulation of up to 44% of the nominal flow rate ($Q = 0.66 \div 1.1 \cdot Q_{BEP}$). This modification therefore also opens a greater potential for the use of PAT as a replacement for a throttle valve.

The following Table 3 summarizes the absolute values of the performance parameters achieved at BEP. The values were corrected using affine relations to a constant net head of 10 m, 20 m, and 30 m.

From the achieved results, the relative increase in the parameters of the Turbine and the Hybrid variant related to the Original was subsequently determined:

$$\Delta A = 100 \cdot \frac{A_m - A_0}{A_0} \quad (\%) \tag{6}$$

where A_0 is a parameter of the Original and A_m is a parameter of the modification (Turbine or Hybrid). An overview of the relative increases in the performance parameters in comparison with those of the Original is presented in Table 4.

The technical implementation of such modifications is a challenge. Every PAT modification means an increase in price. From this point of view, the Hybrid variant, considering only a modification of the impeller, appears to be the most advantageous. The volute casing and the draft tube do not have to be modified. At present, the problem of impeller manufacturing could be solved with the help of so-called additive technologies, as they can be used to manufacture virtually any geometry. An alternative way is to manufacture only the impeller blades along with the front shroud. This unit can be then glued or welded to the rear shroud. The resultant experience and test results with such 3D printed impellers are presented by Polák [24].

5. Conclusions

The focus of this study is two-fold. The first focus is the presentation of a calculation model for the design of a low specific speed Francis turbine impeller. The second focus is an experimental verification of the results of this model for the design of PAT innovation in order to increase its efficiency. The algorithm of the calculation model combines the original graphic–numerical design of the geometry of the Francis impeller so that it is as user-friendly and clear as possible. The example of the numerical solution described in this article presents the results of the design of particular PAT with an impeller with a diameter of $D_1 = 132$ mm and a specific speed of $Ns = 80$ min^{-1}. A comparison of the geometry characteristics designed by the model with the realized Francis turbine impellers gives a corresponding likeness.

Based on the theoretical results, the manufacture of the impeller proposed by the calculation model was instigated. Thus, the Turbine variant, with a new impeller geometry and modification of the closely adjacent parts (i.e., the volute casing and the draft tube), was created.

Testing on a test circuit at 10 m, 20 m, and 30 m head proved that the Turbine variant has a positive effect on improving the efficiency of PAT—in terms of absolute value, the efficiency increased by up to 10% in optimal operation (BEP). The modification further resulted in a flow rate increase of roughly 8%. Added together, the overall PAT power output was increased by 25%. Due to the changed geometry of the impeller blades, the torque was increased by 20 to 30%. These promising results led to the modification of the calculation model, as well as the construction and testing of another variant—the Hybrid. Its mission was to maintain the positives achieved by the Turbine, but at the same time, to minimize the massive interventions and modifications of the original pump. The results obtained with the Hybrid variant in BEP are as follows: In absolute terms, the efficiency was 10 to 11% higher than that of the unmodified Original variant. The flow rate was about 20% higher. This resulted in an even greater increase in overall power output of 37 to 45%. There was also a significant increase in torque of up to 60%. However, the Hybrid variant had, in BEP, significantly lower shaft speed (approximately by 15%) than the Original. On the other hand, it provided a wider control of the flow range ($Q = 0.66 \div 1.1 \cdot Q_{BEP}$), which is advantageous when using PAT as a throttle valve in WDN. In summary, it can be stated that the modifications proposed by the calculation model have a significantly positive effect on increasing the efficiency of PAT operation.

In addition to the modifications described above, another way to increase the efficiency of PAT is to modify the adjacent parts. This mainly concerns a draft tube. Its significance increases as specific speed increases. Further research specifically on high-speed machines will be focused on solving this problem.

Funding: This research has been supported by the IGA 2020:31130/1312/3115 Analysis of liquid flow in hydrodynamic pump and in pump as turbine.

Institutional Review Board Statement: Not applicable.

Informed Consent Statement: Not applicable.

Data Availability Statement: The data presented in this study are openly available at [10.5293/IJFMS. 202015.8.3.169].

Conflicts of Interest: The author declares no conflict of interest.

Nomenclature

A	measured value
B	impeller width on inlet, m
BEP	best efficiency point
c	absolute velocity of water, m·s^{-1}
D	impeller diameter, m
FC	frequency converter
FP	feed pump
g	gravitational acceleration, m·s^{-2}
H	net head, m
L	blade length, m
N	rotational speed, min^{-1}
Ns	specific speed, min^{-1}
P	power output, W
PAT	pump as turbine
Q	flow rate, L·s^{-1}
T	torque, N·m
u	circumferential velocity of impeller, m·s^{-1}
w	relative velocity of water, m·s^{-1}
WDN	water distribution network
Y	specific energy, J·kg^{-1}

Subscripts and Superscripts

e	external
i	internal
M	model
T	turbine

u	circumferential component
1	inlet
2	outlet

Greek Symbols

α	angle between circumferential and absolute velocity: deg
β	angle between relative and circumferential velocity, deg
ρ	density of water, kg·m^{-3}
η	total efficiency, 1, %

References

1. Thoma, D.; Kittredge, C.P. Centrifugal pumps operated under abnormal conditions. *J. Power Sources* **1931**, *73*, 881–884.
2. Carravetta, A.; Derakhshan, H.S.; Ramos, H.M. Pumps as turbines—Fundamentals and Applications. In *Springer Tracts in Mechanical Engineering*; Springer International Publishing: Cham, Switzerland, 2018; 236p, ISBN 978-3-319-67506-0.
3. Williams, A.A. Pumps as turbines for low cost micro hydro power. *Renew. Energy* **1996**, *9*, 1227–1234. [CrossRef]
4. Venturini, M.; Alvisi, S.; Simani, S.; Manservigi, L. Energy production by means of pumps as turbines in water distribution networks. *Energies* **2017**, *10*, 1666. [CrossRef]
5. Stefanizzi, M.; Capurso, T.; Balacco, G.; Binetti, M.; Torresi, M.; Camporeale, S.M. Pump as turbine for throttling energy recovery in water distribution networks. *AIP Conf. Proc.* **2019**, *2191*, 020142. [CrossRef]
6. Balacco, G. Performance Prediction of a Pump as Turbine: Sensitivity Analysis Based on Artificial Neural Networks and Evolutionary Polynomial Regression. *Energies* **2018**, *11*, 3497. [CrossRef]
7. Stefanizzi, M.; Torresi, M.; Fortunato, B.; Camporeale, S.M. Experimental investigation and performance prediction modeling of a single stage centrifugal pump operating as turbine. *Energy Procedia* **2017**, *126*, 589–596. [CrossRef]
8. Derakhshan, S.; Nourbakhsh, A. Theoretical, numerical and experimental investigation of centrifugal pumps in reverse operation. *Exp. Therm. Fluid Sci.* **2008**, *32*, 1620–1627. [CrossRef]
9. Barbarelli, S.; Amelio, M.; Florio, G. Experimental activity at test rig validating correlations to select pumps running as turbines in microhydro plants. *Energy Convers. Manag.* **2017**, *149*, 781–797. [CrossRef]
10. Kramer, M.; Terheiden, K.; Wieprecht, S. Pumps as turbines for efficient energy recovery in water supply networks. *Renew. Energy* **2018**, *122*, 17–25. [CrossRef]
11. Polák, M. The Influence of Changing Hydropower Potential on Performance Parameters of Pumps in Turbine Mode. *Energies* **2019**, *12*, 2103. [CrossRef]
12. Singh, P. Optimization of the Internal Hydraulics and of System Design for Pumps as Turbines with Field Implementation and Evaluation. Ph.D. Thesis, University of Karlsruhe, Karlsruhe, Germany, 2005.
13. Singh, P.; Nestmann, F. Internal hydraulic analysis of impeller rounding in centrifugal pumps as turbines. *Exp. Therm. Fluid Sci.* **2011**, *35*, 121–134. [CrossRef]
14. Doshi, A.; Channiwala, S.; Singh, P. Inlet impeller rounding in pumps as turbines: An experimental study to investigate the relative effects of blade and shroud rounding. *Exp. Therm. Fluid Sci.* **2017**, *82*, 333–348. [CrossRef]
15. Capurso, T.; Bergamini, L.; Camporeale, S.M.; Fortunato, B.; Torresi, M. CFD analysis of the performance of a novel impeller for a double suction centrifugal pump working as a turbine. In Proceedings of the 12th European Conference on Turbomachinery Fluid dynamics & Thermodynamics ETC13, Lausanne, Switzerland, 8–12 April 2019.
16. Giosio, D.R.; Henderson, A.D.; Walker, J.M.; Brandner, P.A.; Sargison, J.E.; Gautam, P. Design and performance evaluation of a pump-as-turbine micro-hydro test facility with incorporated inlet flow control. *Renew. Energy* **2015**, *78*, 1–6. [CrossRef]
17. Frosina, E.; Buono, D.; Senatore, A. A performance prediction method for pumps as turbines (PAT) using a computational fluid dynamics (CFD) modeling approach. *Energies* **2017**, *10*, 103. [CrossRef]
18. Nechleba, M. *Hydraulic Turbines—Their Design and Equipment*, 2nd ed.; STNL Prague: Prague, Czech Republic, 1962. (In Czech)
19. Gülich, J.F. *Centrifugal Pumps*, 3rd ed.; Springer: Berlin, Germany, 2008; 1116p, ISBN 978-3-642-40113-8.
20. Nielsen, T.K. Simulation model for Francis and reversible pump turbines. *Int. J. Fluid Mach. Syst.* **2015**, *8*, 169–182. [CrossRef]
21. Bednář, J. *Turbines—Small Hydropower Plants*; Marcela Bednářová: Blansko, Czech Republic, 2013; 360p, ISBN 978-80-905437-0-6. (In Czech)
22. Iliev, I.; Trivedi, C.; Dahlhaug, O.G. Simplified hydrodynamic analysis on the general shape of the hill charts of Francis turbines using shroud-streamline modeling. *J. Phys. Conf. Ser.* **2018**, *1042*, 012003. [CrossRef]
23. European Committee for Standardization. *Rotodynamic Pumps—Hydraulic Performance Acceptance Tests—Grades 1, 2 and 3*; ČSN EN ISO 9906; European Committee for Standardization: Brussels, Belgium, 2013. (In Czech)
24. Polák, M. Behaviour of 3D printed impellers in performance tests of hydrodynamic pump. In Proceedings of the 7th International Conference on Trends in Agricultural Engineering, Prague, Czech Republic, 17–20 September 2019; pp. 447–552.

Article

Application of CFD to the Design of Manifolds Employed in the Thermodynamic Method to Obtain Efficiency in a Hydraulic Turbine

Erick O. Castañeda Magadán, Gustavo Urquiza Beltrán, Laura L. Castro Gómez * and Juan C. García Castrejón

Centro de Investigación en Ingeniería y Ciencias Aplicadas, Universidad Autónoma del Estado de Morelos, Cuernavaca 62209, Mexico; erick.castanedamag@uaem.edu.mx (E.O.C.M.); gurquiza@uaem.mx (G.U.B.); jcgarcia@uaem.mx (J.C.G.C.)
* Correspondence: lauracg@uaem.mx

Abstract: This study presents the design and implementation of different types of manifolds (sampling system) to measure water flow properties (velocity, pressure, and temperature) through the high- and low-pressure section of a Francis-type low head hydraulic turbine (LHT of 52 m) to calculate it is efficiency using the Thermodynamic Method (TM). The design of the proposed manifolds meets the criteria established in the "International Electrotechnical Commission—60041" Standard for the application of the TM in the turbine. The design of manifolds was coupled to the turbine and tested by the Computational Fluid Dynamics (CFD) application, under the same experimental conditions that were carried out in a power plant, without the need for on-site measurements. CFD analyses were performed at different operating conditions of volumetric flow (between values of 89.67 m^3/s and 35.68 m^3/s) at the inlet of turbine. The mechanical power obtained and the efficiency calculated from the numerical simulations were compared with the experimental measurements by employing the Gibson Method (GM) on the same LTH. The design and testing of manifolds for high- and low-pressure sections in a low head turbine allows for the constant calculation of efficiency, avoiding breaks in the generation of electrical energy, as opposed to other methods, for example, the GM. However, the simulated (TM) and experimental (GM) efficiency curves are similar; therefore, it is proposed that the design of the manifolds is applied in different geometries of low-head turbines.

Keywords: computational fluid dynamics; hydraulic efficiency; Gibson method; manifolds; turbine; thermodynamic method

Citation: Castañeda Magadán, E.O.; Urquiza Beltrán, G.; Castro Gómez, L.L.; García Castrejón, J.C. Application of CFD to the Design of Manifolds Employed in the Thermodynamic Method to Obtain Efficiency in a Hydraulic Turbine. *Energies* **2021**, *14*, 8359. https://doi.org/10.3390/en14248359

Academic Editors: Adam Adamkowski and Anton Bergant

Received: 7 October 2021
Accepted: 7 December 2021
Published: 11 December 2021

Publisher's Note: MDPI stays neutral with regard to jurisdictional claims in published maps and institutional affiliations.

Copyright: © 2021 by the authors. Licensee MDPI, Basel, Switzerland. This article is an open access article distributed under the terms and conditions of the Creative Commons Attribution (CC BY) license (https://creativecommons.org/licenses/by/4.0/).

1. Introduction

The "International Electrotechnical Commission—60041" (IEC—60041) Standard establishes various test development methods to determine the hydraulic performance of different hydraulic turbomachinery, such as the Reel method, Pitot tubes, and Pressure-Time (also called Gibson), among which is the Thermodynamic Method ™. According to the standard, this method allows, in a hydroelectric power station, for the measurement of flow properties extracted in the high- and low-pressure section (inlet and outlet of the turbine or pump, respectively), to calculate the hydraulic efficiency of the turbomachinery. This method is less invasive compared to others, for example, the Pressure-Time method (also called the Gibson method). The Pressure-Time method is accurate and can inexpensively perform indirect flow measurements for low head turbines. However, it could be risky due to the phenomenon used for measurement. The application of TM instead of the Gibson method aims to avoid damage in any component of the hydraulic turbine, such as the penstock, valves, or distributor. In addition, it allows for the calculation of continuous efficiency by simultaneously measuring the interest variables without stopping power energy generation.

The IEC—60041 Standard establishes that the application of TM is limited to specific hydraulic energy values greater than 1000 J/kg (heads higher than 100 m). However, under favorable conditions, the measurement interval could be extended to lower values of the specific hydraulic energy or heads lower than 100 m [1,2].

Given the inherent difficulties in directly measuring the flow that define the hydraulic efficiency (η_h), it is possible to carry out their extractions in manifolds that are especially designed for the determination of temperature, pressure, and velocity in the fluid, installing them in the inlet and outlet sections of the turbine, respectively (Figure 1).

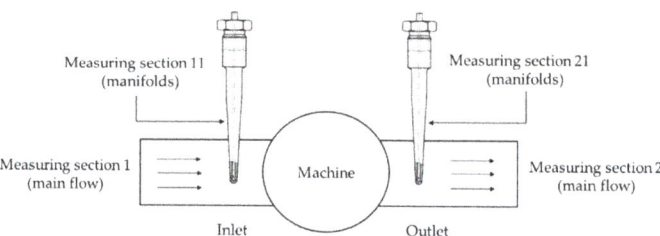

Figure 1. Conceptual diagram showing the location of manifolds to measure flow properties to compute power and efficiency according to IEC—60041.

The manifolds must be designed to ensure that the velocity inside is at a specific interval, so that the flow is uniform when it comes into contact with the installed temperature transducers. This guarantees that the temperature will remain constant inside the manifold and around the sensor. Moreover, the precision and sensitivity of the temperature measurement instruments should be sufficient to provide an indication of a temperature difference of at least 0.001 K between the measurement points. In addition, the temperature of the extracted water should be continuously monitored by thermometers of at least ±0.05 K precision and 0.01 K sensitivity [2]. According to different authors, Pt-100 Resistive Temperature Detectors (RTD's) are commonly used for measurement due to their high stability and precision [3–5].

According to TM, the direct operating procedure or direct method is used to measure the efficiency of the turbine under study. This method measures temperature, velocity, and pressure, extracting water from the penstock at the high-pressure side of the turbine to a manifold with a minimum expansion. Hydraulic losses and friction cause an increase in the temperature of the water passing through the turbine. This phenomenon can be calculated using the specific heat of the water. Although the authors of [6] defined that the decrease in the head in a turbine reduces the temperature difference between the inlet and outlet, they are directly proportional.

On the other hand, although this is a numerical case, in experimental cases, authors such as [4] propose a procedure for the normalization of experimental tests from the opening of the closing control device. After 10 min stabilization in the generator's frequency, the temperature data recording is started by means of Pt-100 type sensors during the first 2 min. At the end, the average value of the temperature difference is calculated (high and low pressure). During this period, the measurements of the other parameters, such as inlet and outlet pressure and power, are simultaneous. This procedure is repeated for different openings of the closing control device, that is, for different load values in the unit, as in the present case.

Hydraulic turbines and the geodesic points where these are installed can present aspects of great complexity, such as installing manifolds on the low-pressure side embedded in concrete tubes. However, with a correct design of collecting tubes that are long enough for sample extraction, the measured temperature values could be considered adequate [7]. In the high-pressure section, the optimal length for penetration of the detraction into the pipe can be calculated. However, the length established by IEC-60041 could be enough [8–11].

IEC-60041 establishes that the design of detraction probes for the high-pressure zone must present the appropriate structural study to avoid total or partial detachment, and that it reaches essential areas such as the runner, causing significant damage. To select the correct materials for the probes that support the loads, the typical properties of the materials used in engineering can be consulted [10,11].

According to [3], the design of a horizontal sampling system at the outlet of the turbine is better than vertical. However, the research is based on a Pelton-type turbine. According to the turbine types, the power distribution and partial flow passage can demonstrate significant differences for the present study.

On the other hand, the system can be designed by two or more means of sampling; for example, a system composed of an arrangement of horizontal tubes with a central mixing chamber, in which the relevant sensors are coupled. Furthermore, perforated tubes are located at the turbine's outlet, and temperature sensor is placed at different heights to measure temperature changes throughout the section.

A hybrid vertical detraction system and a mixing chamber for each tube would reduce the number of sensors required and improve measurement. In addition, the use of perforated tubes for the water samples at the outlet of the turbine omits the presence of elbows to avoid friction losses [12].

The development of accurate instruments allows for the application of TM in low head turbines; for example, most hydroelectric power plants in Mexico have heads lower than 100 m, such as 22 and 76 m. Consequently, the present study focuses on a 52-m head Francis-type hydraulic turbine installed in a hydroelectric plant in México. This has a rotational velocity of 180 RPM (18.84 rad/s) under normal operating conditions, i.e., constant volumetric input flow (between values of 89.67 m³/s and 35.68 m³/s), and a 3.5 m maximum tip diameter for the runner.

With these values, the specific speed in the turbine is calculated according to [13–16], see Equation (1). N is expressed in RPM, Q is the volumetric flow in (m³/s) and H is the head in meters.

$$Ns = N\left(\frac{Q^{0.5}}{H^{0.75}}\right) = \frac{638}{H^{0.512}} \qquad (1)$$

The turbines can be classified according to the specific speed, at the head (H), a range from 50 to 240 m can be found the Francis turbine, and their specific speed is between 51 and 255 dimensionless (Power in kW) [16]. Therefore, the specific speed value for the studied turbine is 87.93, i.e., a Francis slow turbine.

On the other hand, an example comparison of the efficiency calculations in a turbine was performed using the Gibson Method (GM) and the TM at the Gråsjø power plant in Norway, which show differences between the efficiency curves below 0.5%, for the entire range measured below 0.15% and for relative powers between 0.5 and 1.15%. The Gråsjø power plant is equipped with a vertical Francis turbine and has a net height of 50 m [17], which serves as a reference for current research development.

2. Materials and Methods
2.1. Measurement System Design
2.1.1. Manifolds Design for the High-Pressure Section (Inlet)

According to Castro [18] and Urquiza [19], the principal parameters were obtained to design the manifolds used in TM on the turbine´s inlet section. The values shown in Table 1 are the final results of the Gibson method, applied on a 52.54 m head turbine under different working conditions. (Q_T) it is the net volumetric flow, (Q_0) is leakage flow when wicked gates are closed, (P_1) is inlet pressure in the flow of water, (P_m) is the mechanical power energy generated by the runner, (P_e) is the electrical power measurement in the generator, (T_{orque}) is the torque generated by the runner, (η_h) is the hydraulic efficiency of the turbine and (η_g) is the efficiency measured in the generator. The number of manifolds and their positioning is shown in Figure 2. The proposed design is shown in Figure 3 [20].

Table 1. Parameters of the turbine on study [18,19].

Q_T (m³/s)	Q_0 (m³/s)	P_1 (kPa)	P_m (MW)	P_e (MW)	T_{orque} (kN m)	η_h (%)	η_g (%)
89.67	0.7	390.09	31.65	31.05	1679.94	85.10	98.30
82.00	0.7	392.03	30.71	30.12	1630.04	89.80	98.28
76.14	0.7	393.48	29.03	28.45	1540.87	91.16	98.23
68.73	0.7	395.35	26.05	25.50	1382.70	89.91	98.14
60.99	0.7	396.64	22.63	22.10	1201.17	87.84	97.97
52.90	0.7	397.92	19.02	18.51	1009.55	84.92	97.68
46.11	0.7	399.69	15.72	15.23	834.39	80.08	97.26
35.68	0.7	404.70	10.14	9.68	538.22	65.89	96.06

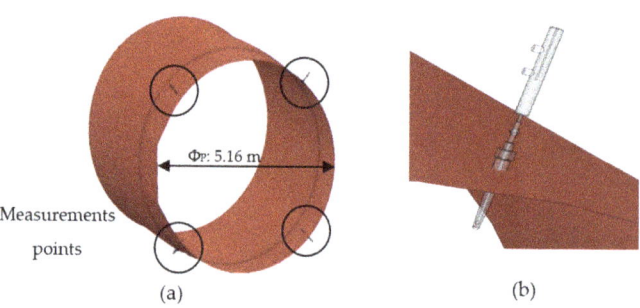

Figure 2. Measurement system, high-pressure section: (**a**) general view, (**b**) upper-right probe and manifold, zoom.

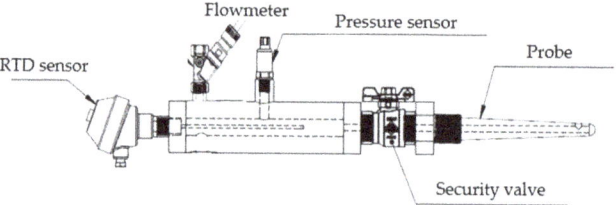

Figure 3. Manifold proposed and instrumentation.

According to [19], for each volumetric flow, the rotational velocity is 180 RPM (18.84 rad/s), and the total deviation of measurements was ±1.6%. It is possible to define the total deviation of measurements of the flow in a systematic way, with Equation (2):

$$\delta_Q = \pm\sqrt{\delta_{\Delta\rho}^2 + \delta_{\Delta A}^2 + \delta_C^2 + \delta_\delta^2 + \delta_{Dp}^2 + \delta_{\Delta pf}^2 + \delta_t^2 + \delta_{Ql}^2 + \delta_{rp}^2} \quad (2)$$

where:

$\delta_{\Delta\rho}$ —Uncertainty regarding the change in water density due to subsequent pressure change.
$\delta_{\Delta A}$—Uncertainty regarding the change of pipe section due to the change in pressure.
δ_C—Uncertainty regarding the determination of the C-value (C = L/A).
δ_ρ—Uncertainty regarding the value of water density.
$\delta_{\Delta p}$—Uncertainty regarding errors in measuring pressure differences between sections of the pressure pipe.
$\delta_{\Delta pf}$—Uncertainty regarding the decrease in pressure in the section of the pipe that generates hydraulic losses.
δ_t—Error relating to measurement over time.

δ_{Ql}—Relative uncertainty of measurement under final conditions by assessing flow intensification (leakage intensification).
δ_{rp}—Error regarding the pressure change log.

The probe intrusion depth in the pressure tube for the extracted water samples is 170 mm, placed diametrically opposite to, or at 90° from, each other. According to Côté [9], the increase in the intrusion length does not represent significant changes between the results obtained with a longer probe (50 mm minimum). The differences between the results obtained with probes of different length were small, and no greater than those obtained with probes of the same length. On the other hand, the intrusion depth of the probe is at an optimum point where the main velocity produces a velocity equal to the average falling velocity of the turbine at the probe inlet. The optimal penetration where this condition is fulfilled is reported for different flow velocity profiles within the penstock [8].

However, the power of the turbine shaft (P_m) or mechanical power has been calculated with Equation (3):

$$P_m = (P_e/\eta_g) - P_f \tag{3}$$

where P_e is the generator active power (measured on site), η_g is the efficiency of the generator (obtained from the manufacturer), and $P_f = (P_{tB} + P_{gB})$ are the losses in the load-bearing block (P_{tB}) and the guide-bearing (P_{gB}). The losses have been calculated in accordance with the IEC 60041 standard.

2.1.2. Manifolds Design for the Low-Pressure Section (Outlet)

For the study of energy transfer in the low-pressure section, the geometry and design parameters were obtained by Castro [18]. The low-pressure section is made up of a rotating domain and a stationary one. The first is made up of the runner, hub and shroud of the turbine; the second is made up of the draft tube, divider and outlet of the section.

According to the standard, the distance of the traction intakes in this section must be located at a distance from the runner of at least five times its maximum diameter; for the turbine in question, the tip diameter of the runner is 3.5 m and the minimum distance required is 17.5 m. However, the manifolds were located farther away than the minimum distanced required to avoid turbulence generated in the walls, close to the division of the draft tube (see Figure 4).

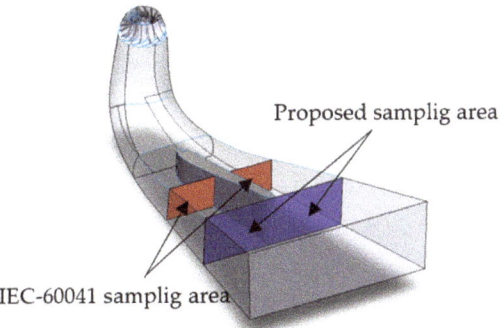

Figure 4. General geometry low section pressure (isometrical view).

Hulaas establishes that, under favorable conditions, the application of TM can be extended to falls of less than 100 m; on the other hand, since it is an inaccessible, closed measurement selection, the only possibility of exploring the temperature is through an intake device located inside the tube. This device consists of at least two tubes that collect partial flows [1,2].

Based on Figure 4, four fluid withdrawal intakes were coupled to perform temperature, flow rate and pressure measurements at the outlet of the draft tube; the proposed design is shown in Figure 5.

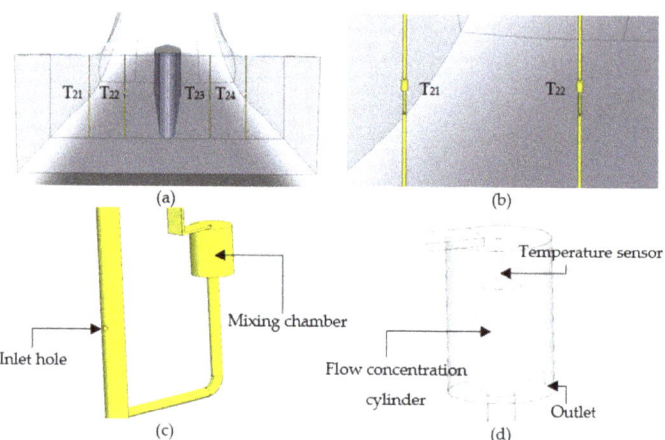

Figure 5. Manifold vessels coupling, outlet section: (**a**) manifolds T_{21}, T_{22}, T_{23} and T_{24}, (**b**) view outlet section left, (**c**) isometric view of manifold vessel, (**d**) mixing chamber (inside).

2.2. Numerical Simulation (CFD)

The computational fluid dynamics (CFD) analysis for the high- and low-pressure sections was performed in commercial software (ANSYS CFX). The domain discretization was performed by ICEM for both domains, and both the numerical calculation, and the post-process were performed by ANSYS CFX.

The discretization of the high-pressure section was of the non-structured tetrahedral type, presenting a total of 1,273,913 elements. In both the high- and low-pressure section, the element unit is millimeters (mm).

For the high-pressure section, the minimum size of the element is 1 mm, and the maximum size is 480 mm. This section includes the temperature sensors, probes, manifolds, inlet, outlet, and penstock.

The discretization for the low-pressure section is also that of the non-structured tetrahedral type, presenting a total of 6,297,796 elements. On the other hand, united with the elements, smaller bodies such as collector tubes (manifolds), mixing chambers, RTD's, and the flow inlet and outlet locations are added. For the low-pressure section, the minimum size of the element is 1 mm, and the maximum size is 600 mm. This section includes the temperature sensors, manifolds, runner, inlet and outlet of turbine, and draft tube, respectively.

For each of the numerical simulations, mass flow conditions calculated from the inlet volumetric flow were established.

According to [21], some turbulence models, such as k−Epsilon, are only valid for fully developed turbulence, and do not perform well in the area close to the wall. Two ways of dealing with the near-wall region are usually proposed.

One way is to integrate the turbulence with the wall, where turbulence models are modified to enable the viscosity-affected region to be resolved with all the mesh down to the wall, including the viscous sublayer. When using a modified low-Reynolds turbulence model to solve the near-wall region, the first cell center must be placed in the viscous sublayer (preferably y+ = 1), leading to the requirement of abundant mesh cells. Thus, substantial computational resources are required.

Another way is to use the so-called wall functions, which can model the near-wall region. When using the wall functions approach, there is no need to resolve the boundary layer, causing a significant reduction in the mesh size and the computational domain. Then:
- First, grid cell need to be 30 < y+ < 300. If this is too low, the model is invalid. If this is too high, the wall is not properly resolved.
- The high-Re model (Standard k−Epsilon, RNG k−epsilon) can be used.
- This method is used when there is greater interest in the mixing than the forces on the wall.

For the present case, the absolute distance from the wall in temperature sensors (walls of greater interest) is 0.97 mm (y), the Re number is 3998.2, the skin friction (C_f) is 0.013, the Wall shear stress (τ_w) is 2.44 Pa, the friction velocity ($u*$) is 0.049 m/s and the y+ value is 47. As the y+ value is in the range 30 < y+ < 300, both the turbulence model k-Epsilon and mesh are applicable for the study.

2.2.1. High Pressure Section

The high-pressure domain (penstock, Figure 6) was established as a stationary numerical analysis, with a k-Epsilon turbulence model and the Total Energy model to obtain temperature changes at strategic points in the domain. The fluid temperature at the inlet was 25 °C, and the walls of the study domain were defined as adiabatic.

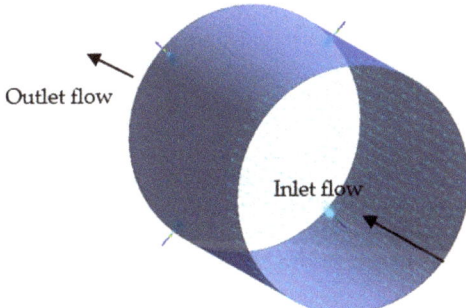

Figure 6. CFD, Post-processing. High-pressure section: Isometric view.

The boundary condition at the input was established as a mass flow rate and the outlet was established as a pressure outlet. Both the inlet and outlet conditions are presented in Table 1; for example, the first simulation is a development to 89,418.9 kg/s (89.67 m^3/s) and 390 kPa values, respectively. A total of 2000 iterations were established, with a convergence criterion of residual type "RMS", with a value of 1×10^{-6} and, for energy, a value of 1×10^{-4}.

The post-processing of the interest variable in the software shows the water temperature inside the manifolds (Figure 7), and the temperature on the surface of the RTD instrument through color contours (Figure 8), in which the higher value corresponds to the red color and the minor to the blue. The RTD sensor, a simulated surface within the study domain, directly obtains the necessary resolution for temperature measurement. The dimensions of the simulated sensor are 4 mm in diameter and 152 mm long [20]. Proper mixing of the fluid is confirmed by means of the temperature contours inside the manifolds, and a constant temperature is ensured. The maximum temperature of the fluid inside the manifolds is 25.1 °C, and the maximum temperature on the surface of the RTD sensor is 25.09 °C.

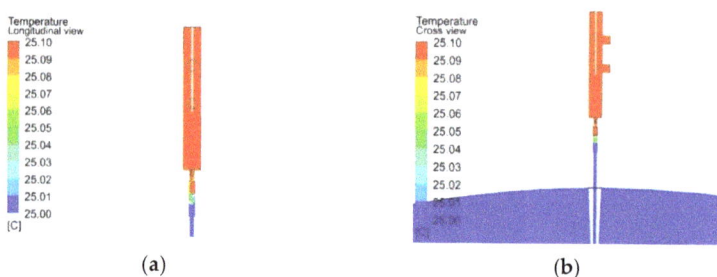

Figure 7. Internal temperature vessel, high-pressure section: (**a**) Longitudinal view, (**b**) Cross view.

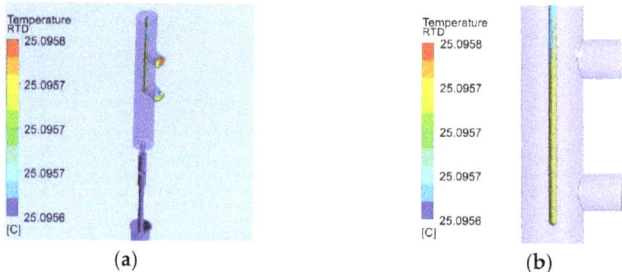

Figure 8. RTD temperature, high-pressure section: (**a**) Isometric view, (**b**) Longitudinal view (zoom).

According to the standard, at the manifold outlet, the volumetric flow must be between 0.1×10^{-3} and 0.5×10^{-3} m^3/s; therefore, the expected velocity range will be between 0.29 m/s and 1.46 m/s, respectively, since the outlet diameter of the manifolds is 0.02 m. Figure 9 shows the outlet velocity of the manifolds using colored contours. The obtained results confirm the values that are allowed by the standard.

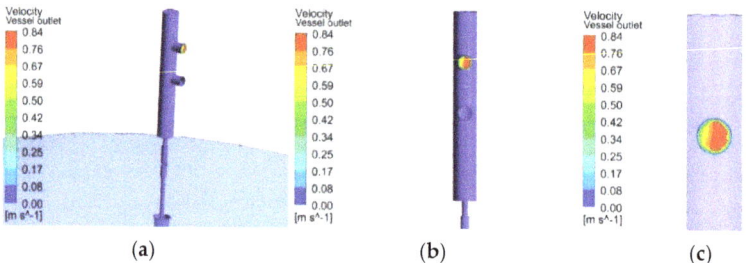

Figure 9. Velocity outlet, high-pressure section: (**a**) Isometric view, (**b**) Front view, (**c**) location velocity outlet (zoom).

On the other hand, Figure 10 shows the pressure contours at a location where a relevant sensor is physically attached.

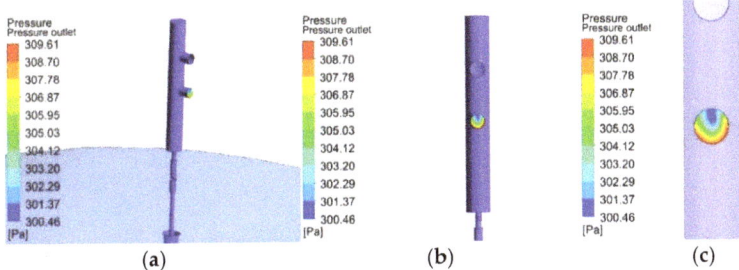

Figure 10. Pressure location, high-pressure section: (**a**) Isometric view, (**b**) Front view, (**c**) location pressure outlet (zoom).

2.2.2. Low Pressure Section

The CFD in the low-pressure section, as well as in the high-pressure one, used different inlet mass flows (presented in Table 1); however, the pressure at the outlet of the turbine (draft tube) was established as a pressure static outlet or open to the atmosphere. The numerical simulation was of the "turbo-machinery" type, defining a rotating domain (runner) and a stationary domain (draft tube and manifolds). When using two types of domains, it is necessary to establish a new boundary condition, defined as an interface. This configures itself as a "stage" type, since it adapts the results of a domain with movement to a stationary one, in which it is determined to be a "fluid–fluid" interface with corresponding 360° angles. A volumetric flow inlet with a direction based on cylindrical components was defined, a rotational velocity of the runner at 180 rpm and the temperature of the inlet fluid was that obtained at the outlet of the penstock for each of the different cases. The k-Epsilon turbulence model and the Total Energy equation were enabled; similarly, the domain walls were adiabatic, as in the penstock. In both the low- and high-pressure section, one of the most prominent turbulence models, the (k-Epsilon) model, was used. This is implemented in most general purpose CFD codes and is considered the industry standard model. It has proven to be stable and numerically robust and has a well-established regime of predictive capability. Therefore, for general-purpose simulations, the model offers a good compromise in terms of accuracy and robustness.

Within CFX, the turbulence model uses the scalable wall-function approach to improve robustness and accuracy when the near-wall mesh is refined. The scalable wall functions enable solutions to arbitrarily fine near-wall grids, significantly improving standard wall functions. Defined thus, a total of 10,000 iterations were established with a convergence criterion of residual type "RMS" with a value of 1×10^{-6} and, for energy, a value of 1×10^{-4}.

The processing of variables of interest in the software shows the temperature measured by the RTD sensor fitted inside the manifold (Figure 11) at the outlet of the draft tube. The dimensions of the simulated sensor are 4 mm in diameter and 50 mm long.

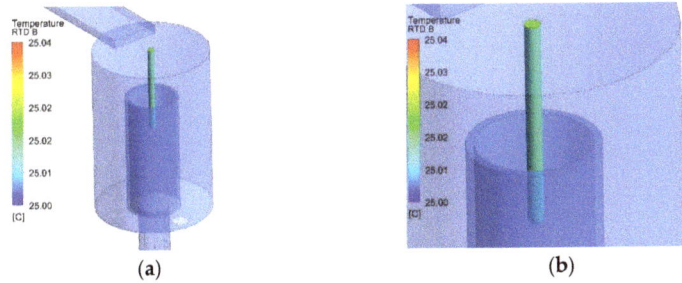

Figure 11. Temperature, low-pressure section: (**a**) Isometric view (**b**) RTD Sensor, zoom.

Figure 12 shows the velocity and pressure at the outlet of the manifold.

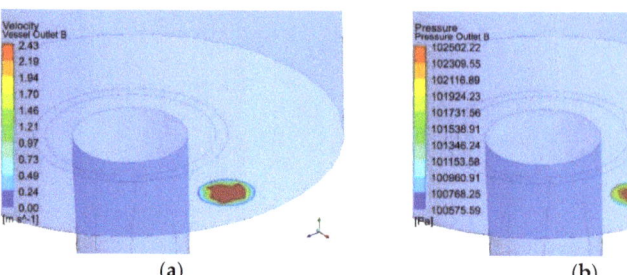

Figure 12. Outlet location, (**a**) Velocity outlet, (**b**) Pressure Outlet.

A view of the flow inlet through velocity vectors to the mixing chamber is shown in Figure 13. The total length of the collecting tubes is 4.06 m, equivalent to the outlet height of the draft tube for correct sampling in the zone, the diameter of the tubes is 30.8 mm or 1 1/2 in., 10 inlet holes to the collection tube with a diameter of 10 mm satisfy the minimum dimensions required by the standard [2].

Figure 13. Internal flow (velocity vectors), low-pressure section.

2.3. Application of Grid Convergence Index (GCI)

According to [22], the computer code used for CFD applications must be fully referenced, and previous code verification studies must be briefly described or cited. Appropriate methods could be selected to validate that CFD results do not depend on the quality or size of the grid. For the present study, the Grid Convergence Index (*GCI*) method was used.

The recommended procedure to calculate the fine-grid convergence index (*GCI*) is based on Equation (4)

$$GCI^{21} = (1.25 e_a^{21})/(r_{21}{}^p - 1) \qquad (4)$$

where $e_a{}^{21}$ is approximated relative error, calculated by Equation (5). ϕ are the values of critical variables. For the present case, ϕ is the temperature (T_{11} or T_{21}) at specific points in specific domains.

$$e_a^{21} = |(\Phi_1 - \Phi_2)/\Phi_1| \qquad (5)$$

$r_{21}{}^p$ is the grid refinement factor $r = h_{coarse}/h_{fine}$. It is desirable that this is greater than 1.3. The 21 subscripts correspond to the relationship between grid 1 (fine) and grid 2 (coarse); see Equation (6)

$$r_{21}{}^p = h_2/h_1 \qquad (6)$$

where "p" is the apparent order of the method used. For estimation of discretization error, it is necessary to define a representative cell, mesh or grid size "h" (mm). For example, Equation (7) is employed for three-dimensional calculations.

$$h = \left[\frac{1}{N} * \sum_{i=1}^{N}(\Delta V_i)^{\left(\frac{1}{3}\right)}\right] \quad (7)$$

ΔV_i is the volume and N is the total number of cells used for the computations. Another method to obtain the size of the grid (h) is analyzing the grid in the software used. This analysis can be conducted according to volume, the maximum/minimum length or the maximum/minimum side or the density of the grid.

In comparison with Equation (4), Roache [23] establishes that the grid convergence index (GCI) is based on Equation (8)

$$GCI_{Ro} = 3|\varepsilon|/(r^p - 1) \quad (8)$$

where ε is equivalent to $e_a{}^{21}$, and r^p is equivalent to $r_{21}{}^p$. A summary and comparison of results for two grids are shown in Tables 2 and 3.

Table 2. Summary of results, high-pressure section.

Grid	ϕ	$e_a{}^{21}$	h	$r_{21}{}^p$	GCI^{21} (%)	GCI_{Ro} (%)
Coarse (2)	25.0957	1.20×10^{-6}	455.38	1.196	3.47×10^{-4}	8.34×10^{-4}
Fine (1)	25.0957		380.65			

Table 3. Summary of results, low-pressure section.

Grid	ϕ	$e_a{}^{21}$	h	$r_{21}{}^p$	GCI^{21} (%)	GCI_{Ro} (%)
Coarse (2)	25.0204	1.22×10^{-5}	816.67	1.917	5.72×10^{-4}	1.37×10^{-3}
Fine (1)	25.0207		426.10			

The grid convergence index (GCI) is adequate when the result is less than 1%, according to Roache. Despite the CGI differences between the authors, a value of less than 1% was obtained for both cases. Due to the presented results, it is possible to carry out the current study with the first generated grid.

2.4. Thermodynamic Method Application

The calculation of Hydraulic Efficiency (η_h) is defined by the ratio of the mechanical power (P_m) and the hydraulic power (P_h) of the turbine, respectively, as in Equation (9).

$$\eta_h = P_m/P_h \quad (9)$$

The mechanical power (P_m) of the turbine is calculated by the specific mechanical energy (E_m), density (ρ) and the volumetric flow (Q_T) that passes through the turbine, as in Equation (10).

$$P_m = E_m * (Q_T * \rho) \quad (10)$$

The hydraulic power (P_h), in contrast with the P_m, is obtained by means of the Specific Hydraulic Energy (E_h), as in Equation (11). The correction factor (ΔP_h) is neglected since Urquiza [8] considered this factor in the presented results.

$$P_h = E_h * (Q_T * \rho) \pm \Delta P_h \quad (11)$$

The E_m was calculated with the variables measured in the manifolds, such as pressure (p), temperature (T) and velocity (v), (see Equation (12)). The reference heights (z) are assigned for each manifold and the isothermal factor ($\hat{a}$), as well as the specific heat (C_p), are obtained from the annexes of IEC 60041, Appendix E physical data, Table EV and EVI [2] (Table 4), and an interpolation of the temperature and average pressure for each of the case studies.

Table 4. Properties of water [2].

	Absolute Pressure (10×10^5 Pa)	
θ (°C)	$\hat{a}$ ($\times 10^{-3}$ m^3/kg)	C_p (J/kg °C)
23	0.9315	4179
24	0.9286	4179
25	0.9257	4179
26	0.9229	4179
27	0.9201	4179

Finally, gravity (g) was obtained from Reference [8]. The subscripts 11 and 21 correspond to the manifolds in the inlet and outlet section, respectively. Similarly, T_1 and T_2 belong to the corresponding sections.

$$E_m = [\hat{a} * (p_{11} - p_{21})] + [C_p * (T_1 - T_2)] + [((v_{11}^2 - v_{21}^2))/2] + [g * (z_{11} - z_{21})] \quad (12)$$

The E_h is obtained by the properties measured in the main water flow (subscripts 1 and 2), Equation (13). Pressure (p), velocity (v) and height (z) are geodetic sampling points or reference points with respect to the height of the sea level at which the turbine is located. ρ, as well as $\hat{a}$ and C_p, are obtained by interpolation.

$$E_h = [((p_1 - p_2))/\rho] + [((v_1^2 - v_2^2))/2] + [g * (z_1 - z_2)] \quad (13)$$

The sampling points are observed in Figure 14, which is a general diagram of the turbine in question (original C.H. Temascal plane), as well as the areas in which the fluid properties are measured.

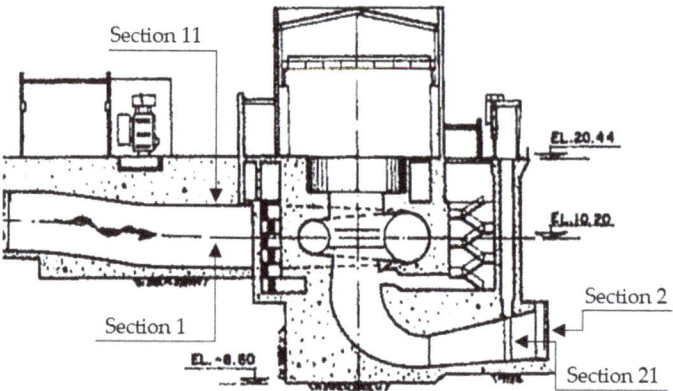

Figure 14. Longitudinal view, measurement points [24].

According to [6], the mechanical energy (E_m) is calculated by Equation (14). In this equation, $\hat{a}$ is an isothermal factor of the water, p_{11}, the inlet pressure in the diffuser, p_{21}, the outlet pressure of the suction tube, T_{11}, the inlet temperature of the suction tube, T_{20}, the outlet temperature of the suction tube aspiration, z_{11}, is a reference point for temperature measurement, and z_{1m} is the reference point for measuring p_{11}.

$$E_m = [\dot{a} * (p_{11} - p_{12})]$$

$$E_m = [C_p * (T_{11} - T_{20})] + [(v_1^2 - v_2^2))/2] + [g * (z_{1m} - z_{11})] \tag{14}$$

However, the variables for the present study were adapted to the previously established conditions, defining E_m as Equation (15).

$$E_m = [Cp * (T_1 - T_2)] + [(v_{11}^2 - v_{21}^2))/2] + [g * (z_{11} - z_{21})] \tag{15}$$

3. Results
3.1. Results of Thermodynamic Method
3.1.1. High-Pressure Section

For each of the different conditions and working sections, the temperature, velocity and pressure in the manifolds were obtained as required by IEC 60041. Similarly, the amount of volumetric flow that exits the manifolds located on the penstock and draft pipe was tested. As it is a stationary type of simulation, the value of temperature, pressure and velocity is obtained by exporting a series of values provided by the software in each of the locations of interest at the end of the numerical calculation (high- and low-pressure section). This series of values is averaged and shown below.

Table 5 contains the average temperature values in the four manifolds; Table 6 contains the average velocity and pressure values of the manifolds. Section 14.3.1 "General"; of the IEC-60041 standard establishes that the thermodynamic method for the average yield is based on the laws of thermodynamics, using the thermodynamic temperature ϑ in Kelvin (K). In case of temperature differences, the temperature can be directly expressed in Celsius (°C) degrees, as $\vartheta_1 - \vartheta_2 = \theta_1 - \theta_2$ [2].

Table 5. Manifold´s temperature, high-pressure section.

Q_T (m³/s)	T_{11} (°C)	T_{12} (°C)	T_{13} (°C)	T_{14} (°C)	T_1 (°C)
89.67	25.095	25.095	25.095	25.095	25.095
82.00	25.095	25.095	25.095	25.095	25.095
76.14	25.095	25.095	25.095	25.095	25.095
68.73	25.096	25.096	25.096	25.096	25.096
60.99	25.096	25.096	25.096	25.096	25.096
52.90	25.096	25.096	25.096	25.096	25.096
46.11	25.096	25.096	25.096	25.096	25.096
35.68	25.097	25.097	25.097	25.097	25.097

Table 6. Manifold's velocity and pressure, high-pressure section.

Q_T (m³/s)	P_{11} (Pa)	v_{11} (m/s)
89.67	314.22	0.70
82.00	301.12	0.66
76.14	303.74	0.68
68.73	294.34	0.67
60.99	268.95	0.70
52.90	287.85	0.66
46.11	251.58	0.67
35.68	254.11	0.68

3.1.2. Low-Pressure Section

The analysis of results in the low-pressure section (runner and draft tube) involves a comparison of the mechanical power and torque generated by the turbine for each flow condition (Table 7) in the software.

Table 7. Comparison between mechanical power and torque, reported vs. simulated.

Q_T (m³/s)	$P_{M\ Reported}$ (MW)	$P_{M\ Simulated}$ (MW)	Torque $_{Reported}$ (kN m)	Torque $_{Simulated}$ (kN m)
89.67	31.65	31.58	1679.94	1676.13
82.00	30.71	30.66	1630.04	1627.58
76.14	29.03	28.96	1540.87	1537.15
68.73	26.05	25.99	1382.70	1379.33
60.99	22.63	22.58	1201.17	1198.73
52.90	19.02	18.97	1009.55	1006.96
46.11	15.72	15.67	834.39	831.56
35.68	10.14	10.12	538.22	537.32

By demonstrating the same mechanical power and torque conditions, the results in the draft tube can be analyzed. The manifolds attached to the draft tube acquired samples of the main flow (water) to obtain the energy distribution at different points. Variables such as temperature, velocity and pressure, obtained in each of the containers, are shown in Tables 8 and 9.

Table 8. Manifold´s temperature, low-pressure section.

Q_T (m³/s)	T_{21} (°C)	T_{22} (°C)	T_{23} (°C)	T_{24} (°C)	T_2 (°C)
89.67	25.023	25.017	25.019	25.022	25.020
82.00	25.018	25.014	25.011	25.013	25.014
76.14	25.012	25.011	25.008	25.009	25.010
68.73	25.008	25.008	25.008	25.007	25.008
60.99	25.008	25.010	25.007	25.007	25.008
52.90	25.009	25.011	25.009	25.008	25.010
46.11	25.013	25.014	25.012	25.011	25.013
35.68	25.020	25.021	25.018	25.017	25.019

Table 9. Manifold´s velocity and pressure, low-pressure section.

Q_T (m³/s)	P_{21} (Pa)	v_{21} (m/s)
89.67	99,385.15	1.31
82.00	99,503.34	1.25
76.14	99,843.35	1.15
68.73	100,511.12	0.89
60.99	100,265.66	1.02
52.90	99,748.05	0.98
46.11	99,441.40	0.94

4. Discussion

The results obtained in the low-pressure section (draft tube) show that the direction of runner rotation (clockwise) and the geometry of the draft tube discharges water from a turbine, in addition to acting as an energy-recovery device, helping to improve the overall performance of the unit. It can also allow the downstream water level to be lower or higher than the equatorial plane of the turbine, depending on the needs of the facility. The draft tube, due to its divergent shape, causes a deceleration in the velocity of the water leaving the turbine, converting the kinetic energy of the fluid into pressure energy (Figure 15) [18].

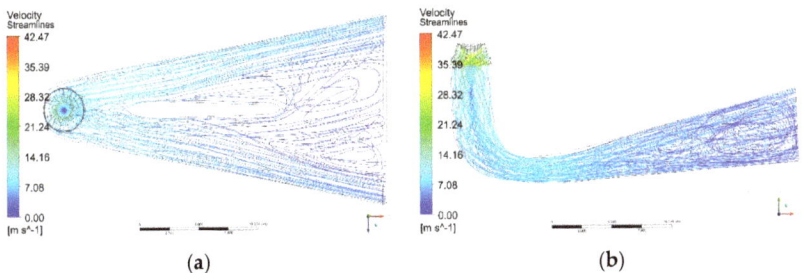

Figure 15. Velocity streamlines on the complete turbine, (**a**) upper view, (**b**) lateral View.

By coupling the manifolds in the draft tube, the flow distribution is affected, causing recirculation or vorticity in the area in which manifolds are located. The location of the manifolds is suggested by IEC-60041. Depending on the dimensions of probes, vorticity can be created behind the probes and then dissipated. The flow disturbance will be downstream once velocity, pressure, and temperature variables have been measured, so they cannot influence efficiency calculations. Therefore, the average temperatures in the manifolds T_{22} and T_{23} are slightly higher than the average temperature of T_{21} and T_{24}, as derived from the flow distribution behavior in the turbine (Figure 16).

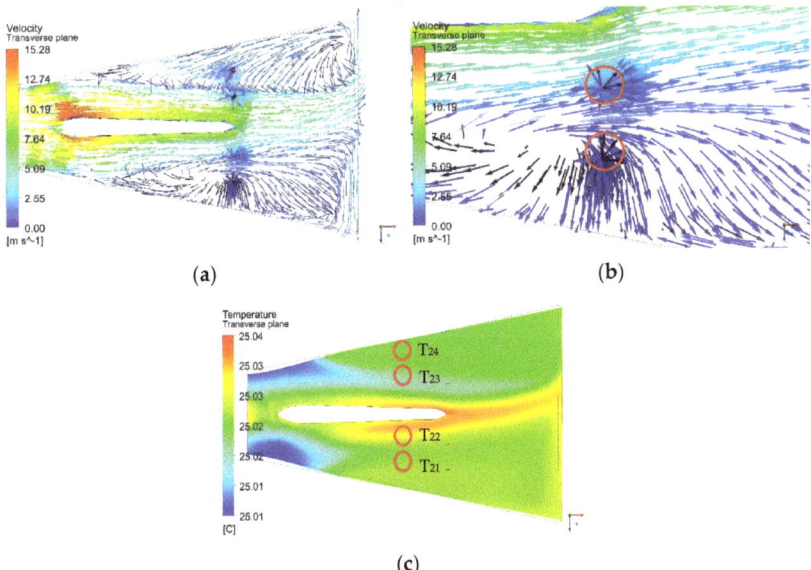

Figure 16. Manifold´s in the draft tube, (**a**) Recirculation flow (normalized symbols), (**b**) Recirculation flow in manifolds, left section "zoom" (normalized symbols) (**c**) Temperature contour.

The summary of results obtained from the temperature differences $T_1 - T_2$ (ΔT), E_m, E_h, P_m, P_h and η_h, for different cases is presented in Table 10. Figures 17 and 18 show the main comparison of the results, between what was reported in [18,24] and the current case study.

Table 10. Summary of results, application of Thermodynamic Method.

Q_T (m³/s)	ΔT (°C) [1]	E_m (J/kg)	E_h (J/kg)	P_m (MW)	P_h (MW)	η_h (%)
89.67	0.075	336.04	420.12	30.05	37.57	79.99
82.00	0.081	363.26	420.26	29.71	34.37	86.44
76.14	0.085	379.30	421.10	28.80	31.98	90.07
68.73	0.087	389.71	423.14	26.71	29.01	92.10
60.99	0.087	388.17	424.21	23.61	25.80	91.50
52.90	0.086	383.80	424.16	20.25	22.38	90.48
46.11	0.083	370.69	425.20	17.05	19.55	87.18
35.68	0.077	347.91	429.30	12.38	15.28	81.04

[1] ΔT: Temperature difference between measured sections ($T_1 - T_2$).

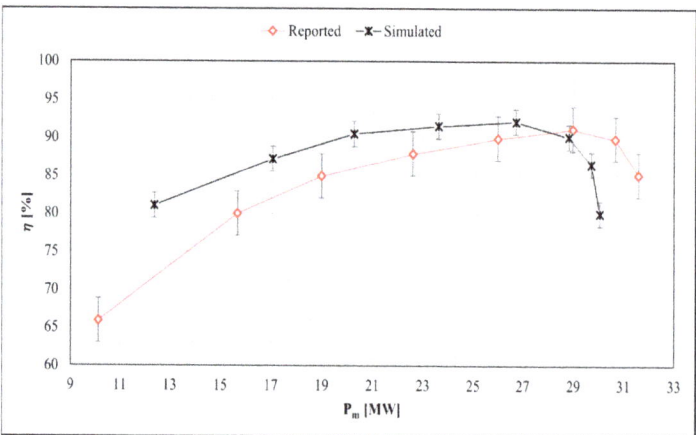

Figure 17. Comparison, Reported hydraulic efficiency (Gibson method) vs. Simulated hydraulic efficiency.

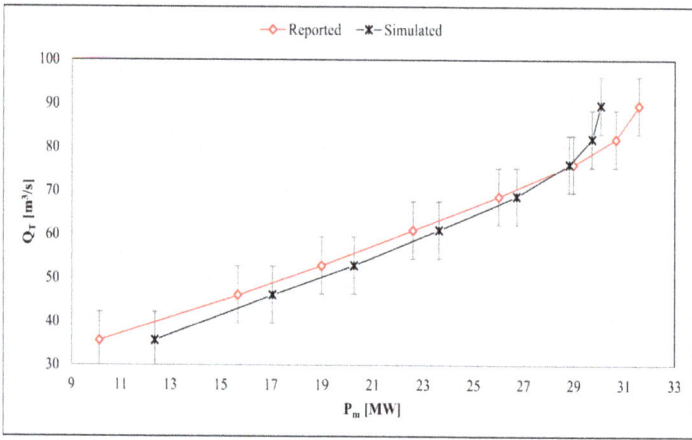

Figure 18. Comparison of mechanical power generated, reported (Gibson method) vs. simulated.

CFD simulations are a proven tool to investigate hydraulic turbine performance, while measurements of some parameters, such as flow or pressure, are common in calculations of their efficiency. In the present study, the design of manifolds and CFD applications contribute to the assay, with sampling system (manifolds) and experimental measurement times in the power plant, complying with the criteria established to apply the TM to low-load turbines.

Experimental studies report that the water temperature at the turbomachine outlet must be higher than that at the inlet. With a lower temperature difference between the measurement sections, the maximum hydraulic efficiency is presented. According to those mentioned above [3], the difference between the efficiency curves is around 0.5%; however, for the present study, the maximum and minimum differences in efficiency are 15.12% and 1.09%, respectively, for the Gibson method (reported). As one of the most important variables for the study is the temperature on surfaces of principal components, such as the runner, penstock, draft tube, etc., and these are unknown, the domain was specified as adiabatic. As a result, there is a low-temperature increase in the water between the high- and low-pressure sections. These cause a low-energy exchange and higher efficiency than expected. If the temperature in these components was known, the boundary conditions could be set differently, and a lower efficiency would be expected in different cases. Likewise, the efficiency would present results closer to those reported. The hydraulic efficiency of the turbine is susceptible to temperature changes between one section and another. This sensitivity is presented with values up to 0.0001 K; the assumed temperature, or a change in temperature in any of the components, has a direct effect on efficiency.

The simulated TM presented differences in the mechanical power and efficiency; however, the behavior of the generated curve shows the same tendency as the curve in the experimental data obtained using the Gibson method (reported), presenting a gradual increase in efficiency until a maximum point is reached. This subsequently decreases. The results obtained for each operating condition are similar to those reported by the Gibson method, meaning an adequate comparison for the study of the proposed manifolds design, considering the head limits (less than 100 m), the amount of maximum volumetric input flow (89.67 m^3/s), the type of turbine (Francis slow) and the specific speed of the turbomachine (less than 110). In future studies, the authors recommend developing transitory simulations for other operating conditions, as well as using the experimental test to measure temperature in the main components, and set different variables in the numerical simulations.

According to [3,12], the present study used a hybrid vertical detraction system and a mixing chamber for each tube, reducing the number of sensors that are required to facilitate installation in the low-pressure section. In addition, the manifolds proposed in the low-pressure section are compatible at different outlet heights for the draft tube, as it is only necessary to adjust the tube length.

5. Conclusions

Based on the location of the manifolds in the input and output sections, the proposed design of manifolds to measure properties of the main flow of a Francis-type low-head hydraulic turbine meet with the requirements suggested by the IEC—60041 Standard to carry out the Thermodynamic Method (TM) employing Computational Fluid Dynamics (CFD).

The distance from the turbine center to the measuring section is essential. The minimum distance set in the standard [2] is five times its maximum diameter, and the measurements show that it should be the absolute minimum. According to Figure 3, a shorter distance could improve energy distribution.

Using a mixing chamber inside the draft tube allows for a direct measurement of temperature in the principal flow at the outlet. In addition, inside the mixing chamber, there is a water flow concentrator, which helps to direct the flow into the temperature sensor, obtaining a direct measurement. The IEC-60041 establishes that the minimum number of tubes consists of two units that collect partial flows. However, increasing the number of tubes and manifolds at the outlet makes it possible to improve the temperature measurements. In this case, four manifolds were used in the low-pressure section. In both the left and right section, two manifolds were installed after the division to avoid a high recirculation or vorticity in the area in which manifolds are located.

On the other hand, the results obtained from the mechanical power and torque in the turbine runner were identical to those reported by the Gibson method (GM); however, the efficiency between the above methods is similar. To obtain results that are closer to reality, the numerical simulations used in CFD must be supplied from as many boundary conditions as possible (actual conditions). It is necessary to set the temperature on the surface of principal components so that the main flow of water makes contact via its passage through the turbomachine to the efficiency results, with the application of TM.

The efficiency calculation is higher under particular volumetric flow conditions (35.68 m^3/s and 68.73 m^3/s) compared to the efficiency reported when applying the GM. The maximum efficiency generated by the turbine applying the TM was 92.10%, corresponding to a flow of 68.73 m^3/s. After the maximum efficiency point, the TM's efficiency is lower than the GM's.

Author Contributions: Conceptualization: L.L.C.G.; Investigation: E.O.C.M. and L.L.C.G.; Methodology: L.L.C.G.; Project administration: G.U.B.; Resources: G.U.B.; Software: L.L.C.G.; Supervision: G.U.B.; Writing—original draft preparation: E.O.C.M.; Writing—review & editing: L.L.C.G. and J.C.G.C. All authors have read and agreed to the published version of the manuscript.

Funding: This work is partly supported by the National Council for Science and Technology [Conacyt], CVU Number: 707755.

Acknowledgments: To Arturo Nava Torres, for his unconditional collaboration in the presented project. To the "Centro de Investigación en Ingeniería y Ciencias Aplicadas (CIICAp)", for all facilities provided during my stay.

Conflicts of Interest: The authors declare no conflict of interest.

Glossary

$\hat{a}$	Isothermal factor of water (m^3/kg)
C_p	Specific heat capacity of water (J/kg °C)
E_h	Specific hydraulic energy (J/kg)
E_m	Specific mechanical energy (J/kg)
g	gravity acceleration (m/s^2)
p_1	Turbine pressure inlet (Pa)
p_{11}	Average pressure vessels, high-pressure section (Pa)
p_2	Turbine pressure outlet (Pa)
p_{21}	Average pressure vessels, low-pressure section (Pa)
P_e	Active generator power (MW)
P_f	Difference in losses in the bearings (%)
P_{gB}	Loss in guide bearing (%)
P_h	Hydraulic power (MW)
P_m	Mechanical power (MW)
P_{tB}	Loss in load bearing (%)
Q_0	Leakage flow (m^3/s)
Q_T	Volumetric flow in turbine (m^3/s)
T_1	Average temperature vessels, high-pressure section (°C)
T_{11}	Temperature, upper-right vessel (°C)
T_{12}	Temperature, upper-left vessel (°C)
T_{13}	Temperature, lower-right vessel (°C)
T_{14}	Temperature, lower-right vessel (°C)
T_2	Average temperature vessels, low-pressure section (°C)
T_{21}	Temperature vessel A (°C)
T_{22}	Temperature vessel B (°C)
T_{23}	Temperature vessel C (°C)
T_{24}	Temperature vessel D (°C)
v_1	Turbine velocity inlet (m/s)

v_{11}	Average velocity vessels, high-pressure section (m/s)
v_2	Turbine velocity outlet (m/s)
v_{21}	Average velocity vessels, low-pressure section (m/s)
z_1	Reference point high-pressure section (m)
z_{11}	Reference point in manifolds, high-pressure section (m)
z_2	Reference point low-pressure section (m)
z_{21}	Reference point in manifolds, low-pressure section (m)
ΔP_h	Hydraulic power correction (W)
θ	Temperature (°C)
Φ_P	Penstock diameter
δ_C	Uncertainty regarding the determination of the C-value (C = L/A) (%)
δ_{Ql}	Relative uncertainty of measurement under final conditions by assessing flow intensification (leakage intensification) (%)
δ_Q	Total deviation of measurements of the flow in a systematic manner (%)
δ_{rp}	Error regarding the pressure change log (%)
δ_t	Error relating to measurement over time (%)
$\delta_{\Delta A}$	Uncertainty regarding the change in pipe section due to the change in pressure (%)
$\delta_{\Delta p}$	Uncertainty regarding errors in measuring pressure differences between sections of the pressure pipe (%)
$\delta_{\Delta pf}$	Uncertainty regarding the decrease in pressure in the section of the pipe that generates hydraulic losses (%)
$\delta_{\Delta \rho}$	Uncertainty regarding the change in water density due to subsequent pressure change (%)
δ_ρ	Uncertainty regarding the value of water density (%)
η_g	Generator efficiency (%)
η_h	Hydraulic efficiency (%)
ρ	Density (kg/m^3)

References

1. Hulaas, H.; Vinnogg, L. Field acceptance tests to determine the hydraulic performance of hydraulic turbines, storage pumps and pump-turbines. Clause 14 Thermodynamic method for measuring efficiency, comments. In Proceedings of the International Group for Hydraulic Efficiency Measurements 2010, Roorkee, India, 21–23 October 2010.
2. International Electrotechnical Commission 60041 (IEC 60041). Thermodynamic method for measuring efficiency. In *Field Acceptance Tests to Determine the Hydraulic Performance of Hydraulic Turbines, Storage Pumps and Pump-Turbines*, 3rd ed.; International Electrotechnical Commission: Geneva, Switzerland, 1991; pp. 293–319.
3. Hulaas, H.; Nilsen, E.; Vinnogg, L. Thermodynamic efficiency measurements of Pelton turbines. Experience from investigation of energy/Temperature distribution in the discharge canal measuring section. In Proceedings of the 7th International Conference on Hydraulic Efficiency Measurements, Milan, Italy, 3–6 September 2008; p. 11.
4. Patil, S.; Verma, H.; Kumar, A. Efficiency measurement of hydro machine by Thermodynamic method. In Proceedings of the 8th International Conference on Hydraulic Efficiency Measurements, Roorkee, India, 21–23 October 2010.
5. Shang, D. Application research on testing efficiency of main drainage pump in coal mine using thermodynamic theories. *Int. J. Rotating Mach.* **2017**, *2017*, 5936506. [CrossRef]
6. Kahraman, G.; Lütfi, Y.H.; Hakan, F.Ö. Evaluation of energy efficiency using thermodynamics analysis in a hydropower plant: A case study. *Renew. Energy* **2009**, *34*, 1458–1465. [CrossRef]
7. Feng, X.; Hequet, T.; Muciaccia, F. Efficiency testing in Tai An (Shandong China) PSPP reversible units by means of thermodynamic method. In Proceedings of the International Group for Hydraulic Efficiency Measurements 2008, Milano, Italy, 3–6 September 2008.
8. Karlicek, R.F. Analysis of uncertainties in the Thermodynamic Method of testing hydraulic turbines. In Proceedings of the IGHEM Seminar, Reno, NV, USA, 28–31 July 1998.
9. Côté, E.; Proulx, G. Experiments with the thermodynamic method. In Proceedings of the International Group for Hydraulic Efficiency Measurements 2012, Trondheim, Norway, 28 June 2012.
10. Gere, J.M.; Goodno, B.J. *Mechanics of Materials*; Cengage: Boston, MA, USA, 2009.
11. Beer, F.; Russell, E.; DeWolf, J.; Mazurek, D. *Mechanics of Materials*; McGraw-Hill Education: New York, NY, USA, 2010.
12. Mangla, M.; Khodre, N. Measurement of turbine efficiency by thermodynamic Method for field acceptance test of hydro turbine and Comparison with model test result. In Proceedings of the International Group for Hydraulic Efficiency Measurements 2010, Roorkee, India, 21–23 October 2010.
13. Lugaresi, A.; Massa, A. Designing Francis turbines: Trends in the last decade. *Water Power Dam Constr.* **1987**, *39*, 23–32.
14. Islam, R.J.; Siam, I.R.; Hasan, R.; Hasan, S.; Islam, F. A Comprehensive Study of Micro-Hydropower Plant and Its Potential in Bangladesh. *Int. Sch. Res. Netw.* **2012**, *2012*, 635396.
15. Hatata, A.Y.; El-Saadawi, M.M.; Saad, S. A feasibility study of small hydro power for selected locations in Egypt. *Energy Strategy Rev.* **2019**, *24*, 300–313. [CrossRef]

16. Prawin, A.M.; Jawahar, C.P. Design of 15 kW Micro Hydro Power Plant for Rural Electrification at Valara. In Proceedings of the 1st International Conference on Power Engineering, Computing and CONtrol, PECCON-2017, Tamil Nadu, India, 2–4 March 2017.
17. Ole, G.D.; Torbjørn, K.N.; Brandåstrø, B.; Håkon, H.F.; Wiborg, E.J.; Hulaas, H. Comparison between pressure-time and thermodynamic efficiency measurements on a low head turbine. In Proceedings of the 6th International Conference on Innovation in Hydraulic Efficiency Measurements, Portland, OR, USA, 30 July–1 August 2006.
18. Castro, L.; Urquiza, G.; Adamkowski, A.; Reggio, M. Experimental and numerical simulations predictions comparison of power and efficiency in hydraulic turbine. *Model. Simul. Eng.* **2011**, *2011*, 146054. [CrossRef]
19. Castañeda, M.E.O.; Castro, G.L.L.; Urquiza, B.G.; Alcántara, M.J. Diseño de un recipiente colector para medición de eficiencia teórica en turbinas hidráulicas. In Proceedings of the SOMIM Conference, Sinaloa, Mexico, 18–20 September 2019.
20. Urquiza, B.G.; Kubiak, S.; Adamkowski, A.; Janicki, W. Condiciones Previas para la Medición de Flujo y Cálculo de Eficiencia de la Unidad No. 4 en la C. H. Temascal, Tech. Rep. 76P/DM/CIICAp. 2005.
21. Lecture 7: Turbulence Modeling Introduction to ANSYS Fluent, Sales Conference Theme and Team Building. Available online: https://www.academia.edu/36090206/Lecture_7_Turbulence_Modeling_Introduction_to_ANSYS_Fluent (accessed on 5 December 2021).
22. Celik, B.I.; Ghia, U.; Roache, P.J.; Freitas, C.J.; Coleman, H.; Raad, P.E. Procedure for estimation and reporting of uncertainty due to discretization in CFD applications. *J. Fluids Eng. Trans. ASME* **2008**, *1*, 130.
23. Roache, P.J. Perspective: A method for uniform reporting of grid refinement studies. *J. Fluids Eng.* **1994**, *116*, 405–413. [CrossRef]
24. Urquiza, B.G.; Kubiak, S.; Adamkowski, A.; Janicki, W. Resultados de Medición de Flujo y Cálculo de Eficiencia de la Unidad No. 4 en la C. H. Temascal, Tech. Rep. 77P/DM/CIICAp. 2005.

Article

Mechanistic Model of an Air Cushion Surge Tank for Hydro Power Plants

Madhusudhan Pandey [1], Dietmar Winkler [1], Kaspar Vereide [2], Roshan Sharma [1] and Bernt Lie [1,*]

[1] Telemark Modeling and Control Center (TMCC), University of South-Eastern Norway (USN), 3918 Porsgrunn, Norway; madhusudhan.pandey@usn.no (M.P.); dietmar.winkler@usn.no (D.W.); roshan.sharma@usn.no (R.S.)

[2] Department of Civil and Environmental Engineering, Norwegian University of Science and Technology, 7034 Trondheim, Norway; kaspar.vereide@ntnu.no

* Correspondence: bernt.lie@usn.no

Abstract: Due to the increasing use of renewable energy sources, and to counter the effects of fossil fuels, renewable dispatchable hydro power can be used for balancing load and generation from intermittent sources (solar and wind). During higher percentage change in load acceptance or rejection in the intermittent grid, the operations of surge tanks are crucial in terms of water mass oscillation and water hammer pressure, and to avoid wear and tear in actuators and other equipment, such as hydro turbines. Surge tanks are broadly classified as open types, with access to open air, and closed types, with a closed volume of pressurized air. Closed surge tanks are considered to have a more flexible operation in terms of suppressing water mass oscillation and water hammer pressure. In this paper, a mechanistic model of an air cushion surge tank (ACST) for hydro power plants is developed based on the ordinary differential equations (ODEs) for mass and momentum balances. The developed mechanistic model of the ACST is a feature extension to an existing open-source hydro power library—OpenHPL. The developed model is validated with experimental data from the Torpa hydro power plant (HPP) in Norway. Results show that the air friction inside the ACST is negligible as compared to the water friction. The results also indicate that a hydro power plant with an ACST is a potential candidate as a flexible hydro power in an interconnected power system grid supplied with intermittent energy sources. Conclusions are drawn based on the simulation results from hydraulic performance of the ACST.

Keywords: air cushion surge tank (ACST); air friction model; flexible hydro power plants; mechanistic model; OpenHPL

Citation: Pandey, M.; Winkler, D.; Vereide, K.; Sharma, R.; Lie, B. Mechanistic Model of an Air Cushion Surge Tank for Hydro Power Plants. *Energies* 2022, *15*, 2824. https://doi.org/10.3390/en15082824

Academic Editors: Adam Adamkowski and Anton Bergant

Received: 17 March 2022
Accepted: 11 April 2022
Published: 13 April 2022

Publisher's Note: MDPI stays neutral with regard to jurisdictional claims in published maps and institutional affiliations.

Copyright: © 2022 by the authors. Licensee MDPI, Basel, Switzerland. This article is an open access article distributed under the terms and conditions of the Creative Commons Attribution (CC BY) license (https://creativecommons.org/licenses/by/4.0/).

1. Introduction

1.1. Background

Electricity generation from renewable energy is increasing because of oil insecurity, climatic concern, the nuclear power debate, and carbon emission prices. In a growing trend of renewable energy, today's power systems are a combination of intermittent and dispatchable renewable sources in a common interconnected grid. Intermittent sources include sources like solar power plants and wind power plants, whose variability can be balanced using a dispatchable renewable source like a hydro power plant, as discussed in [1,2]. In an interconnected power grid with both intermittent and dispatchable sources, a sudden loss in generation from the intermittent sources, for example, shadowing a large number of solar panels as in the case of solar power plants, a shutdown of the wind generators for unacceptable wind velocity as in the case of wind power plants, hydro power plants must be able to operate with a higher percentage of load acceptance to cope with the loss in generation, and to protect the power grid from a blackout. Similarly, when there is a sudden increase in production from the intermittent generation, hydro power plants must be able to operate with a higher percentage of load rejection to cope with grid instability and blackout. This indicates the need for flexible operation of dispatchable hydro power plants. In [3,4], the concept of *flexible hydro power* is coined for the interconnected power grid. Similarly, in [5] cascaded hydro power plants are considered as one of the candidates for flexible hydro power plants. In relation to the concept of flexible hydro power, hydro power plants with open surge tanks are relatively less able to tackle a higher percentage of load acceptance and rejection. However, power plants with ACST are more likely to tackle a higher percentage of load acceptance and rejection as ACST can be placed very near to the turbine. Hydraulic behavior of the open surge tanks studied in [6] outlines their operational limits in terms of their design heights and water hammer effects. As the percentage of load acceptance and rejection increases in the case of the open surge tanks, water mass oscillation inside the surge tanks may exceed the maximum allowed height and the operational limit of the power plant equipment due to an excessive water hammer effect. Similarly, in [7,8] the benefits of ACST with respect to open surge tanks are given.

In this regard, it is of interest to study the hydraulic behavior of an ACST (closed surge tank) with respect to open surge tanks. A simple mechanistic model of an ACST was developed and studied previously in [9] as a feature extension to an open-source hydro power library—OpenHPL. OpenHPL is based on an equation-based language—Modelica. OpenHPL is under development at the University of South-Eastern Norway. This paper primarily focuses on the model improvements from [9], validation of the improved model with experimental data from [10], and hydraulic behavior of an ACST in relation to flexible hydro power plants.

1.2. Previous Work and Contributions

The model of hydraulic transients inside the surge tank is a well-established theory using Newton's second law [11,12]. The use of hydraulic resistances in the inlet of the surge tank helps to reduce water hammer effects. Different types of surge tanks designed with respect to the hydraulic resistances are presented in [13]. The time evolution equations for developing a mechanistic model of the surge tank are given in [14]. The hydraulic resistance at the inlet of different kinds of surge tanks can be studied from [14,15]. Closed surge tanks or ACST are important in terms of suppressing water mass oscillation due to the cushioning of air during hydraulic transients [16]. A hydraulic scale model of an ACST was studied in [10] based on 1D mass and momentum balances. In [17], a simulation study was carried out considering 1D mass and momentum equations for both water and air inside the ACST. In the paper, it is shown that the mass and momentum balances for air inside the ACST can be further simplified with an ideal gas relation. Other studies include the gas seepage theory for air loss through the ACST chamber in [18], a monitoring method for the hydraulic behavior of the ACST in [19], stability analysis of the ACST in [20], etc. The model developed in most of the previous work assumes an adiabatic process for the cushioning of air inside the ACST. The polytropic constant for air γ is considered around 1.4 for almost all the models of the ACST. However, previous work lacks modeling of the ACST with a possible consideration of friction due to air flow inside the ACST during its operation. The following research contributions are provided in this paper:
- a mechanistic model of an ACST, and
- a comparison between the ACST models with and without air friction.

1.3. Outline

Section 2 provides a mechanistic model of an ACST based on mass and momentum balances. In Section 3, model fitting and simulation results are outlined through a case study of the ACST used in Torpa Hydro Power Plant (HPP). Section 4 provides conclusions and future work.

2. Mechanistic Model of ACST

A general schematic and a flow diagram of an ACST is shown in Figure 1. The free water surface inside the surge tank is filled with pressurized air. Figure 1a shows the general schematic of an ACST where the water with volumetric flow rate $\dot{V}$ flows towards the air chamber through the access tunnel with length L_t and diameter D_t. The intake-penstock manifold pressure at the bottom of the tank is represented by p_m, and the air pressure at the air chamber due to the cushioning of the air is represented by p_c. The diameter of the air chamber is D. H is the total height of the surge tank and L is the total vertical slant length of the surge tank. In the figure, h represents the water level inside the tank during the operation of the ACST, and the dotted line in Figure 1a indicates that h is a variable quantity. Figure 1b shows a flow diagram inside the surge tank where F_f is the fluid friction against $\dot{V}$, F_g is the force due to gravity in the downward direction, and $F_g^{\dot{V}}$ is the projection of F_g in the alignment of the flow.

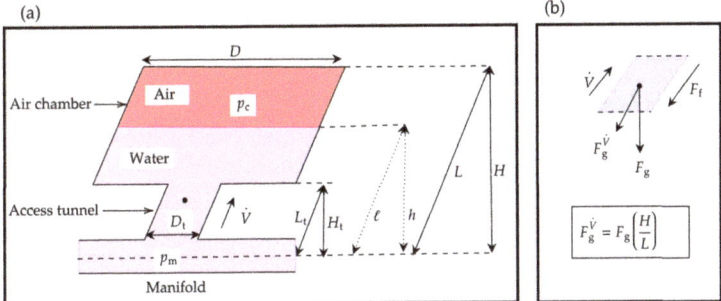

Figure 1. ACST with an access tunnel and an air chamber. (**a**) general schematic of ACST and (**b**) flow diagram.

Models developed in OpenHPL are based on a semi-explicit DAE formulation with a differential equation for the mass and the momentum balances as described in [21] and given by

$$\frac{dm}{dt} = \dot{m} \qquad (1)$$

$$\frac{d\mathcal{M}}{dt} = \dot{\mathcal{M}} + F \qquad (2)$$

where $\dot{m}$ and $\dot{\mathcal{M}}$ represent the mass flow rate and the momentum flow rate, respectively.

Equations (1) and (2) are expressed with a series of algebraic equations as

$$\dot{m} = \rho \dot{V} \qquad (3)$$

$$\mathcal{M} = mv \qquad (4)$$

$$\dot{\mathcal{M}} = \dot{m}v \qquad (5)$$

$$F = F_p - F_g^{\dot{V}} - F_f \qquad (6)$$

where ρ is the density of the water, m is the mass of air and water inside the ACST, v is the average velocity of the flow, V is the volume of the ACST, F is the total force acting in the surge tank, F_p is the pressure force, and F_f is the fluid frictional force. The expressions for all the variables are given in the sequel. A general idea regarding mathematical formulations of these variables is taken from [9].

The total mass inside the surge tank is expressed as

$$m = m_w + m_a \qquad (7)$$

where m_w and m_a are the masses of the water and the air inside the surge tank, respectively. m_a is constant inside the chamber and is determined based on the initial air cushion pressure p_{c0} which is considered to be a design parameter for the hydraulic performance of the surge tank. If h_{c0} is the initial water level inside the surge tank for the initial air cushion pressure p_{c0}, then the expression for the mass of the air inside the surge tank is found from an adiabatic compression and rarefaction of the air inside the surge tank during operation. It is found that for an ACST with a larger diameter, the heat transfer between air and water, air to the walls of the ACST, etc., can be neglected, and an adiabatic process of compression and rarefaction of the air inside the ACST can be assumed [16]. For an adiabatic process with pressure p, volume V, and γ of the air inside the ACST, considering standard temperature and pressure (STP), the relation $pV^\gamma = $ constant is assumed where γ is the ratio of specific heats at constant pressure and at constant volume. The mass of the air is then calculated formulating an ideal gas relation with the initial air pressure p_{c0} and the initial volume $A\left(L - h_{c0}\frac{L}{H}\right)$ given by

$$m_a = \frac{p_{c0} A \left(L - h_{c0}\frac{L}{H}\right) M_a}{RT^\circ} \quad (8)$$

where M_a is the molar mass of air, R is the universal gas constant and T° is the temperature taken at STP. Similarly, A is the area of the air chamber expressed as $A = \pi \frac{D^2}{4}$.

From Equation (2) formulating $p_{c0} V_0^\gamma = p_c V^\gamma$, the air cushion pressure during the operation of the surge tank is given by

$$p_c = p_{c0} \left(\frac{L - h_{c0}\frac{L}{H}}{L - \ell}\right)^\gamma \quad (9)$$

where p_c depends on the length ℓ inside the ACST.

During the operation of the surge tank, the mass of the water inside the surge tank m_w varies according to the variation in h. Thus, the expression for m_w is formulated considering two different scenarios inside the surge tank based on the variation of the water level h. First we consider (i) $h \leq H_t$ and second we consider (ii) $h > H_t$. Furthermore, we also formulate expressions for F_p and F_f for both of the scenarios of the water level h.

2.1. Case $h \leq H_t$

When the water level is up to the tip of the access tunnel or below the tip of the access tunnel, m_w is given by $m_w = \rho A_t \ell$ where ℓ is the slant height for h as shown in Figure 1a. m_w is further expressed as

$$m_w = \rho A_t h \frac{L}{H}. \quad (10)$$

The pressure force F_p is formulated based on the pressure difference at the manifold and the air pressure with an expression

$$F_p = (p_m - p_c) A_t. \quad (11)$$

The frictional force F_f is expressed as

$$F_f = F_{D,w} + F_{D,a} \quad (12)$$

where $F_{D,w}$ is the frictional force formulated for water flow inside the surge tank based on Darcy's friction factor for water, $f_{D,w}$. Similarly, $F_{D,a}$ is the frictional force formulated for air flow inside the surge tank based on Darcy's friction factor for air, $f_{D,a}$. Both $f_{D,w}$ and $f_{D,a}$ are calculated as in [9]. The general expression for Darcy's friction factor f_D is based on Reynolds' number $N_{Re} = \frac{\rho |v| D}{\mu}$ and expressed as

$$f_D = \begin{cases} \frac{64}{N_{Re}} & N_{Re} < 2100 \\ aN_{Re}^3 + bN_{Re}^2 + cN_{Re} + d & 2100 \leq N_{Re} \leq 2300 \\ \frac{1}{\left(2\log_{10}\left(\frac{\varepsilon}{3.7D} + \frac{5.7}{N_{Re}^{0.9}}\right)\right)^2} & N_{Re} > 2300 \end{cases}$$

where μ is the dynamic viscosity of the fluid, ε is the pipe roughness height. For the region $2100 \leq N_{Re} \leq 2300$, f_D is calculated from a cubic interpolation, with the coefficients a, b, c, and d, differentiable at the boundaries. The final expression for F_f is calculated as in [9] given as

$$F_f = \frac{1}{2}\rho v \, |v| \left(A_{w,w}\frac{f_{D,w}}{4} + A_{w,a}\frac{f_{D,a}}{4}\right) \quad (13)$$

where $|v|$ preserves the fluid frictional force against both directions of flow; flow induced from the access tunnel towards the air chamber, and vice-versa. $A_{w,w}$ is the wetted area due to water flow inside the surge tank given by

$$A_{w,w} = \pi D_t \ell \quad (14)$$

and $A_{w,a}$ is the wetted area due to the air during adiabatic compression and rarefaction inside the surge tank, and expressed as

$$A_{w,a} = \pi[D(L - L_t) + D_t(L_t - \ell)]. \quad (15)$$

2.2. Case $h > H_t$

When the water level inside the surge tank is above the access tunnel expression for m_w is formulated by summing the mass of water inside the access tunnel and the mass of water inside the air chamber, and is expressed as

$$m_w = \rho[A_t L_t + A(\ell - L_t)]. \quad (16)$$

For $\ell > L_t$ we consider Figure 2 for finding the total pressure force F_p in the direction of the flow. The calculation of the fluid frictional force is given in Figure 3. From Figure 2, the pressure force F_p is calculated based on the junction pressure p_j between the junction of the access tunnel and the air chamber. p_j is expressed as the sum of the air pressure p_c and the hydrostatic pressure due to the difference in liquid-level $h - H_t$. The junction pressure is then expressed as

$$p_j = p_c + \rho g(\ell - L_t)\frac{H}{L} \quad (17)$$

which relates in the final expression for F_f as

$$F_p = (p_m - p_j)A_t + (p_j - p_c)A. \quad (18)$$

From Figure 2, the overall fluid frictional force F_f is calculated with an expression given as

$$F_f = F_{D,w} + F_\phi + F_{D,a} \quad (19)$$

where $F_{D,w} + F_{D,a}$ is given as

$$F_{D,w} + F_{D,a} = \frac{1}{2}\rho v \, |v| \left(A_{w,w}\frac{f_{D,w}}{4} + A_{w,a}\frac{f_{D,a}}{4}\right)$$

where $A_{w,w} = \pi[D_t L_t + D(\ell - L_t)]$ and $A_{w,a} = \pi D(L - \ell)$; the calculations were similarly performed as in Equations (14) and (15).

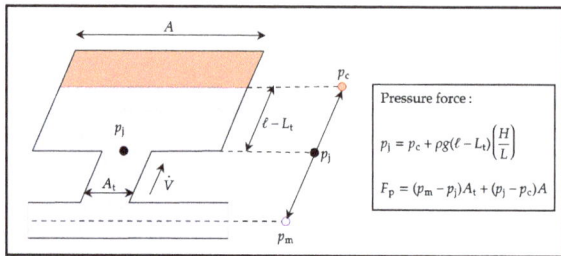

Figure 2. Considering junction pressure p_j for evaluating the overall pressure force F_P in the direction of flow. p_j is the pressure calculated based on the sum of air pressure p_c and hydrostatic pressure due to liquid-level $h - H_t$.

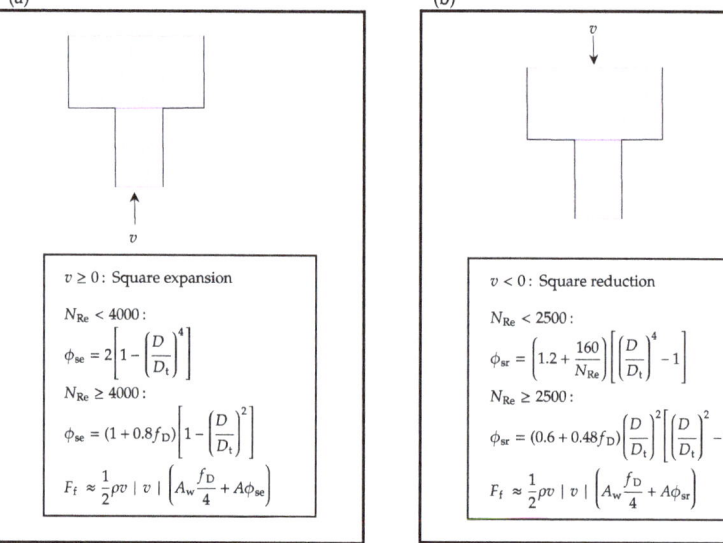

Figure 3. Expressions for fluid frictional force F_f considering (**a**) the square expansion type fitting for the flow towards the chamber through the access tunnel and (**b**) the square reduction type fitting for the flow through the chamber to the access tunnel. In the figures, ϕ_{se} and ϕ_{sr} are the generalized friction factors for the square expansion and the square reduction type fittings, respectively, taken from [15].

In Equation (19), F_ϕ is the fluid frictional force due to water flow from the access tunnel towards the air chamber, and vice-versa. F_ϕ can be expressed in terms of the pressure drop (alternatively can be expressed in terms of the head loss). When the water is flowing *from the access tunnel towards the air chamber*, we consider the pressure drop due to the *square expansion* type of fitting as shown in Figure 3a, and when the water is flowing *from the air chamber towards the access tunnel*, we consider the pressure drop due to the *square reduction* type of fitting as shown in Figure 3b. Thus, F_ϕ is calculated based on the generalized friction factors ϕ_{se} for the square expansion type of fitting and ϕ_{sr} for the square reduction type of fitting. Additionally, for both types of flows as shown in Figure 3, we assume an average cross-sectional area

$$\bar{A} = \frac{A + A_t}{2}.$$

If Δp_ϕ is the pressure drop due to the fittings, there exists a relationship between Δp_ϕ, the average kinetic energy of the fluid per volume $K''' = \frac{1}{2}\rho v \mid v \mid$ and the friction factor $\phi = \{\phi_{se}, \phi_{sr}\}$. The relationship between Δp_ϕ, K''', and ϕ is given by

$$\Delta p_\phi = \phi K'''.$$

The pressure drop Δp_ϕ is related to F_ϕ through the average cross-sectional area $\bar{A}$ and given as

$$F_\phi \approx \Delta p_\phi \bar{A}$$

which can be further expressed as

$$F_\phi \approx \frac{1}{2}\rho v \mid v \mid \bar{A}\phi, \quad \phi = \{\phi_{se}, \phi_{sr}\}.$$

The final expression for overall fluid frictional force F_f is then given as

$$F_f \approx \frac{1}{2}\rho v \mid v \mid \left(A_{w,w} \frac{f_{D,w}}{4} + A_{w,a} \frac{f_{D,a}}{4} + \bar{A}\phi \right) \quad \phi = \{\phi_{se}, \phi_{sr}\}. \tag{20}$$

This completes the expressions for variables m, F_p and F_f for the two scenarios of the liquid level inside the surge tank, viz., $h \leq H_t$ and $h > H_t$. To further complete the information of variables in Equation (6), the expression for F_g^V is calculated as

$$F_g^V = mg\frac{H}{L}, \tag{21}$$

as shown in the flow diagram of Figure 1a. Finally, the mechanistic model of the ACST needs an expression for the average velocity v expressed as

$$v = \frac{\dot{V}}{\bar{A}}. \tag{22}$$

Equations (1)–(6), in addition to other associated algebraic relations from Equations (7)–(22), represent a semi-explicit DAEs formulation for the ACST, and can be modeled in a equation-based modeling language like Modelica. The developed mechanistic model of the ACST is implemented in OpenHPL as a feature extension, and the case study was carried out for Torpa HPP.

3. Case Study

Figure 4a shows the layout diagram of Torpa HPP. Similarly, Figure 4b shows the simulation model of Torpa HPP created in OpenHPL. In Figure 4b, the reservoir model, the intake tunnel model, the penstock model, and the discharge model are developed as in [21]. A detailed model of the penstock considering water compressibility and pipe elasticity can be formulated from [22]. However, we consider the penstock model as a simple pipe model. Similarly, the Francis turbine mechanistic model for the case study is modeled as in [23]. The mechanistic model for the tailrace is taken as an exact mirror replica of the reservoir model.

The dimensions of the ACST shown in Figure 4a are found based on the piezometric diagram for Torpa HPP from [10]. The model developed in Section 2 is based on a cylindrical access tunnel and a cylindrical air chamber. Thus, the hydraulic diameters for the access tunnel D_t and the air chamber D are evaluated based on the volume of air inside the chamber using the operating conditions. Table 1 shows the parameters and the operating conditions of the ACST for Torpa HPP.

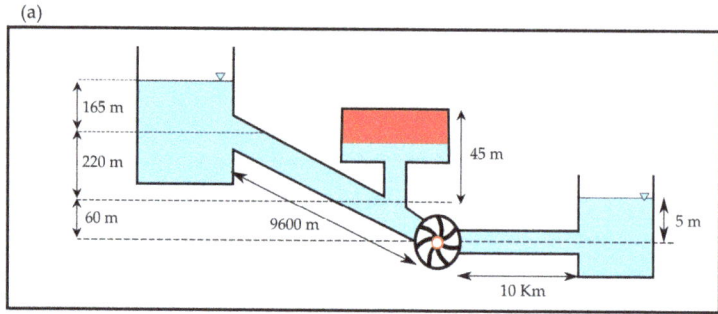
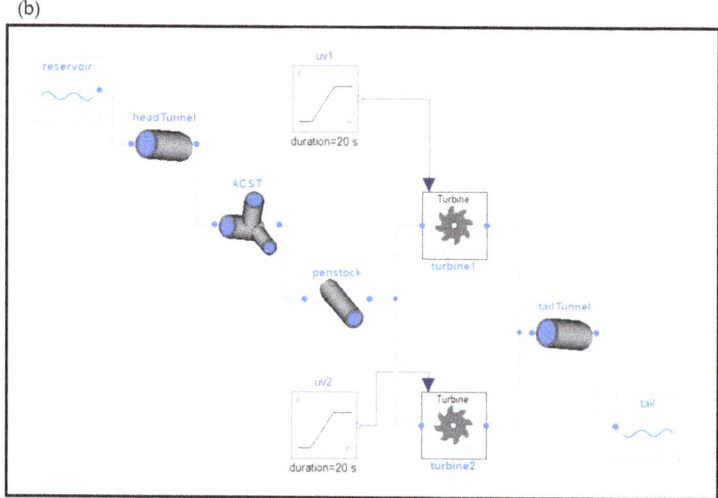

Figure 4. (**a**) Layout diagram for Torpa HPP. Nominal head, nominal discharge, and nominal power output are 445 m, 40 m^3/s and 150 MW, respectively. The ACST has air volume of 13,000 m^3, initially pressurized at $41 \cdot 10^5$ Pa. Similarly, both of the headrace and tailrace tunnels are 7 m in diameter. Torpa HPP consists of two turbine units each rated at 75 MW with rated discharge at 20 m^3/s. Torpa HPP also consists of a tailrace surge tank not shown in the figure. (**b**) Simulation model of Torpa HPP implemented in OpenHPL from the head reservoir to the tail reservoir.

For the model created in Figure 4b, it is of interest to:
1. validate the model with the experimental data from [10],
2. simulate the model considering air friction inside the ACST, and
3. study the hydraulic behavior of the ACST at different load acceptances and rejections.

3.1. Simulation Versus Real Measurements

Figure 5 shows the simulated versus real measurement for Torpa HPP. As shown in Figure 4b, u_{v1} and u_{v2} are the turbine valve signals for the turbine unit-1 and the turbine unit-2, respectively, for controlling the volumetric discharge through the turbines. The input turbine valve signal for unit-1 is given by

$$u_{v1} = \begin{cases} 0.68 & 0 < t \leq 500\,\text{s} \\ \frac{0.68}{50}(t-550) + 0.98 & 500\,\text{s} < t \leq 550\,\text{s} \\ 0.98 & 550\,\text{s} < t \leq 1200\,\text{s} \end{cases},$$

and the input turbine valve signal for unit-2 is given by,

$$u_{v2} = \begin{cases} 0.55 & 0 < t \leq 500\,\text{s} \\ \frac{0.55}{50}(t-550) + 0.93 & 500\,\text{s} < t \leq 550\,\text{s} \\ 0.93 & 550\,\text{s} < t \leq 1200\,\text{s}. \end{cases}$$

For inputs u_{v1} and u_{v2}, the mechanical power outputs for the turbine unit-1 (Figure 5c) and the turbine unit-2 (Figure 5d), the turbines inlet pressure p_{tr} (Figure 5e), and the air pressure inside the surge tank p_c (Figure 5f) are recorded for 1200 s with the measurement samples taken at each second. The air pressure p_c is measured using the pressure sensor PARO scientific 8DP000-S with an error of less than 0.01% of full scale of 6 Mpa, the turbine inlet pressure p_{tr} is measured using the pressure sensor PARO scientific DIQ 73K with an error of less than 0.04% of full scale of 20 Mpa, and the measurements for the mechanical power outputs are provided by the plant owner from Torpa HPP. The information about Torpa HPP and its experimental procedures are taken from [24]. Figure 5 shows that the simulation corresponds well with the real measurements in the case of power productions from the turbines (Figure 5c,d). In the case of the turbine inlet pressure p_{tr} (Figure 5e) there is an steady-state error of 0.6 bar for $0 < t \leq 500$ s. We believe that the steady-state error in p_{tr} for $0 < t \leq 500$ s can be eradicated by the inclusion of detailed geometrical dimensions for the headrace tunnel. In this paper, the headrace tunnel is considerd with a simple slanted pipe geometry as shown in Figure 4a. Similar steady-state error can be seen in the case of the height of water level inside the ACST h (Figure 5g) with negligible error of 0.05 m. In the case of air pressure inside the ACST p_c, the simulation and the measurement data are in good agreement. The measurement sampling rate in the case of water level h, air pressure p_c, and turbine power outputs are slower and oscillatory because the data are only recorded after a minimum change in the measured value, which may be the reason for the steady-state errors and phase difference between the simulation and measurements shown in Figure 5c,d,f,g. In addition, in Figure 5f,g for $800\,\text{s} < t \leq 1200\,\text{s}$, the simulated values have poorly damped oscillation while the measurement quickly reaches a steady value. The simulated and the experimental dynamics of the variables (p_c and h) are not captured well because of the slower and oscillatory sampling rate of the sensors. The simulation and the real measurements are matched by manual tuning of pipe roughness height of the headrace tunnel ($\varepsilon \approx 0.4$ mm), hydraulic diameter of the access tunnel $D_t \approx 15$ m, and hydraulic diameter of the air chamber $D \approx 24$ m.

Table 1. Parameters and operating conditions of the ACST for Torpa HPP.

Quantity	Symbol	Value
Hydraulic diameter of the throat	D_t	15 m
Hydraulic diameter of the chamber	D	24 m
Length of the throat	L_t	29 m
Total height	H	50 m
Total length	L	58 m
Pipe roughness height	ε	0.9 mm
Total volume	–	$17 \cdot 10^3\,\text{m}^3$
Operating temperature	T°	293 K
Adiabatic exponent for air at STP	γ	1.4
Molar mass of air at STP	M_a	$29 \cdot 10^{-3}\,\text{kg mol}^{-1}$
Universal gas constant	R	$8.314\,\text{JK}^{-1}\,\text{mol}^{-1}$
Initial pressure of air	$p_c(0) = p_{c0}$	$41 \cdot 10^5$ Pa
Initial water level	$h(0) = h_{c0}$	27 m
Initial volume of air	V_0	$13 \cdot 10^3\,\text{m}^3$

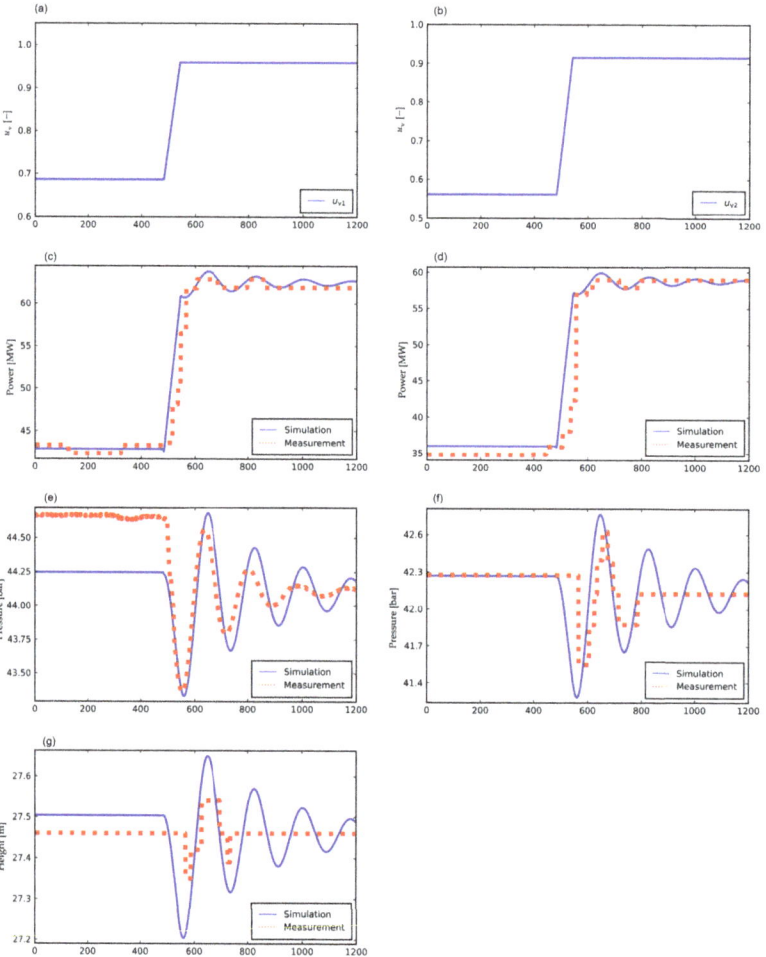

Figure 5. Simulation versus real measurements for Torpa HPP, (**a**) turbine valve signal for unit-1, (**b**) turbine valve signal for unit-2, (**c**) power output for unit-1, (**d**) power output for unit-2, (**e**) inlet pressure of the turbine units or the outlet pressure of the penstock, (**f**) air cushion pressure inside the ACST, and (**g**) height of water level inside the ACST.

3.2. Effect of Air Friction Inside ACST

We now consider Torpa HPP with each of the turbine units rated at 75 MW as a single entity, for simplification, with 150 MW with input u_v as the turbine valve signal. This simplification is made for studying the hydraulic behavior of the ACST in terms of the air friction inside the ACST, and the operation of Torpa HPP with respect to load acceptance and rejection (Section 3.3). Only simulated results will be presented in the sequel.

The air friction force $F_{D,a}$ modeled using Darcy's friction factor f_D inside the ACST of Torpa HPP is considered using Equation (12) for the case of water level $h \leq H_t$, and using Equation (19) for the case of water level $h > H_t$. The input to the turbine with valve signal u_v for the simulation purpose is given by

$$u_v = \begin{cases} 0.5 & 0 < t \leq 500\,\text{s} \\ 0.95 & 500\,\text{s} < t \leq 1500\,\text{s} \end{cases}$$

where the hydro-turbine is loaded from half-load to nominal load at time $t = 500\,\text{s}$.

Figure 6 shows hydraulic behavior of the ACST for the turbine loading from 50% to 95%. Figure 6b–d show the water level h inside the ACST, the air cushion pressure p_c, and the inlet turbine pressure p_{tr}, respectively, for the ACST modeled with and without the air friction consideration. From Figure 6c, we see that the differences in air cushion pressure p_c for the ACST modeled with and without the air friction consideration is in the order of $10^{-5}\,\text{bar} = 1\,\text{Pa}$, even for the turbine loaded from half load to the nominal operation. This is because of the fact that fluid frictional force F_f depends on Darcy's friction factor f_D, and f_D depends on Reynolds' number $N_{Re} = \frac{\rho|v|D}{\mu}$ where μ is the dynamic viscosity of the fluid. At STP, $\mu_{air} = 1.81 \cdot 10^{-5}\,\text{Pa}\cdot\text{s}$ and $\mu_{water} = 8.90 \cdot 10^{-4}\,\text{Pa}\cdot\text{s}$ which can be approximated as $\mu_{water} \approx 100\,\mu_{air}$.

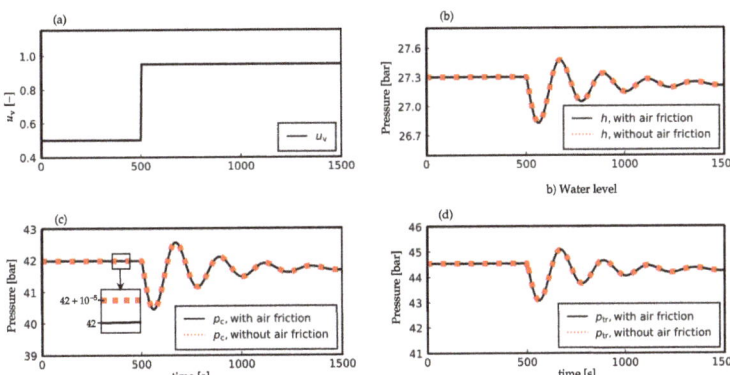

Figure 6. ACST model with and without frictional force due to the air inside ACST for Torpa HPP, (**a**) turbine valve signal u_v, (**b**) water level h inside ACST, (**c**) air cushion pressure p_c, and (**d**) turbine inlet pressure p_{tr}.

3.3. Operations of ACST in Load Acceptance and Rejection

Load acceptance and rejection are created by changing the turbine valve signal u_v from one operating condition to another operating condition, and are described in the sequel.

3.3.1. Load Acceptances

We consider Torpa HPP running at *no load* condition for a time period of 500 s. At $t = 500\,\text{s}$, a different load acceptance condition is created by changing the turbine valve signal u_v, and the hydraulic behavior of the ACST is observed for the next 1500 s. The turbine valve signal u_v is generated as

$$u_v = \begin{cases} 0 & 0 < t \leq 500\,\text{s} \\ u_{va} & 500\,\text{s} < t \leq 2000\,\text{s} \end{cases}$$

where $u_{va} \in \{0.25, 0.5, 0.75, 1.0\}$ for load acceptances of 25%, 50%, 75%, and 100%, respectively. For a total load acceptance (TLA) the load acceptance is 100%.

3.3.2. Load Rejections

In contrast to the load acceptances, we now consider Torpa HPP running at *full load* condition for a time period of 500 s. At $t = 500\,\text{s}$, a different load rejection condition is created by changing the turbine valve signal u_v, and the hydraulic behavior of the ACST is observed for the next 1500 s. The turbine valve signal u_v is generated as

$$u_v = \begin{cases} 1.0 & 0 < t \leq 500\,\text{s} \\ u_{vr} & 500\,\text{s} < t \leq 2000\,\text{s} \end{cases}$$

where $u_{vr} \in \{0.75, 0.5, 0.25, 0.0\}$ for load rejections of 25%, 50%, 75%, and 100%, respectively. For a total load rejection (TLR), the load rejection is 100%.

Figure 7 shows hydraulic performance of the ACST during load acceptances and rejections for Torpa HPP. Figure 7a,c,e,g shows the turbine valve signal u_v, the air pressure p_c, the turbine inlet pressure p_{tr} and the water level inside ACST h, respectively, for the different percentage change in the load acceptances. Similarly, Figure 7b,d,f,h shows u_v, p_c, p_{tr} and h, respectively, for the different percentage change in the load rejections.

Figure 7a shows the turbine valve signal generated for load acceptances of 25%, 50%, 75%, and 100%. Figure 7c, at $t = 500\,\text{s}$, shows that from the no load operation to TLA, the difference in the air pressure p_c inside the ACST is around 4 bar. Similarly, Figure 7e shows that the difference in turbine inlet pressure p_{tr} is around 3 bar, and Figure 7e shows that the difference in the water level h inside the ACST is around 1 m. In addition, Figure 7c shows that the difference in p_c from no load operation to 25% load acceptance, 50% load acceptance and 75% load acceptance are around 1 bar, 2 bar and 3 bar, respectively. Similarly, results can be obtained for p_{tr} (Figure 7e) and h (Figure 7g). For p_c, p_{tr} and h oscillation dies out as the time progresses for $t > 500\,\text{s}$.

Figure 7b shows the turbine valve signal generated for load rejections of 25%, 50%, 75%, and 100%. Figure 7d, at $t = 500\,\text{s}$, shows that from full load operation to TLR, the difference in p_c is around 4 bar as similar in the case of TLA. Similarly, the difference is around 3 bar in the case of p_{tr}, as shown in Figure 7f. The difference in h from full load operation to TLR is also 1 m, as in the case of TLA. Similarly, from Figure 7d, the difference in p_c from full load operation to load rejections of 25%, 50% and 75% are around 1 bar, 2 bar and 3 bar, respectively. Similar results can be obtained for p_{tr} (Figure 7f) and h (Figure 7h). For p_c, p_{tr} and h, oscillation dies out for $t > 500\,\text{s}$, similar to the case of load acceptances. However, the oscillation dies out sooner in the case of TLA than TLR.

3.3.3. ACST as a Flexible Hydro Power

The results for Figure 7 show hydraulic behavior of the ACST in the case of load acceptance and rejection. The difference in the water level is around 1 m for both TLA and TLR. Similarly, the difference in the air pressure is around 4 bar for both TLA and TLR. Referring to the results on the hydraulic performance of the ACST from Section 3.3 and the study carried out for different types of open surge tanks in [6] clearly indicates that ACST has a robust performance on suppressing water mass oscillation and water hammer pressure during a higher percentage of load acceptances and rejections, unlike different types of open surge tanks. Since one of the prominent requirements of a flexible hydro power plant is to have a robust operation under various load acceptances and rejections, a hydro power plant operated with ACST makes it a potential candidate for participating in the concept of flexible hydro power.

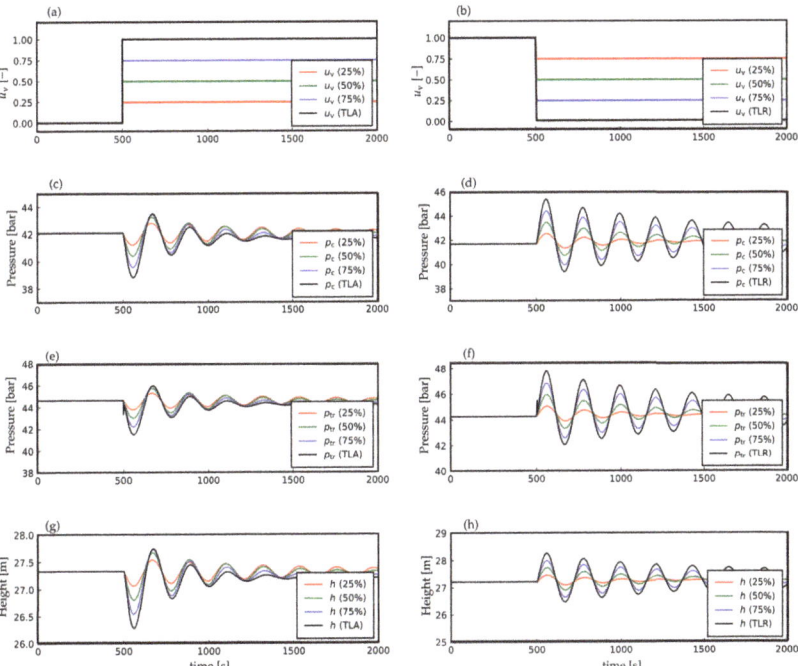

Figure 7. Hydraulic performance of the ACST for Torpa HPP for the different percentage change in the load acceptances and the load rejections, (**a**) turbine valve signal u_v as an input to the load acceptances, (**b**) turbine valve signal u_v as an input to the load rejections, (**c**) air pressure p_c for the load acceptances, (**d**) air pressure p_c for the load rejections, (**e**) turbine inlet pressure p_{tr} for the load acceptances, (**f**) turbine inlet pressure p_{tr} for the load rejections, (**g**) water level inside the ACST h for the load acceptances, and (**h**) water level inside the ACST for the load rejections.

4. Conclusions and Future Work

A mechanistic model of an ACST has been developed considering an access tunnel connected to an air chamber. The difference in diameters of the access tunnel and the air chamber has been taken into consideration. The model is further enhanced with the inclusion of Darcy's friction force for air inside the ACST. Model fitting is done for the 150 MW Torpa HPP. The experimental data and the model simulation were matched by manual tuning of pipe roughness height of the headrace tunnel, and hydraulic diameters of the access tunnel and the air chamber of the ACST. Apart from the model fitting, simulation results show that the effect of air friction inside the ACST is negligible as compared to water friction. The simulation studies carried out for load acceptance and rejection show the robust hydraulic behaviors of the ACST in terms of suppressing water mass oscillation and water hammer pressure, which indicate that a hydro power plant with ACST makes it a potential candidate for flexible hydro power in case of an energy-mix (intermittent and dispatchable sources) interconnected power grid.

Future work includes the study of the hydraulic behavior of ACST in interconnected grids supplied with intermittent generation. In addition, the model for ACST can be improved using Lagrangian computational fluid dynamics. For the Lagrangian approach, the meshless discretization technique smoothed particle hydrodynamics (SPH) can be used to handle coupling between the free water surface and air inside the ACST [25,26].

Author Contributions: Conceptualization, M.P., K.V., R.S. and B.L.; methodology, M.P., R.S. and B.L.; software, M.P. and D.W.; validation, M.P., K.V. and B.L.; formal analysis, M.P.; investigation, M.P.; resources, M.P., D.W. and K.V.; writing—original draft preparation, M.P.; writing—review and editing, M.P.; visualization, M.P. and B.L.; supervision, D.W., K.V. and B.L. All authors have read and agreed to the published version of the manuscript.

Funding: This research received no external funding.

Institutional Review Board Statement: Not applicable.

Informed Consent Statement: Not applicable.

Data Availability Statement: Not applicable.

Acknowledgments: Help and discussions with Liubomyr Vytvytsky, ABB Oslo, regarding model tuning is gratefully acknowledged.

Conflicts of Interest: The authors declare no conflict of interest.

References

1. Pandey, M.; Winkler, D.; Sharma, R.; Lie, B. Using MPC to Balance Intermittent Wind and Solar Power with Hydro Power in Microgrids. *Energies* **2021**, *14*, 874. [CrossRef]
2. Pandey, M.; Lie, B. The Role of Hydropower Simulation in Smart Energy Systems. In Proceedings of the 2020 IEEE 7th International Conference on Energy Smart Systems (ESS), Kyiv, Ukraine, 12–14 May 2020 ; pp. 392–397.
3. Charmasson, J.; Belsnes, M.; Andersen, O.; Eloranta, A.; Graabak, I.; Korpås, M.; Helland, I.; Sundt, H.; Wolfgang, O. *Roadmap for Large-Scale Balancing and Energy Storage from Norwegian Hydropower: Opportunities, Challanges and Needs until 2050*; SINTEF Energi AS: Trondheim, Norway, 2018.
4. Huertas-Hernando, D.; Farahmand, H.; Holttinen, H.; Kiviluoma, J.; Rinne, E.; Söder, L.; Milligan, M.; Ibanez, E.; Martínez, S.M.; Gomez-Lazaro, E.; et al. Hydro power flexibility for power systems with variable renewable energy sources: An IEA Task 25 collaboration. *Wiley Interdiscip. Rev. Energy Environ.* **2017**, *6*, e220. [CrossRef]
5. Graabak, I.; Korpås, M.; Jaehnert, S.; Belsnes, M. Balancing future variable wind and solar power production in Central-West Europe with Norwegian hydropower. *Energy* **2019**, *168*, 870–882. [CrossRef]
6. Pandey, M.; Lie, B. The influence of surge tanks on the water hammer effect at different hydro power discharge rates. In Proceedings of the SIMS 2020, Oulu, Finland, 22–24 September 2020; Linköping University Electronic Press: Linköping, Sweden, 2020; pp. 125–130.
7. Vereide, K.; Richter, W.; Zenz, G.; Lia, L. Surge Tank Research in Austria and Norway. *Wasserwirtschaft* **2015**, *1*, 58–62. [CrossRef]
8. Vereide, K.; Lia, L.; Nielsen, T. Physical modelling of hydropower waterway with air cushion surge chamber. In Proceedings of the 5th International Symposium on Hydraulic Structures, Brisbane, Australia, 25–27 June 2014.
9. Pandey, M.; Lie, B. Mechanistic modeling of different types of surge tanks and draft tubes for hydropower plants. In Proceedings of the SIMS 2020, Oulu, Finland, 22–24 September 2020; Linköping University Electronic Press: Linköping, Sweden, 2020; pp. 131–138.
10. Vereide, K.; Lia, L.; Nielsen, T.K. Hydraulic scale modelling and thermodynamics of mass oscillations in closed surge tanks. *J. Hydraul. Res.* **2015**, *53*, 519–524. [CrossRef]
11. Mosonyi, E. *Water Power Development: High-Head Power Plants*; Akadémiai kiadó: Budapest, Hungary, 1965; Volume 2.
12. Pickford, J. *Analysis of Water Surge*; Taylor & Francis: Abingdon, UK, 1969.
13. Jaeger, C. Present trends in surge tank design. *Proc. Inst. Mech. Eng.* **1954**, *168*, 91–124. [CrossRef]
14. Guo, J.; Woldeyesus, K.; Zhang, J.; Ju, X. Time evolution of water surface oscillations in surge tanks. *J. Hydraul. Res.* **2017**, *55*, 657–667. [CrossRef]
15. Lydersen, A. *Fluid Flow and Heat Transfer*; John Wiley & Sons Incorporated: Hoboken, NJ, USA, 1979.
16. Vereide, K.V. Hydraulics and Thermodynamics of Closed Surge Tanks for Hydropower Plants. Ph.D. Thesis, NTNU, Trondheim, Norway, 2016.
17. Wang, C.; Yang, J.; Nilsson, H. Simulation of water level fluctuations in a hydraulic system using a coupled liquid-gas model. *Water* **2015**, *7*, 4446–4476. [CrossRef]
18. Yulong, L. Studies on gas loss of air cushion surge chamber based on gas seepage theory. In Proceedings of the 2011 International Conference on Electric Technology and Civil Engineering (ICETCE), Lushan, China, 22–24 April 2011; pp. 723–725.
19. Ou, C.; Liu, D.; Li, L. Research on dynamic properties of long pipeline monitoring system of air cushion surge chamber. In Proceedings of the 2009 Asia-Pacific Power and Energy Engineering Conference, Wuhan, China, 27–31 March 2009; pp. 1–4.
20. Yang, X.L.; Kung, C.S. Stability of air-cushion surge tanks with throttling. *J. Hydraul. Res.* **1992**, *30*, 835–850. [CrossRef]
21. Vytvytskyi, L. *User's Guide for the Open Hydropower Library (OpenHPL)*; University of South-Eastern Norway, Porsgrunn, Norway, 2019.

22. Vytvytsky, L.; Lie, B. Comparison of elastic vs. inelastic penstock model using OpenModelica. In Proceedings of the 58th Conference on Simulation and Modelling (SIMS 58), Reykjavik, Iceland, 25–27 September 2017; Linköping University Electronic Press: Linköping, Sweden, 2017; Volume 138, pp. 20–28. [CrossRef]
23. Vytvytskyi, L.; Lie, B. Mechanistic model for Francis turbines in OpenModelica. *IFAC-PapersOnLine* **2018**, *51*, 103–108. [CrossRef]
24. Vereide, K.; Svingen, B.; Nielsen, T.K.; Lia, L. The effect of surge tank throttling on governor stability, power control, and hydraulic transients in hydropower plants. *IEEE Trans. Energy Convers.* **2016**, *32*, 91–98. [CrossRef]
25. Rakhsha, M.; Kees, C.E.; Negrut, D. Lagrangian vs. Eulerian: An analysis of two solution methods for free-surface flows and fluid solid interaction problems. *Fluids* **2021**, *6*, 460. [CrossRef]
26. Bimbato, A.M.; Alcântara Pereira, L.A.; Hirata, M.H. Study of surface roughness effect on a bluff body—The formation of asymmetric separation bubbles. *Energies* **2020**, *13*, 6094. [CrossRef]

MDPI
St. Alban-Anlage 66
4052 Basel
Switzerland
Tel. +41 61 683 77 34
Fax +41 61 302 89 18
www.mdpi.com

Energies Editorial Office
E-mail: energies@mdpi.com
www.mdpi.com/journal/energies

www.ingramcontent.com/pod-product-compliance
Lightning Source LLC
LaVergne TN
LVHW070603100526
838202LV00012B/554